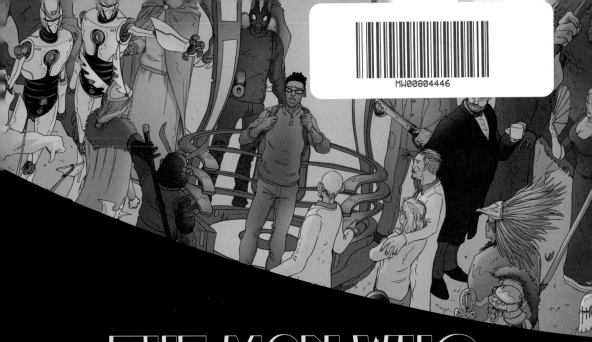

THE MAN WHO F#&%ED UP TIME

JOHN LAYMAN

KARL MOSTERT

DEE CUNNIFFE

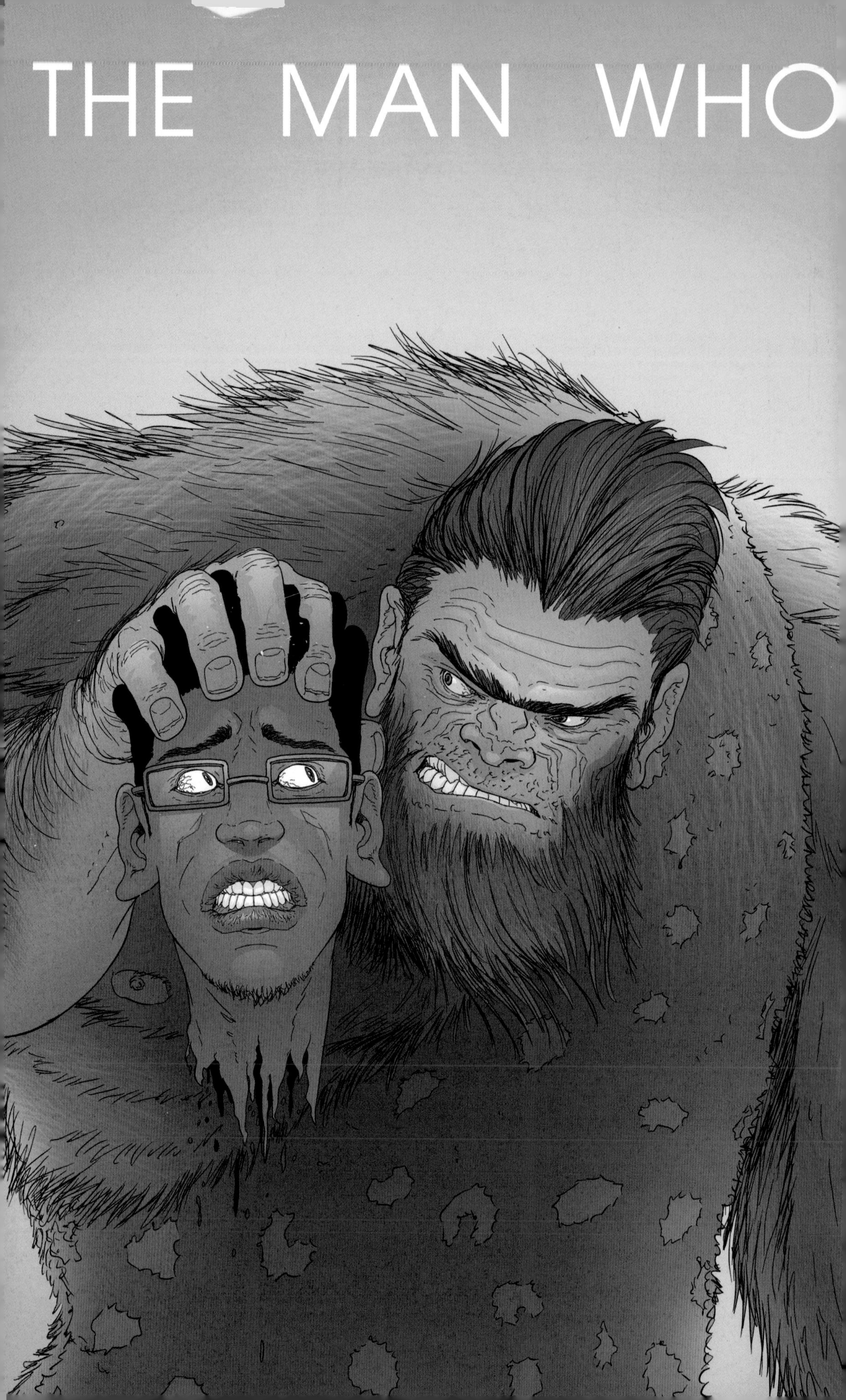
THE MAN WHO

F#€%ED UP TIME

JOHN LAYMAN writer
KARL MOSTERT artist

DEE CUNNIFFE colorist

JOHN LAYMAN letterer

KARL MOSTERT w/ DEE CUNNIFFE front & original series covers

JOHN McCREA w/ ENRICA EREN ANGIOLIN, ANDREW ROBINSON & LARRY STROMAN variant covers

JARED K. FLETCHER logo designer

COREY BREEN book designer

MIKE MARTS editor

created by JOHN LAYMAN & KARL MOSTERT

AFTERSHOCK™

MIKE MARTS - Editor-in-Chief • JOE PRUETT - Publisher/CCO • LEE KRAMER - President • JON KRAMER - Chief Executive Officer
STEVE ROTTERDAM - SVP, Sales & Marketing • DAN SHIRES - VP, Film & Television UK • CHRISTINA HARRINGTON - Managing Editor
MARC HAMMOND - Sr. Retail Sales Development Manager • RUTHANN THOMPSON - Sr. Retailer Relations Manager
KATHERINE JAMISON - Marketing Manager • KELLY DIODATI - Ambassador Outreach Manager • BLAKE STOCKER - Director of Finance
AARON MARION - Publicist • LISA MOODY - Finance • RYAN CARROLL - Development Coordinator • JAWAD QURESHI - Technology Advisor/Strategist
RACHEL PINNELAS - Social Community Manager • CHARLES PRITCHETT - Design & Production Manager • COREY BREEN - Collections Production
TEDDY LEO - Editorial Assistant • STEPHANIE CASEBIER & SARAH PRUETT - Publishing Assistants

AfterShock Logo Design by COMICRAFT
Publicity: contact AARON MARION (aaron@publichausagency.com) & RYAN CROY (ryan@publichausagency.com) at PUBLICHAUS
Special thanks to: ATOM! FREEMAN, IRA KURGAN, MARINE KSADZHIKYAN, KEITH MANZZELLA, STEPHANIE MEADOR, ANTONIA LIANOS & ED ZAREMBA

PRINTED IN KOREA. First Printing: December 2020. 10 9 8 7 6 5 4 3 2 1

AFTERSHOCKCOMICS.COM Follow us on social media

I N T R O D U C T I O N

There is no story more headache-inducing than a time-travel story.

When I pitched THE MAN WHO F#&%ED UP TIME to my friends at AfterShock, it was a deceptively simple premise: "Guy goes back a week in time and makes *slight* changes to the past, only to see *tremendous* changes when he returns to the present." In a case of life imitating art, as the timeline got more complex for poor series star Sean Bennett, explaining it and keeping things straight got even more complex for poor old series writer John Layman!

There's a point when things get so bad for Sean Bennett, when keeping track of the various timelines and escalating insanity is so crazy, he's ready to give up and pack things in. I don't want to say things ever got *that* bad for me when writing the story...but have I mentioned there is no story more headache-inducing than a time-travel story?

Kinda wish I had a time machine now, so me—Present-Day Layman—could go back to when Past-Layman was drowning his sorrows in some bar, wondering how he was *possibly* going to finish this increasingly crazy (and possibly convoluted) story.

I'd let Past-Layman know that everything would be all right, that thanks to artist Karl Mostert and colorist Dee Cunniffe, the book would look so good it didn't completely *have* to make sense, and that editors Christina Harrington and Mike Marts would have Past-Layman's back every step of the way. This book is going to work out *just* the way it was planned to, and be something you're terribly proud of in the end. You're going to like this book quite a lot when it's complete, and you think readers will, too.

Even if I had that time machine to go back, I wouldn't change a dang thing about THE MAN WHO F#&%ED UP TIME. But, y'know, had I known that from the start, it might have gotten rid of some of those headaches!

JOHN LAYMAN
October 2020

1

THE HERE AND NOW

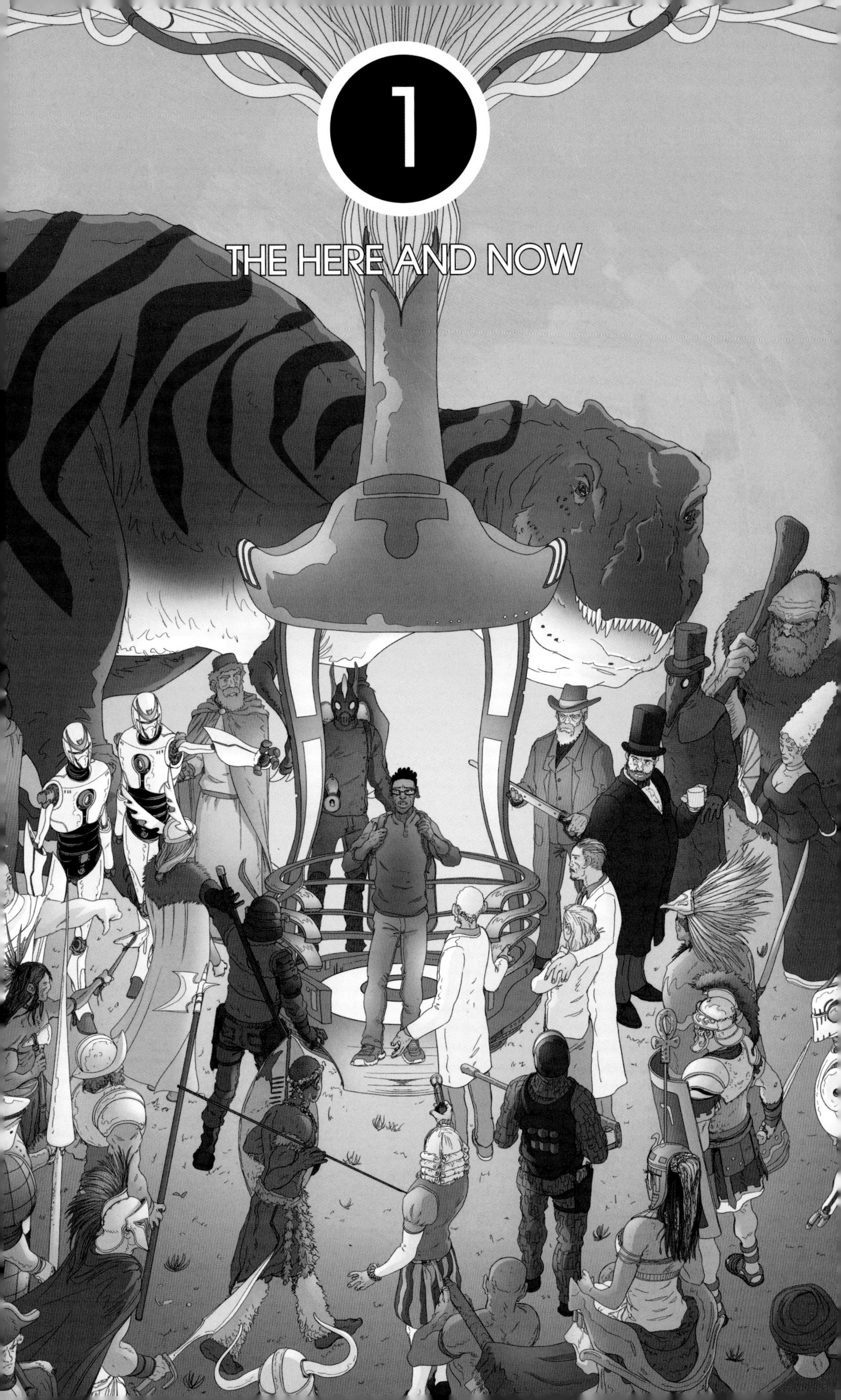

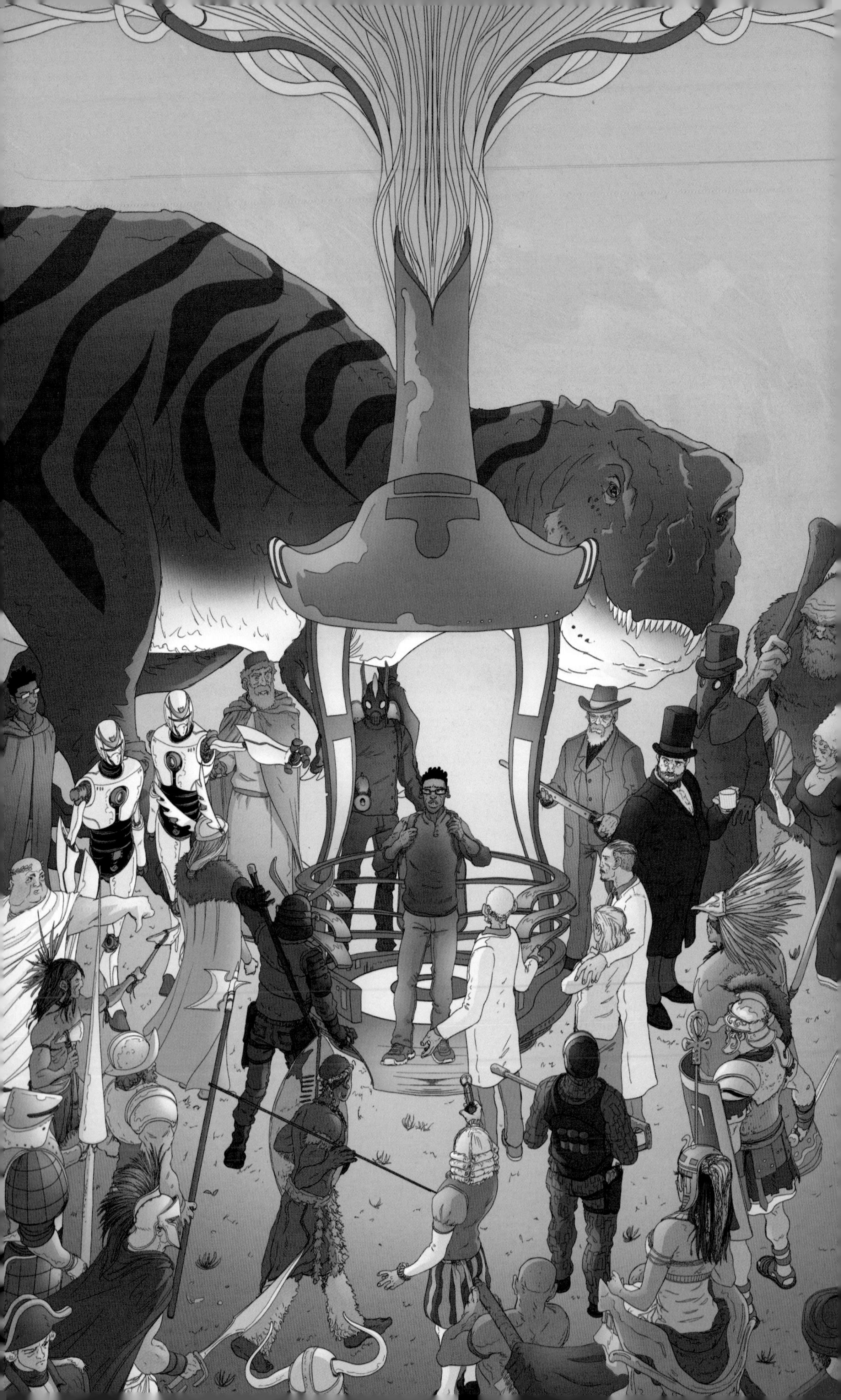

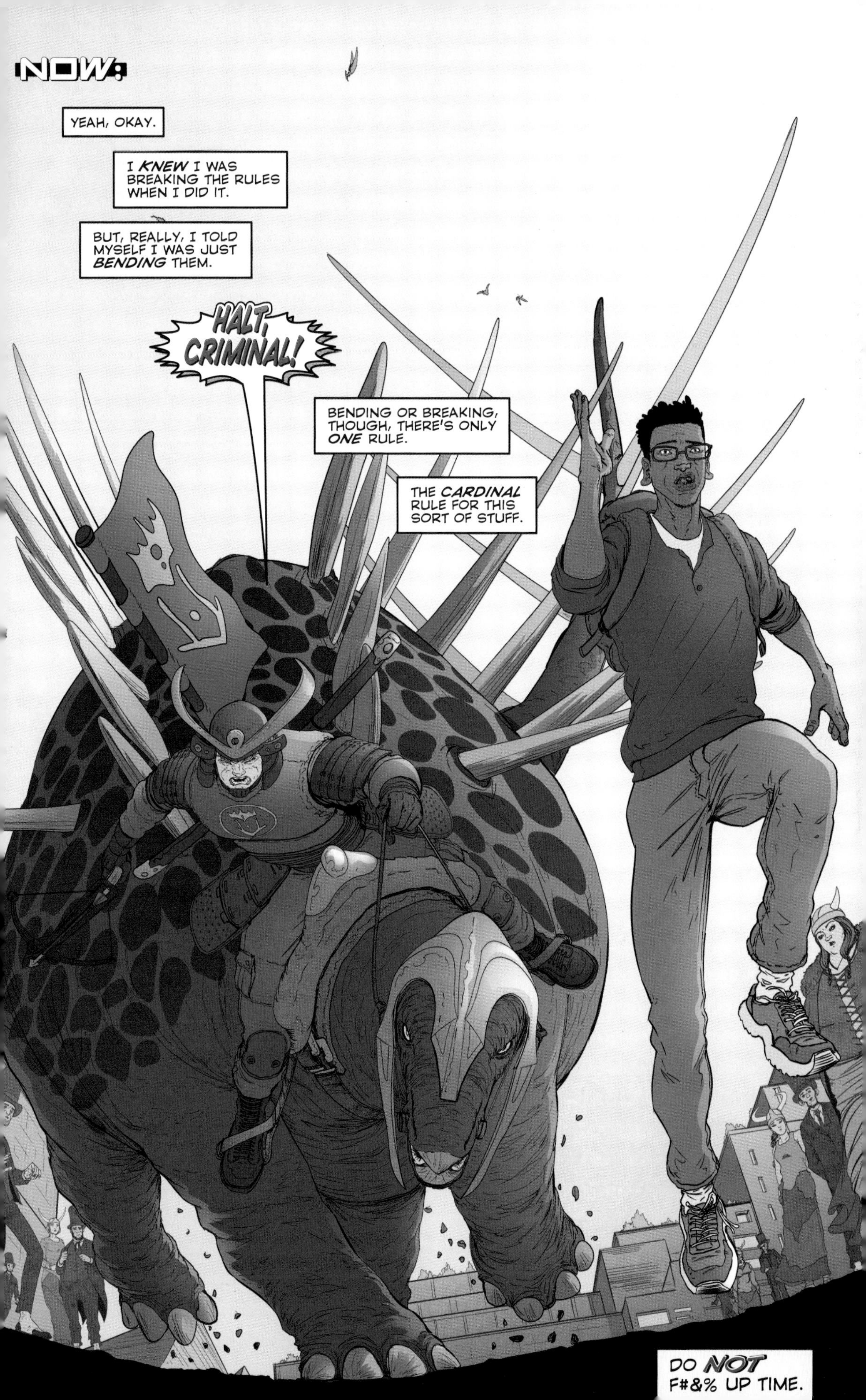
NOW:
YEAH, OKAY.
I KNEW I WAS BREAKING THE RULES WHEN I DID IT.
BUT, REALLY, I TOLD MYSELF I WAS JUST BENDING THEM.
HALT, CRIMINAL!
BENDING OR BREAKING, THOUGH, THERE'S ONLY ONE RULE.
THE CARDINAL RULE FOR THIS SORT OF STUFF.
DO NOT F#&% UP TIME.

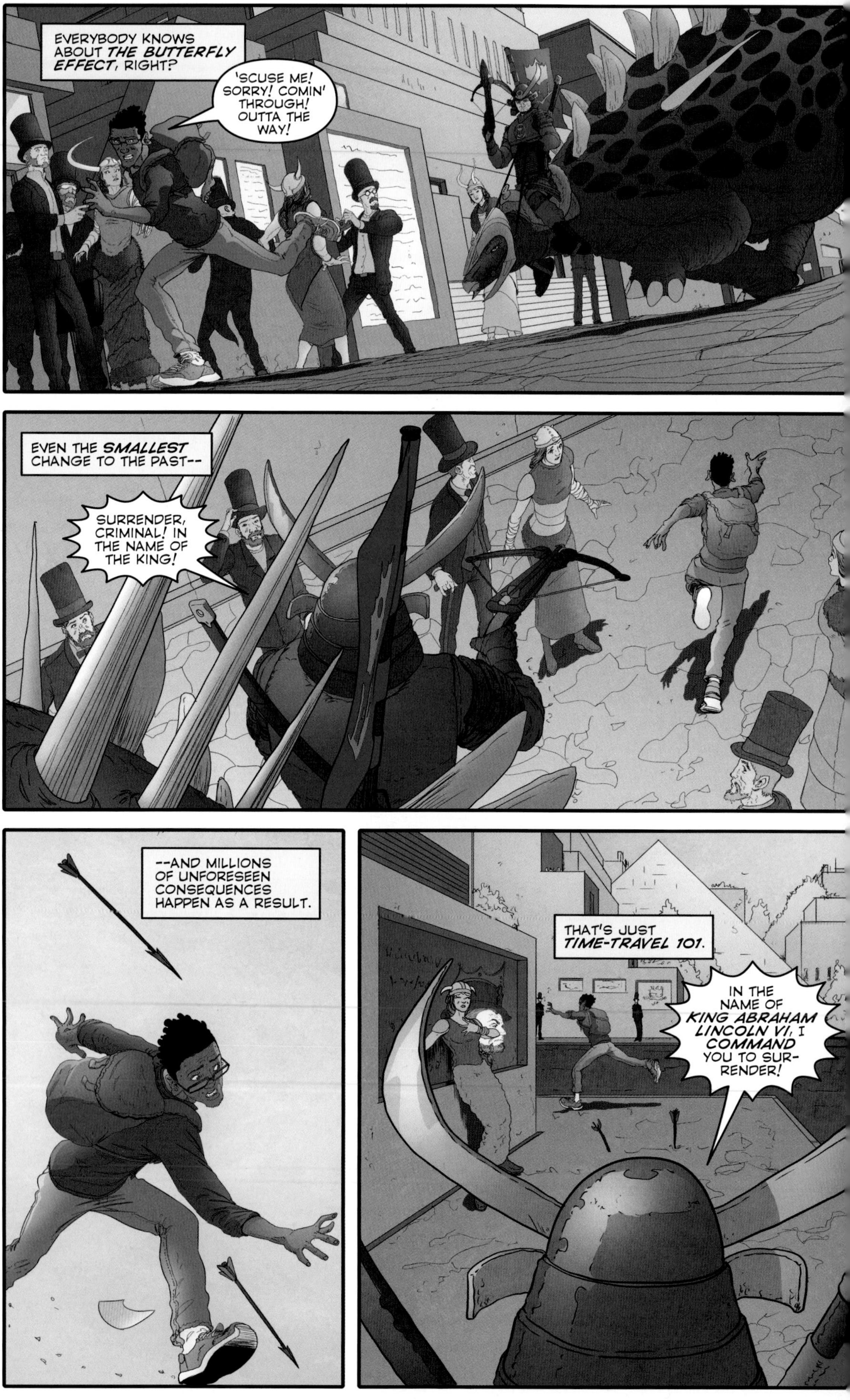
EVERYBODY KNOWS ABOUT THE BUTTERFLY EFFECT, RIGHT?
'SCUSE ME! SORRY! COMIN' THROUGH! OUTTA THE WAY!
EVEN THE SMALLEST CHANGE TO THE PAST--
SURRENDER, CRIMINAL! IN THE NAME OF THE KING!
--AND MILLIONS OF UNFORESEEN CONSEQUENCES HAPPEN AS A RESULT.
THAT'S JUST TIME-TRAVEL 101.
IN THE NAME OF KING ABRAHAM LINCOLN VI, I COMMAND YOU TO SURRENDER!

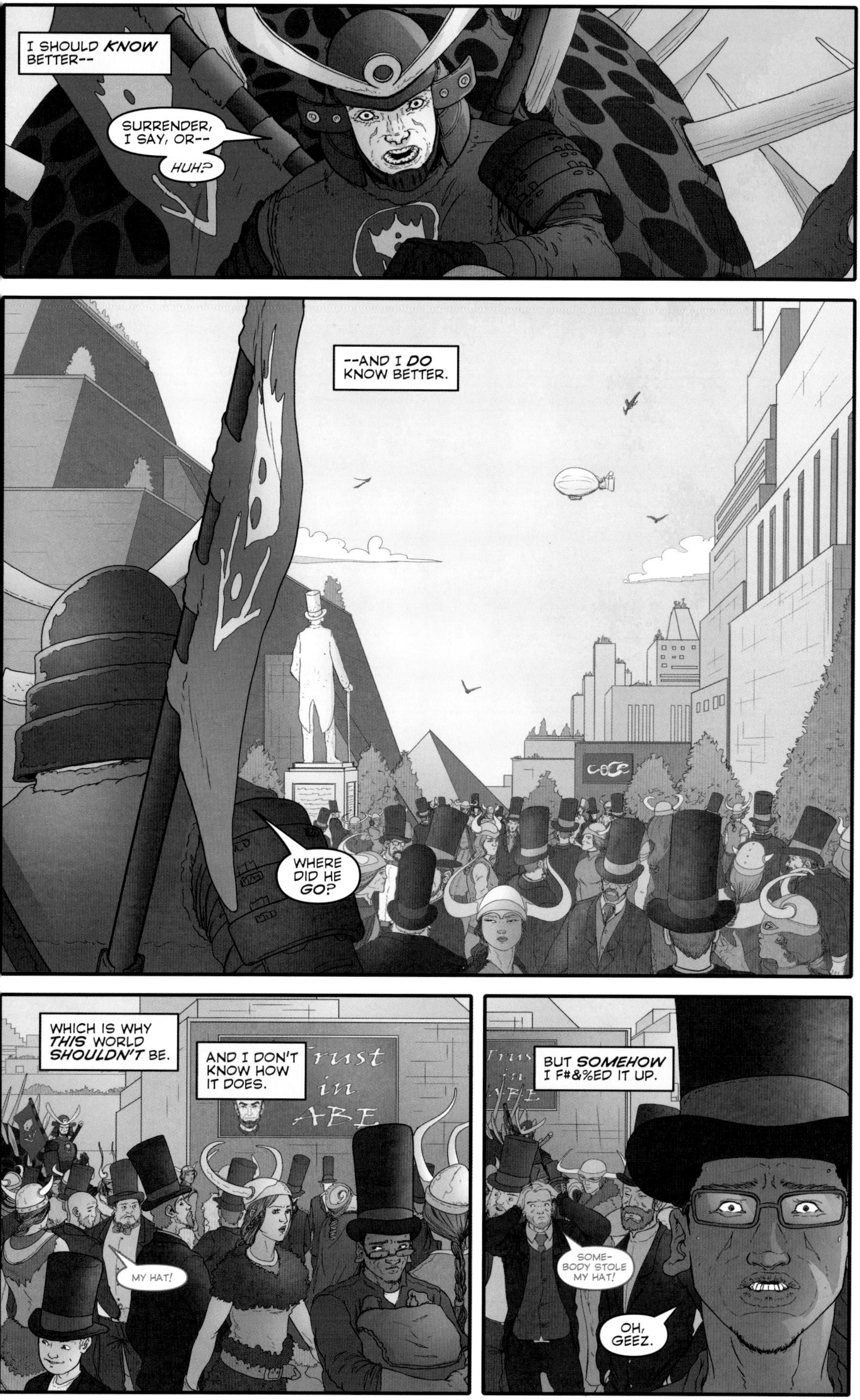

I SHOULD *KNOW* BETTER--
SURRENDER, I SAY, OR--
HUH?
--AND I *DO* KNOW BETTER.
WHERE DID HE *GO?*
WHICH IS WHY *THIS* WORLD *SHOULDN'T* BE.
AND I DON'T KNOW HOW IT DOES.
Trust in ABE
MY HAT!
BUT *SOMEHOW* I F#&%ED IT UP.
SOME-BODY STOLE MY HAT!
OH, GEEZ.

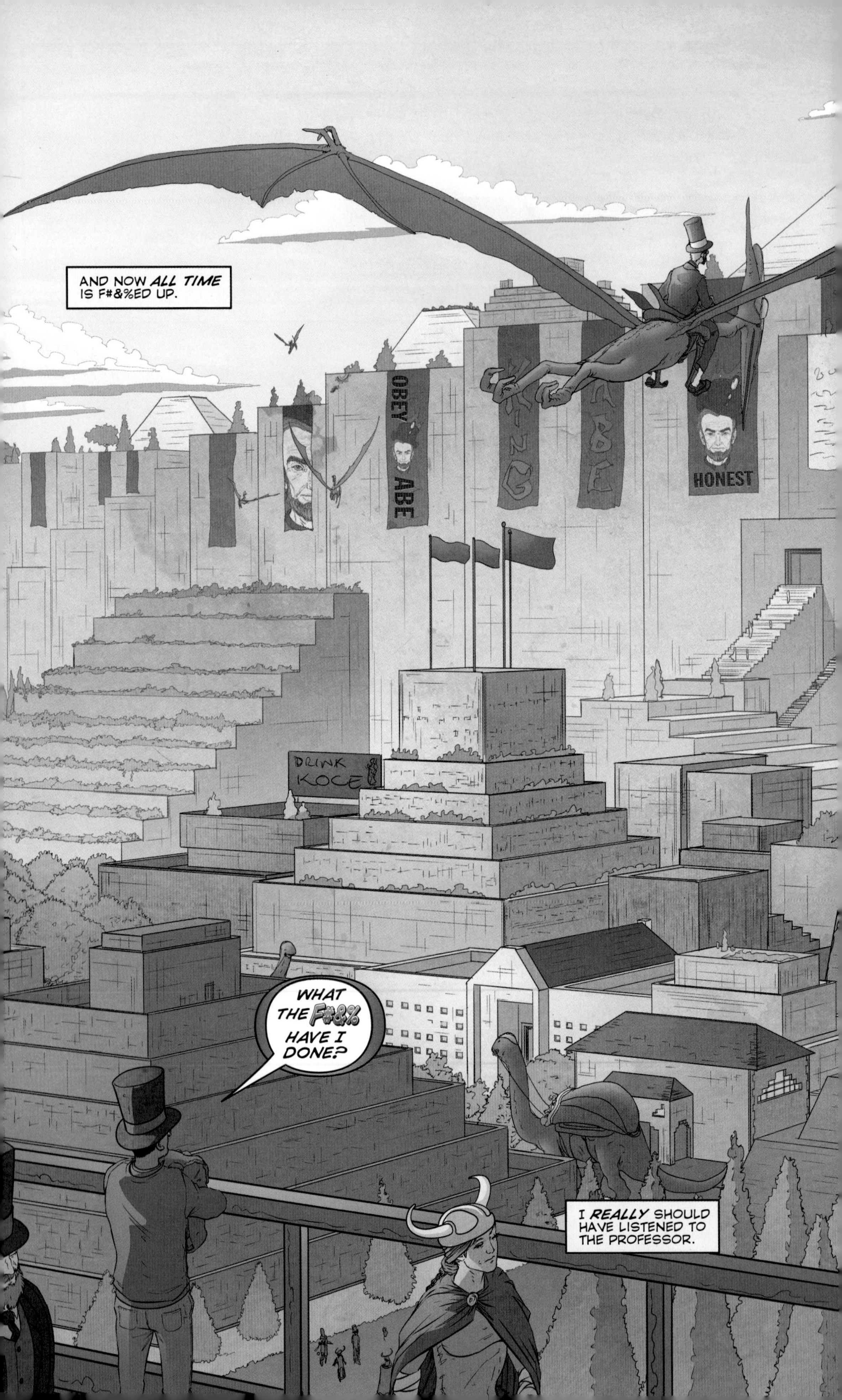
AND NOW *ALL TIME* IS F#&%ED UP.
OBEY ABE
KING ABE
HONEST
DRINK KOCE
WHAT THE F#&% HAVE I DONE?
I *REALLY* SHOULD HAVE LISTENED TO THE PROFESSOR.

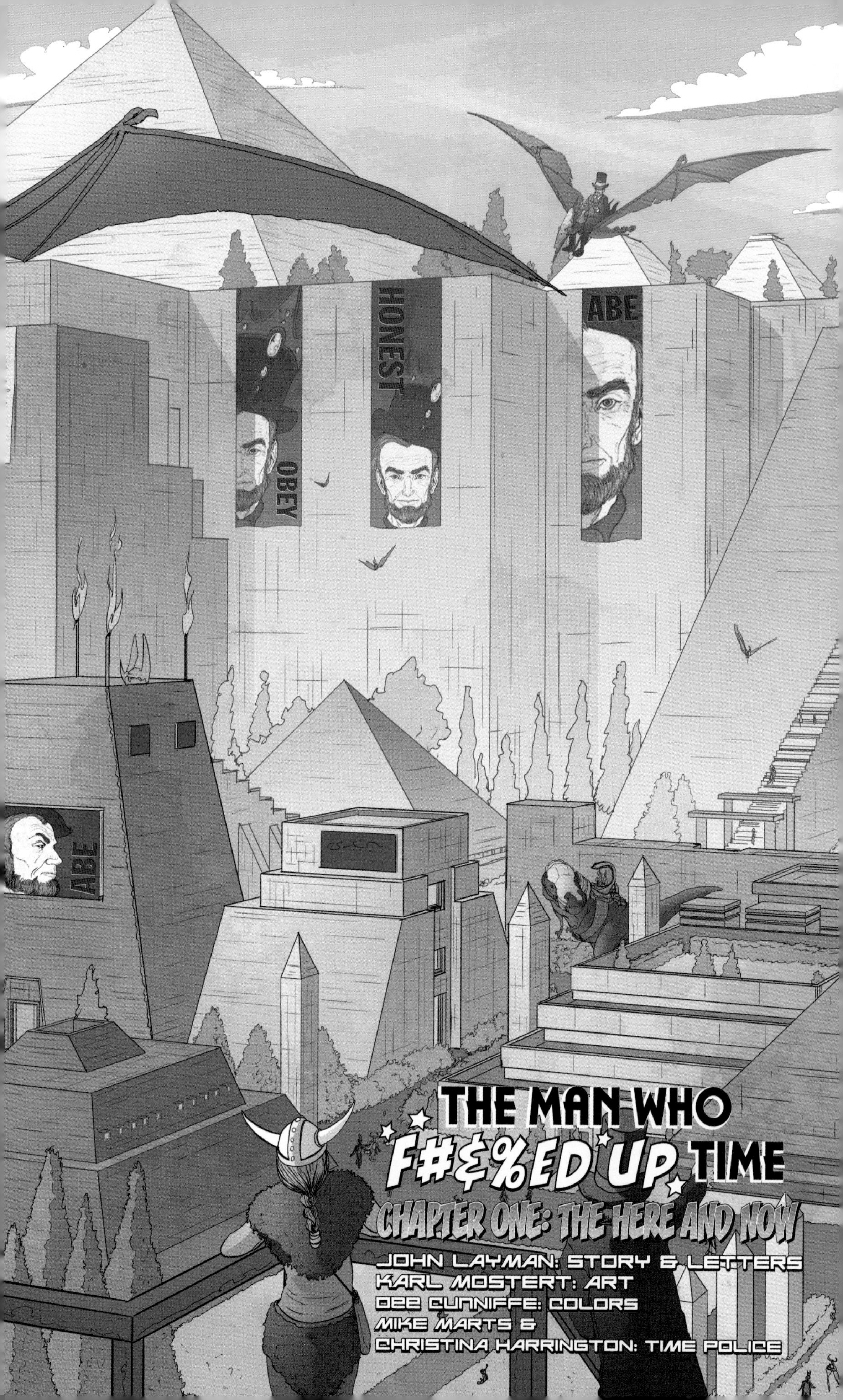
OBEY
HONEST
ABE
ABE
THE MAN WHO F#&%ED UP TIME
CHAPTER ONE: THE HERE AND NOW
JOHN LAYMAN: STORY & LETTERS
KARL MOSTERT: ART
DEB CUNNIFFE: COLORS
MIKE MARTS &
CHRISTINA HARRINGTON: TIME POLICE

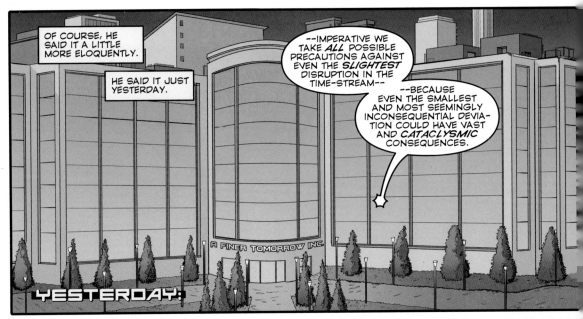

OF COURSE, HE SAID IT A LITTLE MORE ELOQUENTLY.

HE SAID IT JUST YESTERDAY.

--IMPERATIVE WE TAKE *ALL* POSSIBLE PRECAUTIONS AGAINST EVEN THE *SLIGHTEST* DISRUPTION IN THE TIME-STREAM--

--BECAUSE EVEN THE SMALLEST AND MOST SEEMINGLY INCONSEQUENTIAL DEVIATION COULD HAVE VAST AND *CATACLYSMIC* CONSEQUENCES.

A FINER TOMORROW INC.

YESTERDAY:

THAT'S *PROFESSOR KENDRICKS*--IN CHARGE OF THE TEMPORAL PHYSICS DEPARTMENT AT *A FINER TOMORROW LABORATORIES*.

I BELIEVE WE ARE READY.

PROFESSOR STOOCH AND *DR. COOKE* ARE THE OTHER PROJECT LEADS.

WHICH IS TO SAY THE THREE OF THEM MORE OR LESS *ARE* THE TEMPORAL PHYSICS DEPARTMENT.

SYSTEMS CHECK COMPLETE.

FIRE 'ER UP.

ALONG WITH *ME*.

SEAN BENNETT.

LAB ASSISTANT.

GOOD TO GO, SIR.

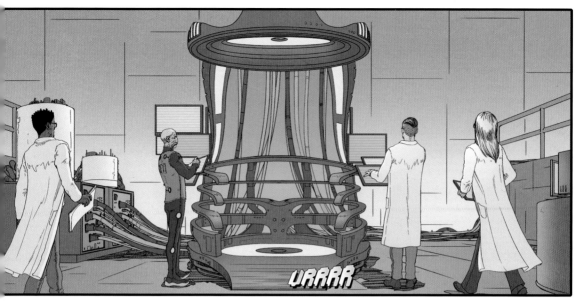

URRRR

URRRRRRRRRR

TWO MILLION YEARS EARLIER:

RRRRRRR

PLUCK

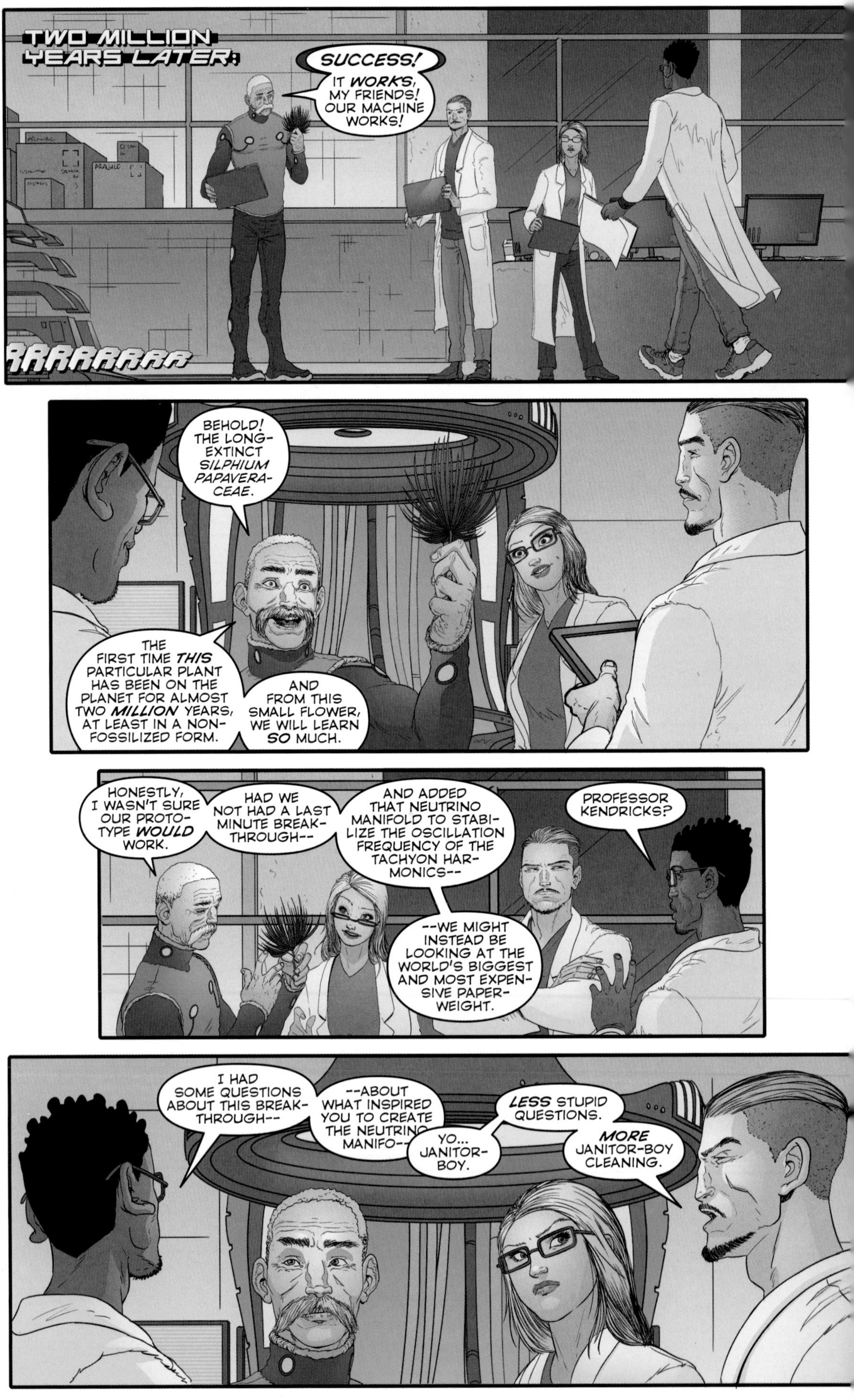
TWO MILLION YEARS LATER:
SUCCESS! IT WORKS, MY FRIENDS! OUR MACHINE WORKS!
RRRRRRRRR
BEHOLD! THE LONG-EXTINCT SILPHIUM PAPAVERACEAE.
THE FIRST TIME THIS PARTICULAR PLANT HAS BEEN ON THE PLANET FOR ALMOST TWO MILLION YEARS, AT LEAST IN A NON-FOSSILIZED FORM.
AND FROM THIS SMALL FLOWER, WE WILL LEARN SO MUCH.
HONESTLY, I WASN'T SURE OUR PROTOTYPE WOULD WORK.
HAD WE NOT HAD A LAST MINUTE BREAKTHROUGH--
AND ADDED THAT NEUTRINO MANIFOLD TO STABILIZE THE OSCILLATION FREQUENCY OF THE TACHYON HARMONICS--
--WE MIGHT INSTEAD BE LOOKING AT THE WORLD'S BIGGEST AND MOST EXPENSIVE PAPERWEIGHT.
PROFESSOR KENDRICKS?
I HAD SOME QUESTIONS ABOUT THIS BREAKTHROUGH--
--ABOUT WHAT INSPIRED YOU TO CREATE THE NEUTRINO MANIFO--
YO... JANITOR-BOY.
LESS STUPID QUESTIONS.
MORE JANITOR-BOY CLEANING.

I'M A *LAB ASSISTANT*, GRANT.

NOT A JANITOR.

THAT'S *DR. COOKE* TO YOU, SEAN. OR, IF YOU'D PREFER, "LAB ASSISTANT" BENNETT.

NOW, DR. COOKE, THIS *REALLY* ISN'T NECESSARY.

I ENJOY YOUNG MR. BENNETT'S ENTHUSIASM AND NATURAL CURIO--

I'M SURE YOU *DO*, PROFESSOR, BUT YOU'VE GOT *WORK* TO DO.

AND SO DOES *HE*.

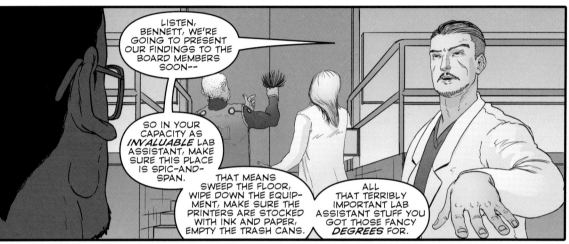

LISTEN, BENNETT, WE'RE GOING TO PRESENT OUR FINDINGS TO THE BOARD MEMBERS SOON--

SO IN YOUR CAPACITY AS *INVALUABLE* LAB ASSISTANT, MAKE SURE THIS PLACE IS SPIC-AND-SPAN.

THAT MEANS SWEEP THE FLOOR, WIPE DOWN THE EQUIPMENT, MAKE SURE THE PRINTERS ARE STOCKED WITH INK AND PAPER, EMPTY THE TRASH CANS.

ALL THAT TERRIBLY IMPORTANT LAB ASSISTANT STUFF YOU GOT THOSE FANCY *DEGREES* FOR.

OH, *THAT'S* RIGHT.

I'M THE ONE WITH THE DEGREES.

YOU'RE THE *DROPOUT*.

ONE MORE THING...

MAKE SURE YOU TIDY UP MY DESK BEFORE YOU *CLOCK OUT* FOR THE NIGHT.

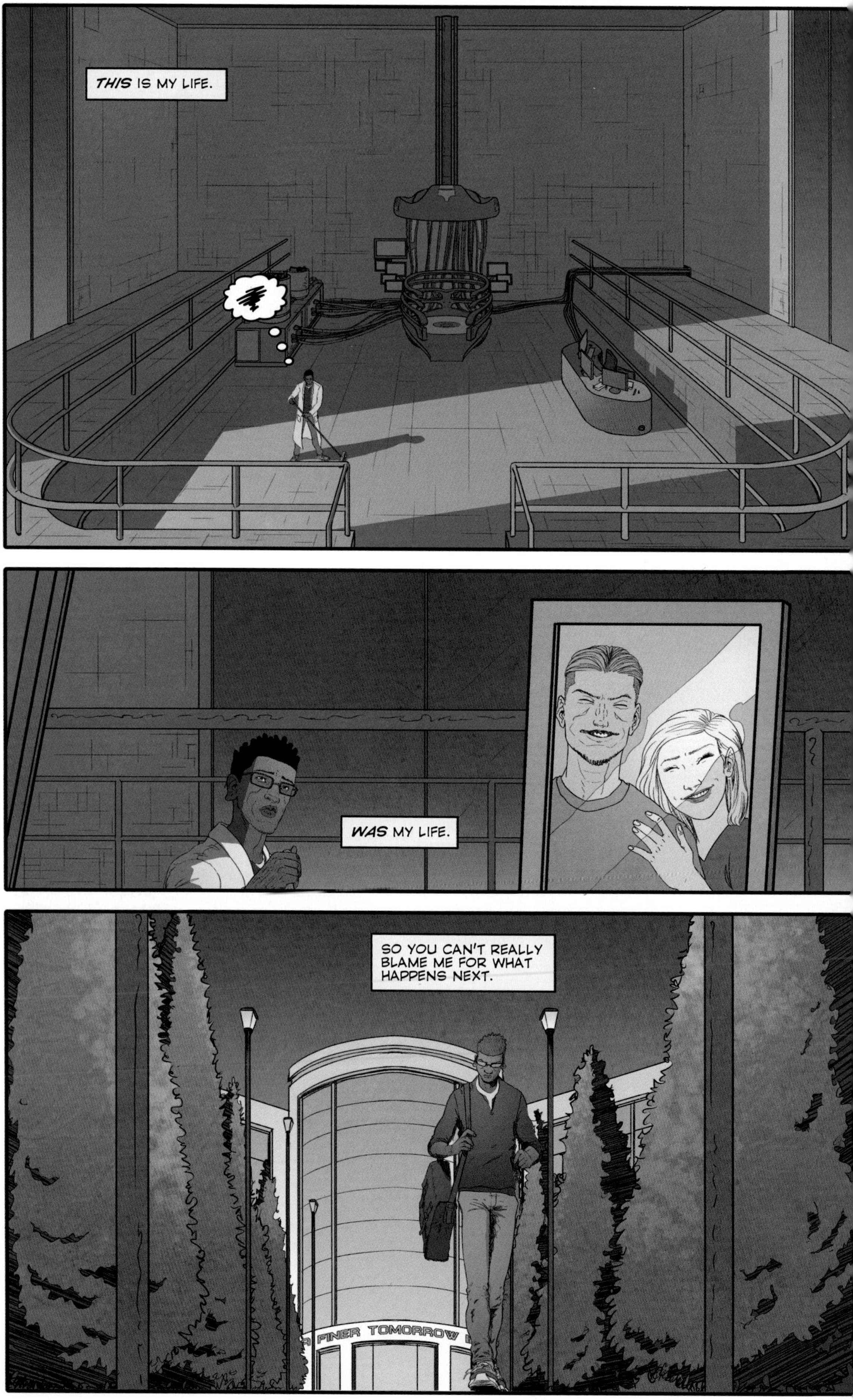
THIS IS MY LIFE.
WAS MY LIFE.
SO YOU CAN'T REALLY BLAME ME FOR WHAT HAPPENS NEXT.
FINER TOMORROW

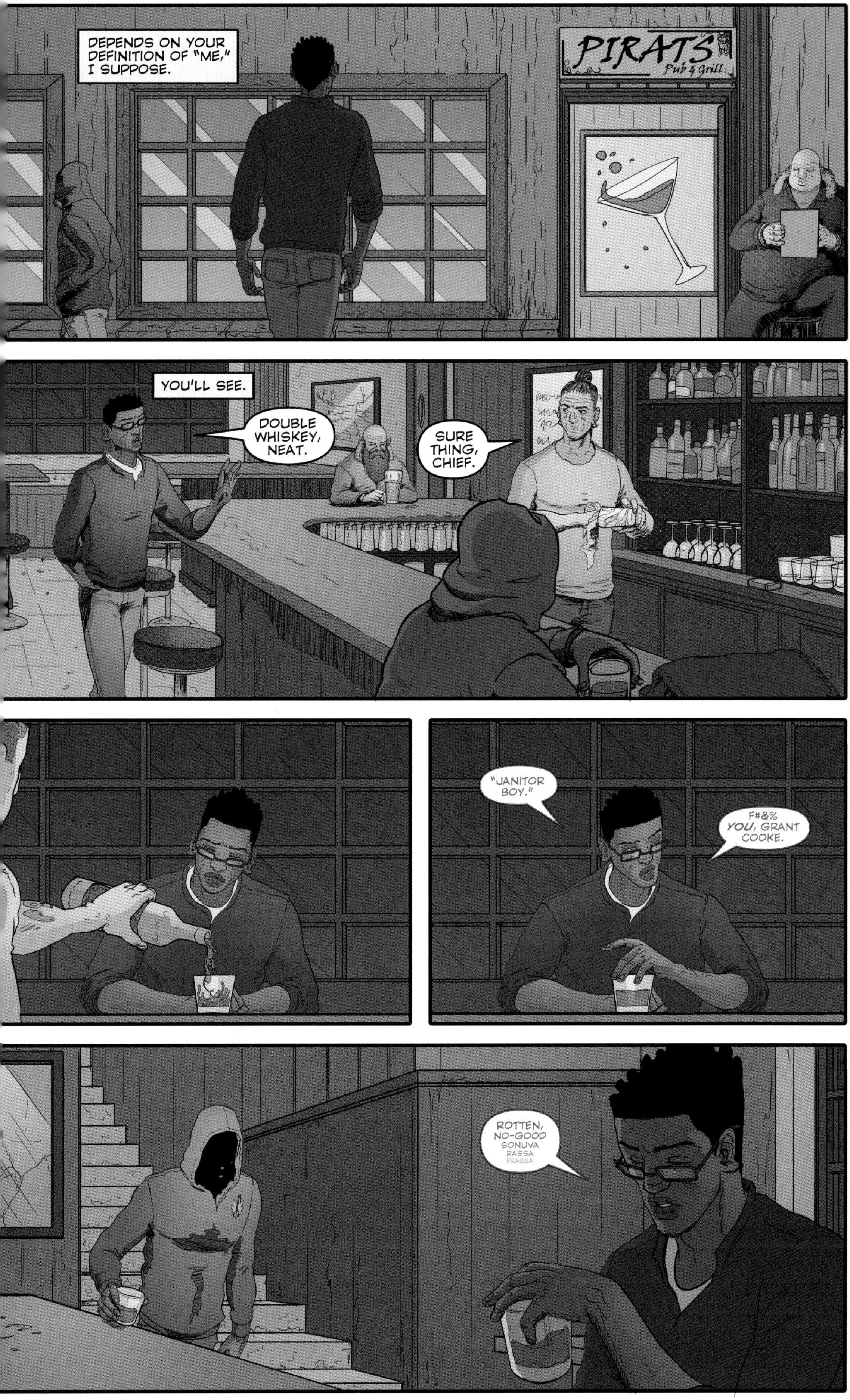
DEPENDS ON YOUR DEFINITION OF "ME," I SUPPOSE.
PIRATS
Pub & Grill
YOU'LL SEE.
DOUBLE WHISKEY, NEAT.
SURE THING, CHIEF.
"JANITOR BOY."
F#&% YOU, GRANT COOKE.
ROTTEN, NO-GOOD SONUVA RASSA FRASSA

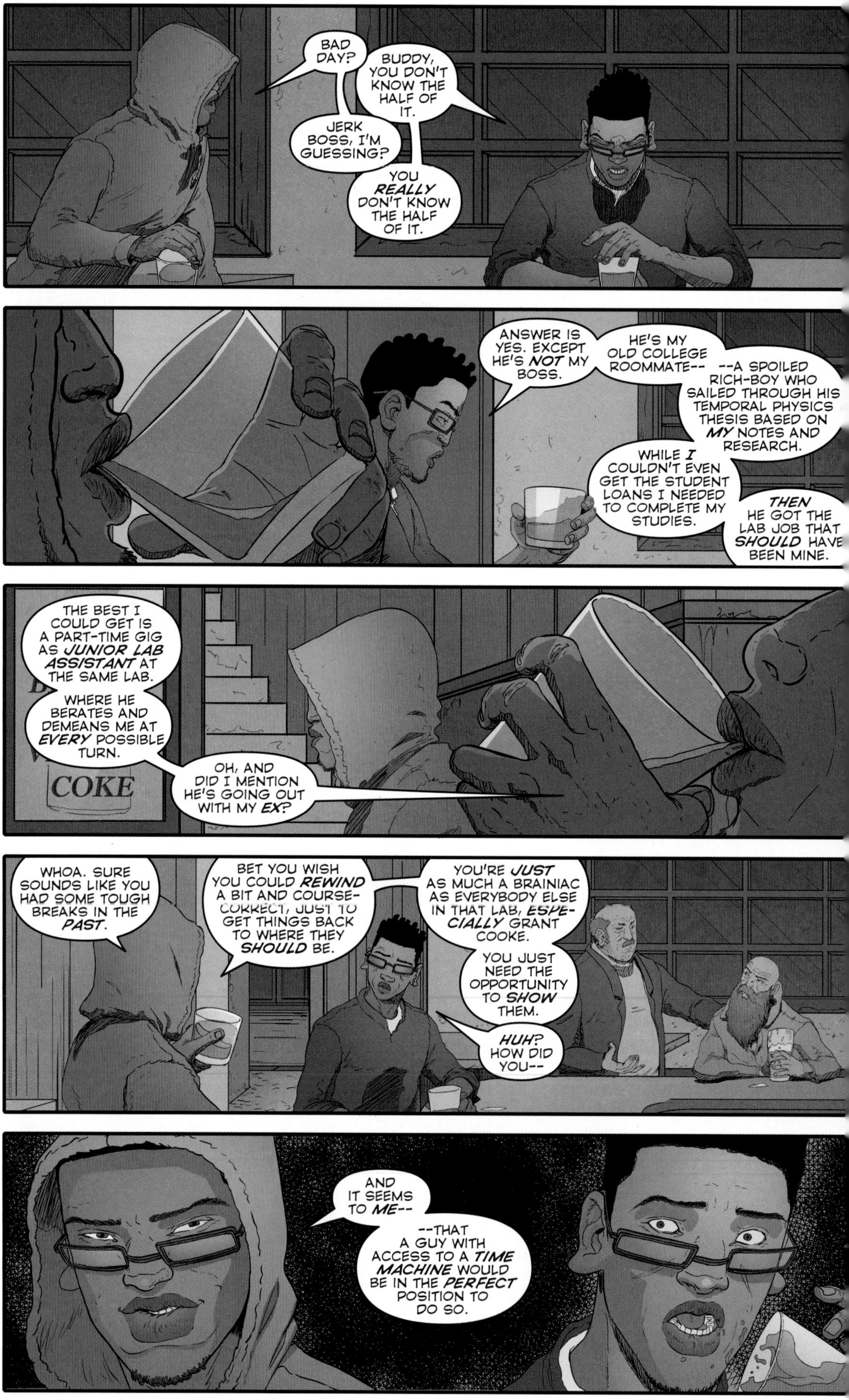
BAD DAY?
BUDDY, YOU DON'T KNOW THE HALF OF IT.
JERK BOSS, I'M GUESSING?
YOU *REALLY* DON'T KNOW THE HALF OF IT.
ANSWER IS YES. EXCEPT HE'S *NOT* MY BOSS.
HE'S MY OLD COLLEGE ROOMMATE--
--A SPOILED RICH-BOY WHO SAILED THROUGH HIS TEMPORAL PHYSICS THESIS BASED ON *MY* NOTES AND RESEARCH.
WHILE *I* COULDN'T EVEN GET THE STUDENT LOANS I NEEDED TO COMPLETE MY STUDIES.
THEN HE GOT THE LAB JOB THAT *SHOULD* HAVE BEEN MINE.
THE BEST I COULD GET IS A PART-TIME GIG AS *JUNIOR LAB ASSISTANT* AT THE SAME LAB.
WHERE HE BERATES AND DEMEANS ME AT *EVERY* POSSIBLE TURN.
COKE
OH, AND DID I MENTION HE'S GOING OUT WITH MY *EX*?
WHOA. SURE SOUNDS LIKE YOU HAD SOME TOUGH BREAKS IN THE *PAST*.
BET YOU WISH YOU COULD *REWIND* A BIT AND COURSE-CORRECT, JUST TO GET THINGS BACK TO WHERE THEY *SHOULD* BE.
YOU'RE *JUST* AS MUCH A BRAINIAC AS EVERYBODY ELSE IN THAT LAB, *ESPECIALLY* GRANT COOKE.
YOU JUST NEED THE OPPORTUNITY TO *SHOW* THEM.
HUH? HOW DID YOU--
AND IT SEEMS TO *ME*--
--THAT A GUY WITH ACCESS TO A *TIME MACHINE* WOULD BE IN THE *PERFECT* POSITION TO DO SO.

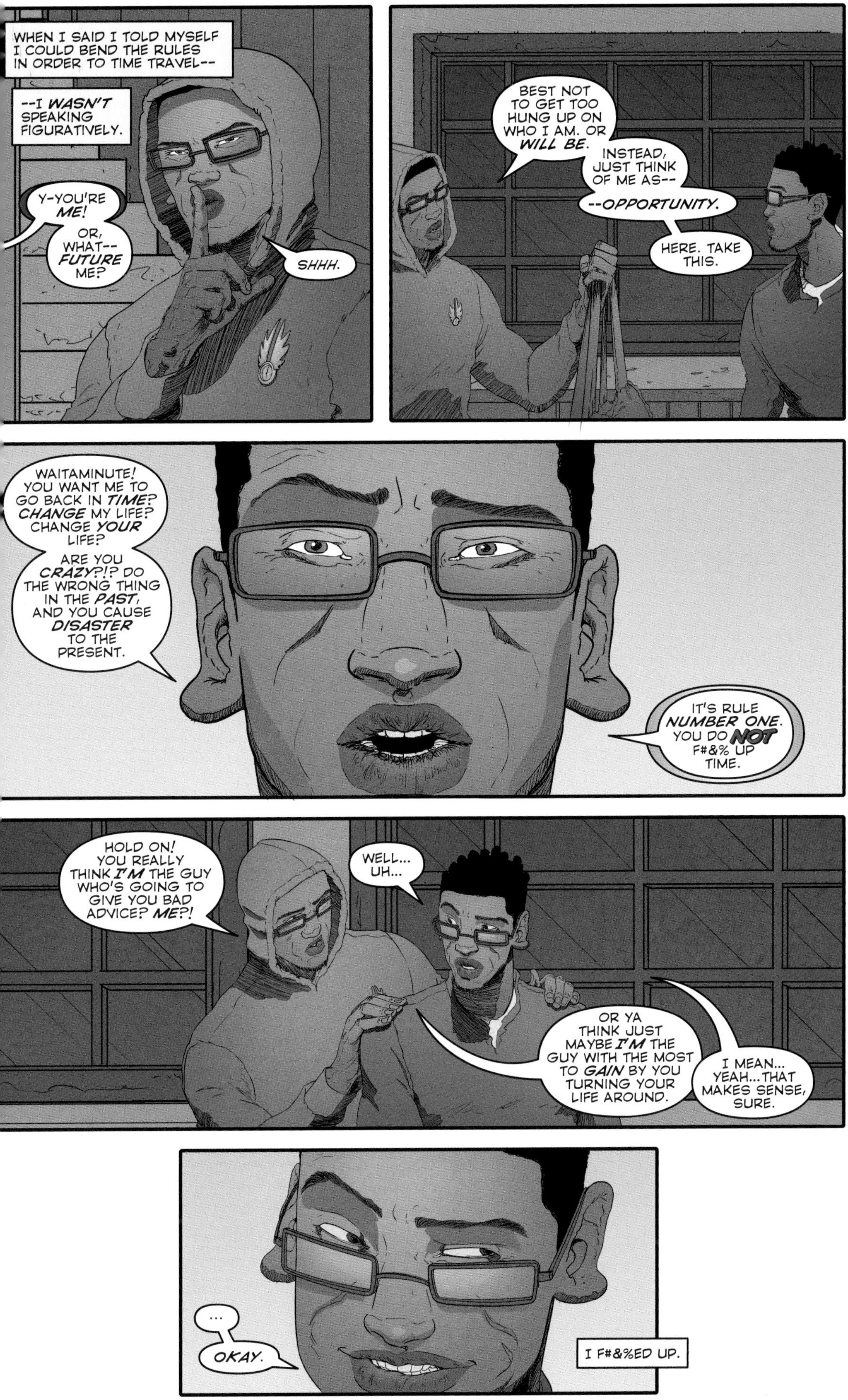
WHEN I SAID I TOLD MYSELF I COULD BEND THE RULES IN ORDER TO TIME TRAVEL--
--I WASN'T SPEAKING FIGURATIVELY.
Y-YOU'RE ME!
OR, WHAT-- FUTURE ME?
SHHH.
BEST NOT TO GET TOO HUNG UP ON WHO I AM. OR WILL BE.
INSTEAD, JUST THINK OF ME AS--
--OPPORTUNITY.
HERE. TAKE THIS.
WAITAMINUTE! YOU WANT ME TO GO BACK IN TIME? CHANGE MY LIFE? CHANGE YOUR LIFE?
ARE YOU CRAZY?!? DO THE WRONG THING IN THE PAST, AND YOU CAUSE DISASTER TO THE PRESENT.
IT'S RULE NUMBER ONE. YOU DO NOT F#&% UP TIME.
HOLD ON! YOU REALLY THINK I'M THE GUY WHO'S GOING TO GIVE YOU BAD ADVICE? ME?!
WELL... UH...
OR YA THINK JUST MAYBE I'M THE GUY WITH THE MOST TO GAIN BY YOU TURNING YOUR LIFE AROUND.
I MEAN... YEAH...THAT MAKES SENSE, SURE.
...
OKAY.
I F#&%ED UP.

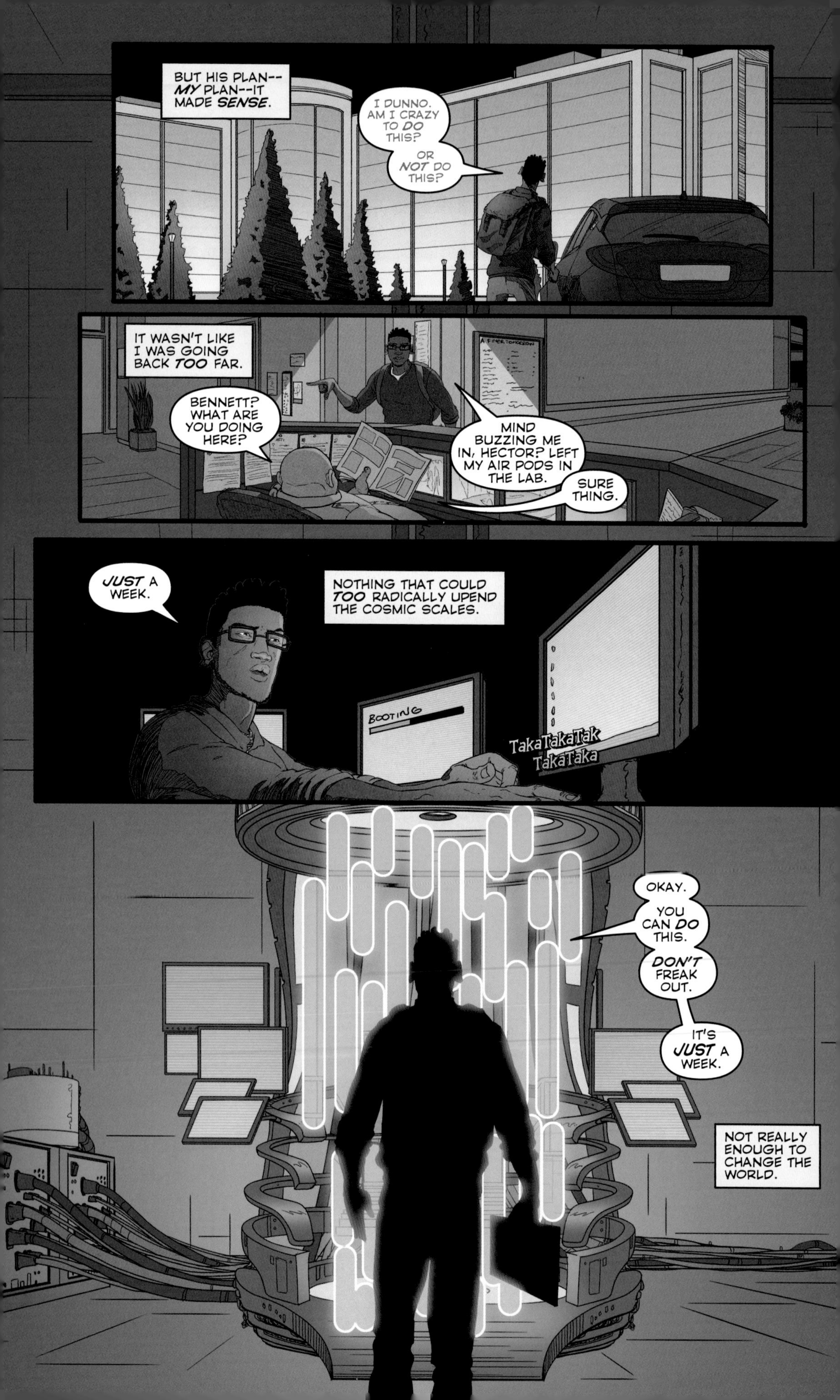

BUT HIS PLAN--MY PLAN--IT MADE SENSE.
I DUNNO. AM I CRAZY TO DO THIS?
OR NOT DO THIS?
IT WASN'T LIKE I WAS GOING BACK TOO FAR.
BENNETT? WHAT ARE YOU DOING HERE?
MIND BUZZING ME IN, HECTOR? LEFT MY AIR PODS IN THE LAB.
SURE THING.
JUST A WEEK.
NOTHING THAT COULD TOO RADICALLY UPEND THE COSMIC SCALES.
BOOTING
TakaTakaTak TakaTaka
OKAY.
YOU CAN DO THIS.
DON'T FREAK OUT.
IT'S JUST A WEEK.
NOT REALLY ENOUGH TO CHANGE THE WORLD.

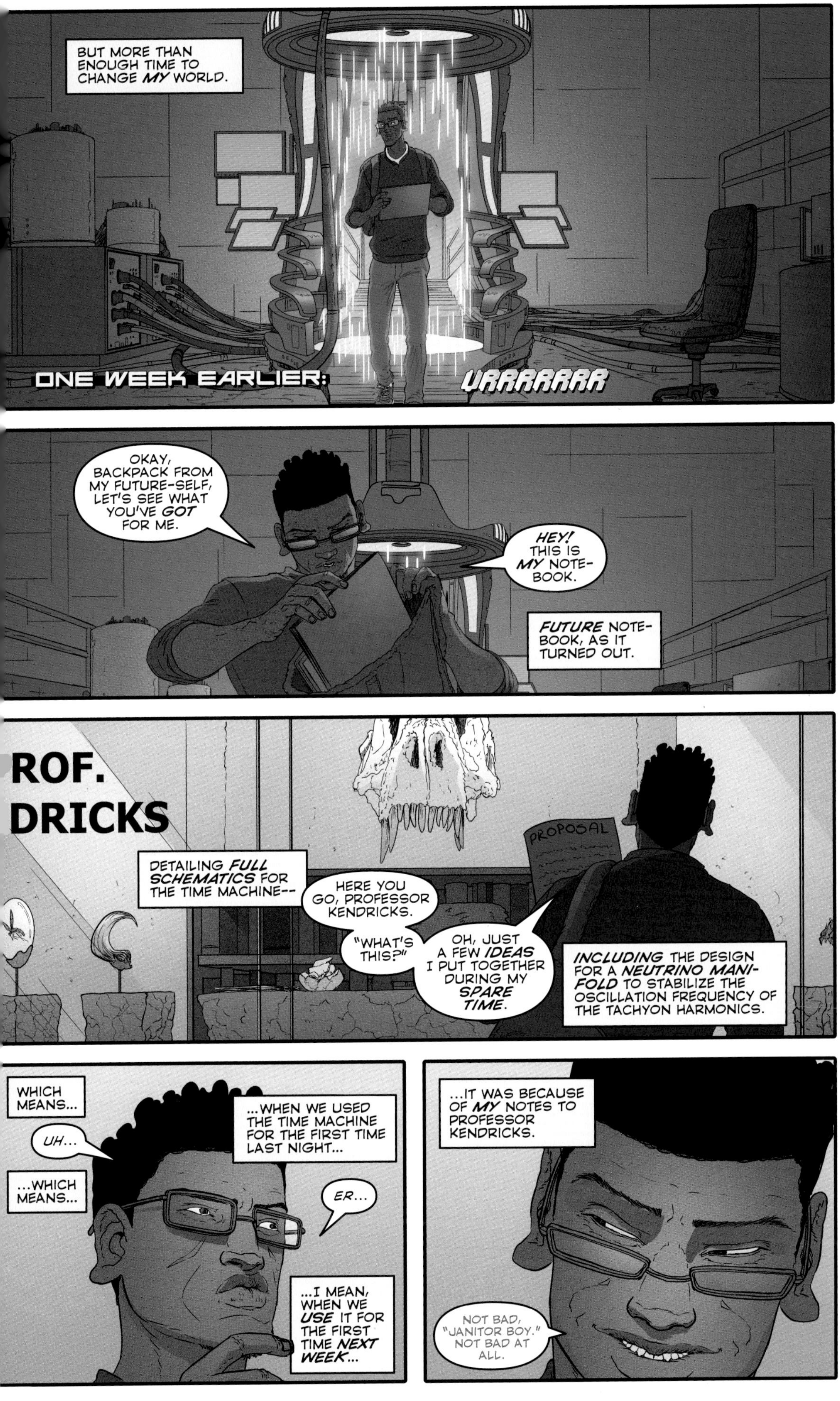

BUT MORE THAN ENOUGH TIME TO CHANGE MY WORLD.
ONE WEEK EARLIER:
URRRRRRR
OKAY, BACKPACK FROM MY FUTURE-SELF, LET'S SEE WHAT YOU'VE GOT FOR ME.
HEY! THIS IS MY NOTE-BOOK.
FUTURE NOTE-BOOK, AS IT TURNED OUT.
ROF. DRICKS
PROPOSAL
DETAILING FULL SCHEMATICS FOR THE TIME MACHINE--
HERE YOU GO, PROFESSOR KENDRICKS.
"WHAT'S THIS?"
OH, JUST A FEW IDEAS I PUT TOGETHER DURING MY SPARE TIME.
INCLUDING THE DESIGN FOR A NEUTRINO MANI-FOLD TO STABILIZE THE OSCILLATION FREQUENCY OF THE TACHYON HARMONICS.
WHICH MEANS...
UH...
...WHEN WE USED THE TIME MACHINE FOR THE FIRST TIME LAST NIGHT...
...WHICH MEANS...
ER...
...I MEAN, WHEN WE USE IT FOR THE FIRST TIME NEXT WEEK...
...IT WAS BECAUSE OF MY NOTES TO PROFESSOR KENDRICKS.
NOT BAD, "JANITOR BOY." NOT BAD AT ALL.

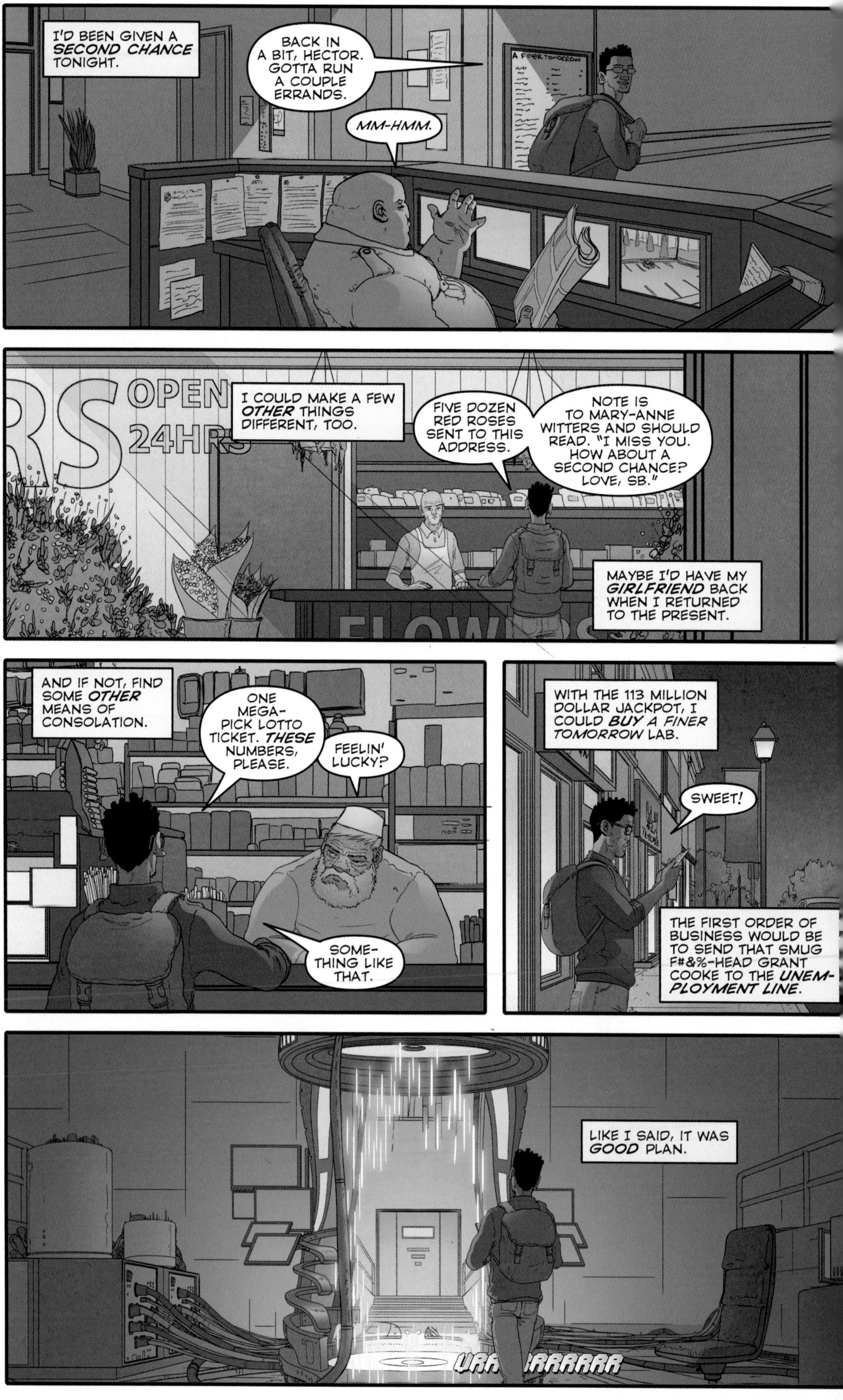
I'D BEEN GIVEN A SECOND CHANCE TONIGHT.
BACK IN A BIT, HECTOR. GOTTA RUN A COUPLE ERRANDS.
MM-HMM.
A FINER TOMORROW
OPEN 24HRS
I COULD MAKE A FEW OTHER THINGS DIFFERENT, TOO.
FIVE DOZEN RED ROSES SENT TO THIS ADDRESS.
NOTE IS TO MARY-ANNE WITTERS AND SHOULD READ. "I MISS YOU. HOW ABOUT A SECOND CHANCE? LOVE, SB."
MAYBE I'D HAVE MY GIRLFRIEND BACK WHEN I RETURNED TO THE PRESENT.
AND IF NOT, FIND SOME OTHER MEANS OF CONSOLATION.
ONE MEGA-PICK LOTTO TICKET. THESE NUMBERS, PLEASE.
FEELIN' LUCKY?
SOME-THING LIKE THAT.
WITH THE 113 MILLION DOLLAR JACKPOT, I COULD BUY A FINER TOMORROW LAB.
SWEET!
THE FIRST ORDER OF BUSINESS WOULD BE TO SEND THAT SMUG F#&%-HEAD GRANT COOKE TO THE UNEMPLOYMENT LINE.
LIKE I SAID, IT WAS GOOD PLAN.
URR IRRRRRRR

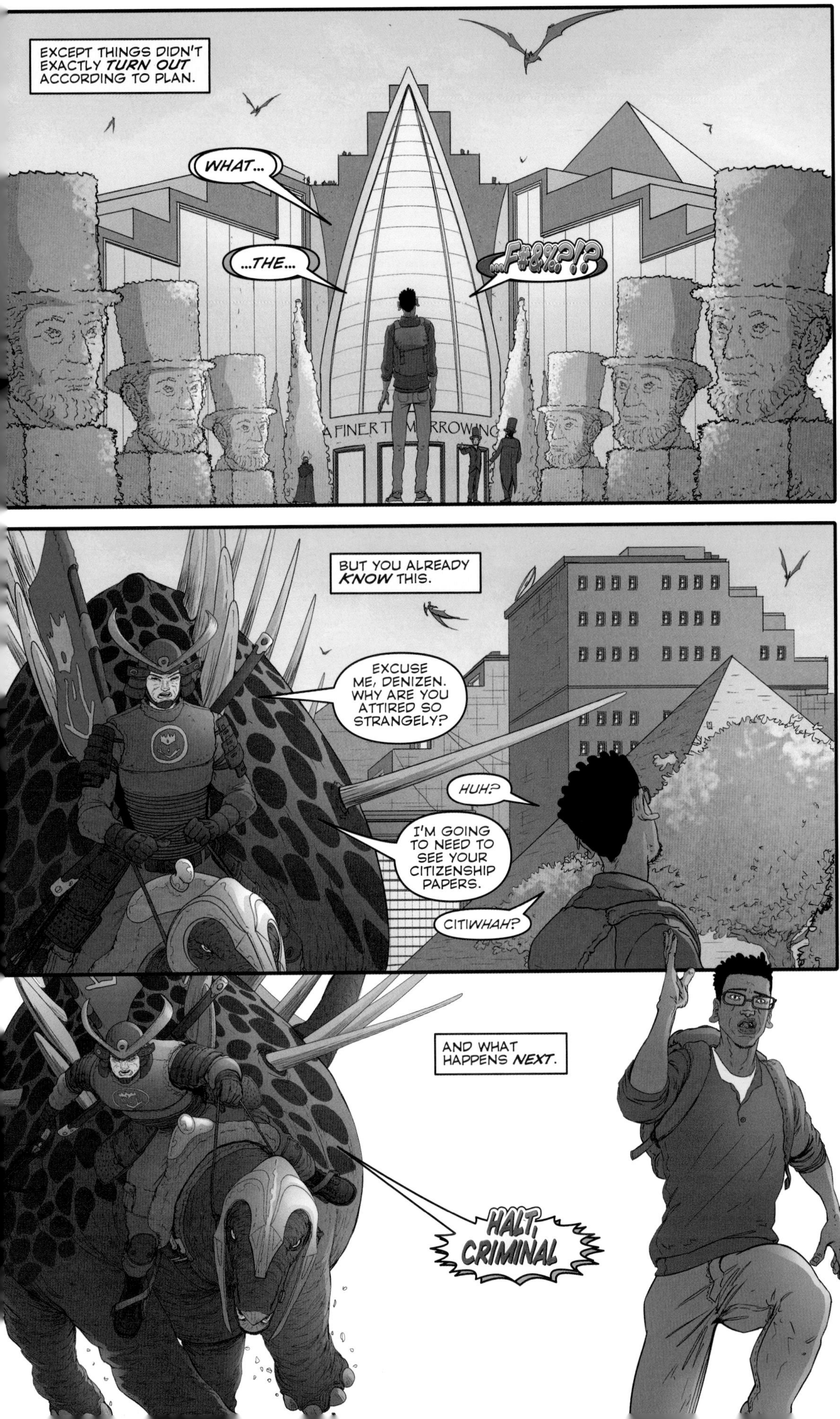
EXCEPT THINGS DIDN'T EXACTLY TURN OUT ACCORDING TO PLAN.
WHAT...
...THE...
...F#&%?!?
A FINER T MORROWING
BUT YOU ALREADY KNOW THIS.
EXCUSE ME, DENIZEN. WHY ARE YOU ATTIRED SO STRANGELY?
HUH?
I'M GOING TO NEED TO SEE YOUR CITIZENSHIP PAPERS.
CITIWHAH?
AND WHAT HAPPENS NEXT.
HALT, CRIMINAL

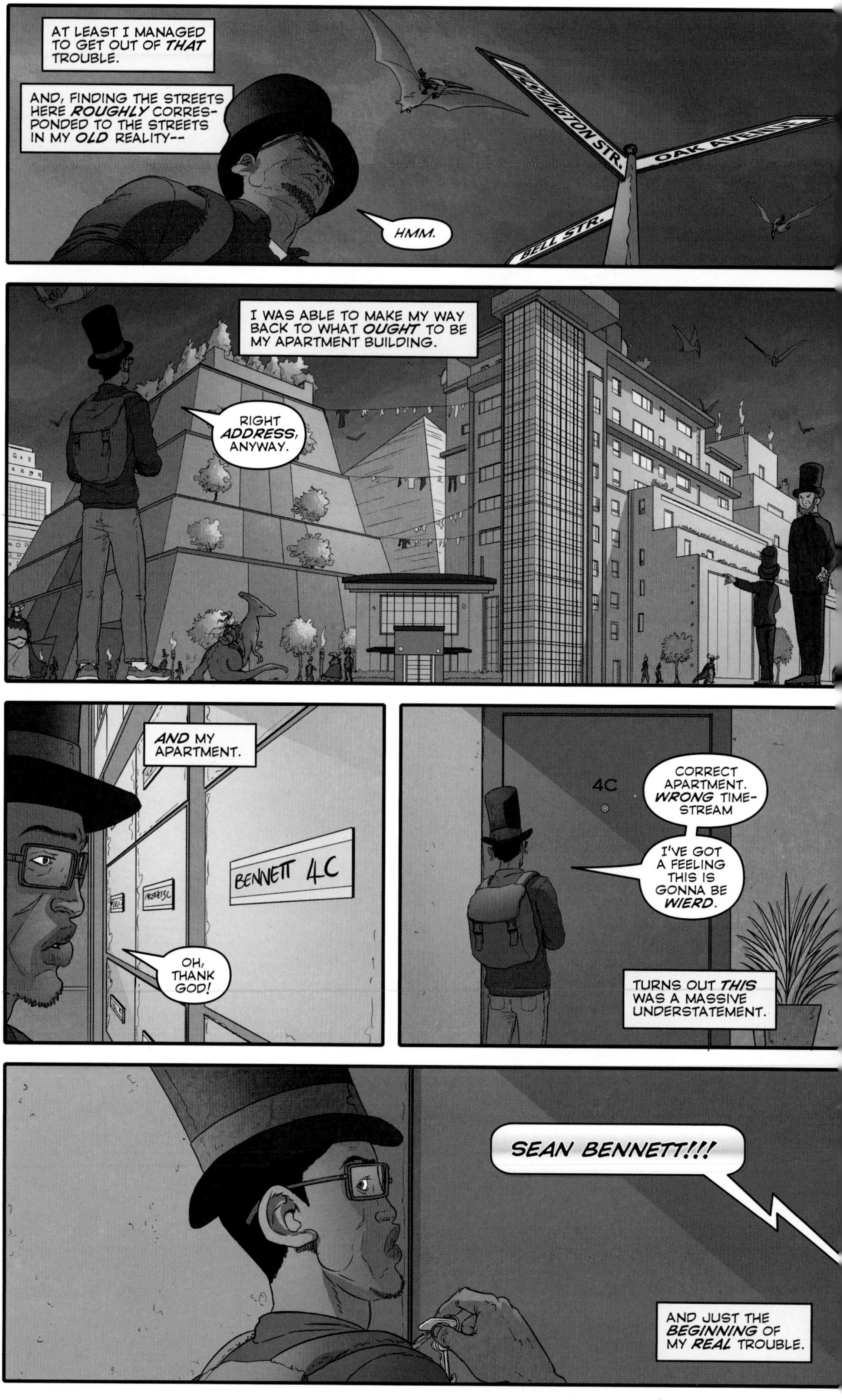
AT LEAST I MANAGED TO GET OUT OF THAT TROUBLE.
AND, FINDING THE STREETS HERE ROUGHLY CORRESPONDED TO THE STREETS IN MY OLD REALITY--
WASHINGTON STR.
OAK AVENUE
BELL STR.
HMM.
I WAS ABLE TO MAKE MY WAY BACK TO WHAT OUGHT TO BE MY APARTMENT BUILDING.
RIGHT ADDRESS, ANYWAY.
AND MY APARTMENT.
BENNETT 4C
OH, THANK GOD!
4C
CORRECT APARTMENT. WRONG TIME-STREAM
I'VE GOT A FEELING THIS IS GONNA BE WIERD.
TURNS OUT THIS WAS A MASSIVE UNDERSTATEMENT.
SEAN BENNETT!!!
AND JUST THE BEGINNING OF MY REAL TROUBLE.

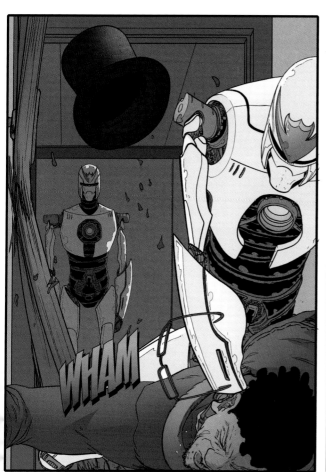

WHAM

WHA-- WHAT'S HAPPENING?

WHO *ARE* YOU?

FUTURE POLICE.

TEMPORAL CRIME PREVENTION.

YOU'VE MADE UNAUTHORIZED *ALTERATIONS* TO THE TIME-STREAM.

FELONY ALTERATIONS.

WE'RE GOING TO GIVE YOU *TWO DAYS* TO REPAIR THE DAMAGE YOU'VE DONE.

EVERY LAST *BIT* OF IT.

OR *ELSE*.

O-OR ELSE?

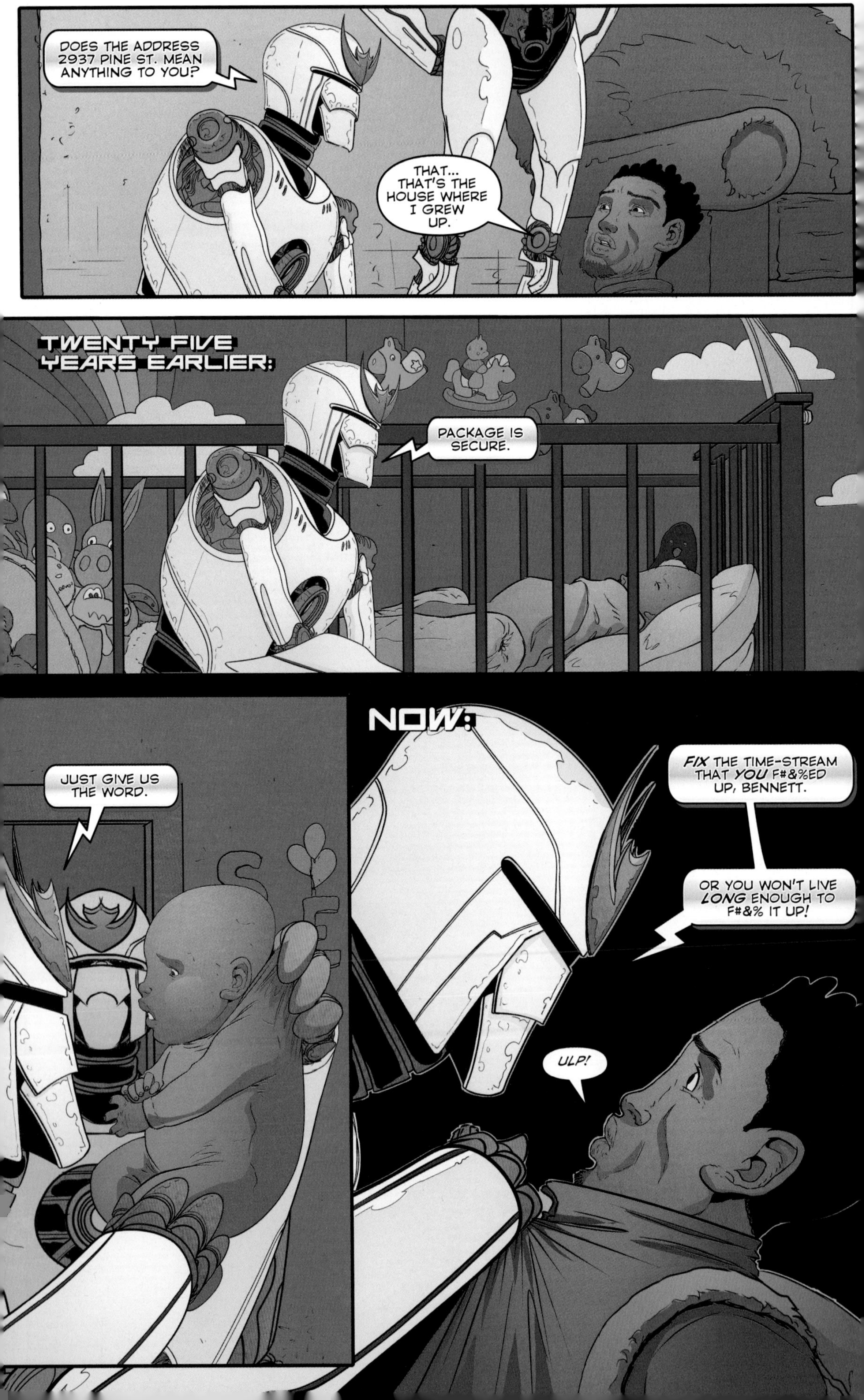
DOES THE ADDRESS 2937 PINE ST. MEAN ANYTHING TO YOU?
THAT... THAT'S THE HOUSE WHERE I GREW UP.
TWENTY FIVE YEARS EARLIER:
PACKAGE IS SECURE.
JUST GIVE US THE WORD.
NOW:
FIX THE TIME-STREAM THAT YOU F#&%ED UP, BENNETT.
OR YOU WON'T LIVE LONG ENOUGH TO F#&% IT UP!
ULP!

2

JUST IN TIME

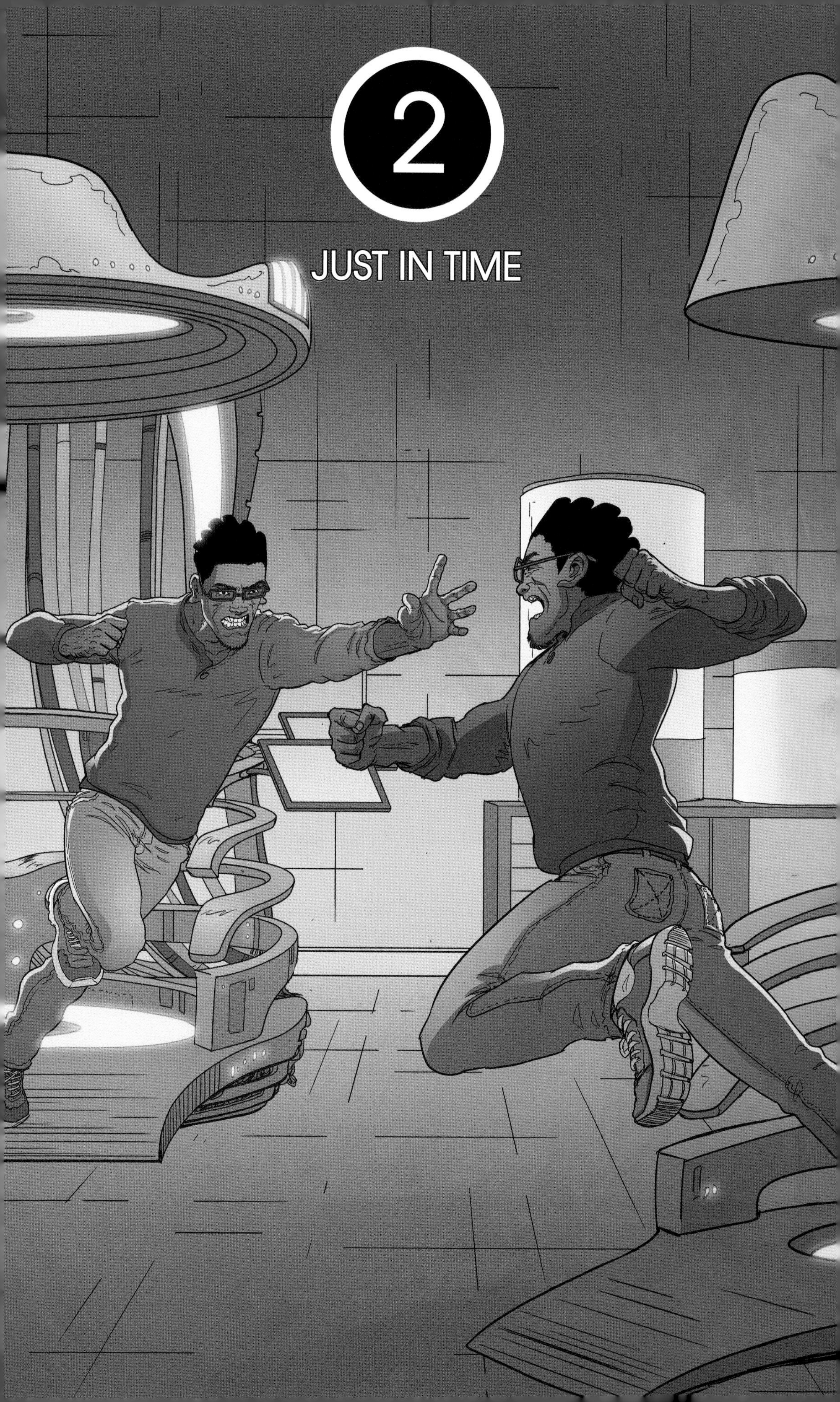

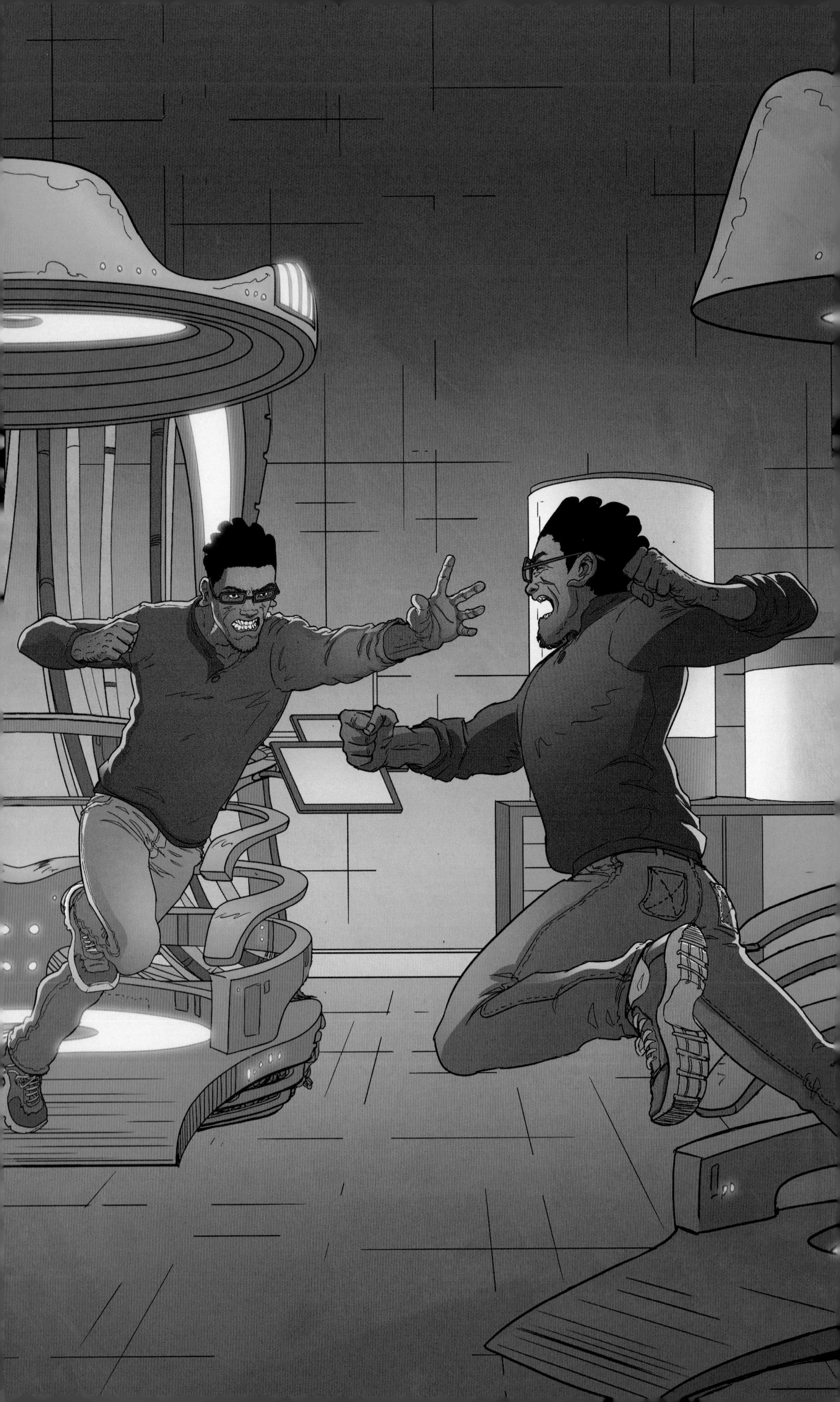

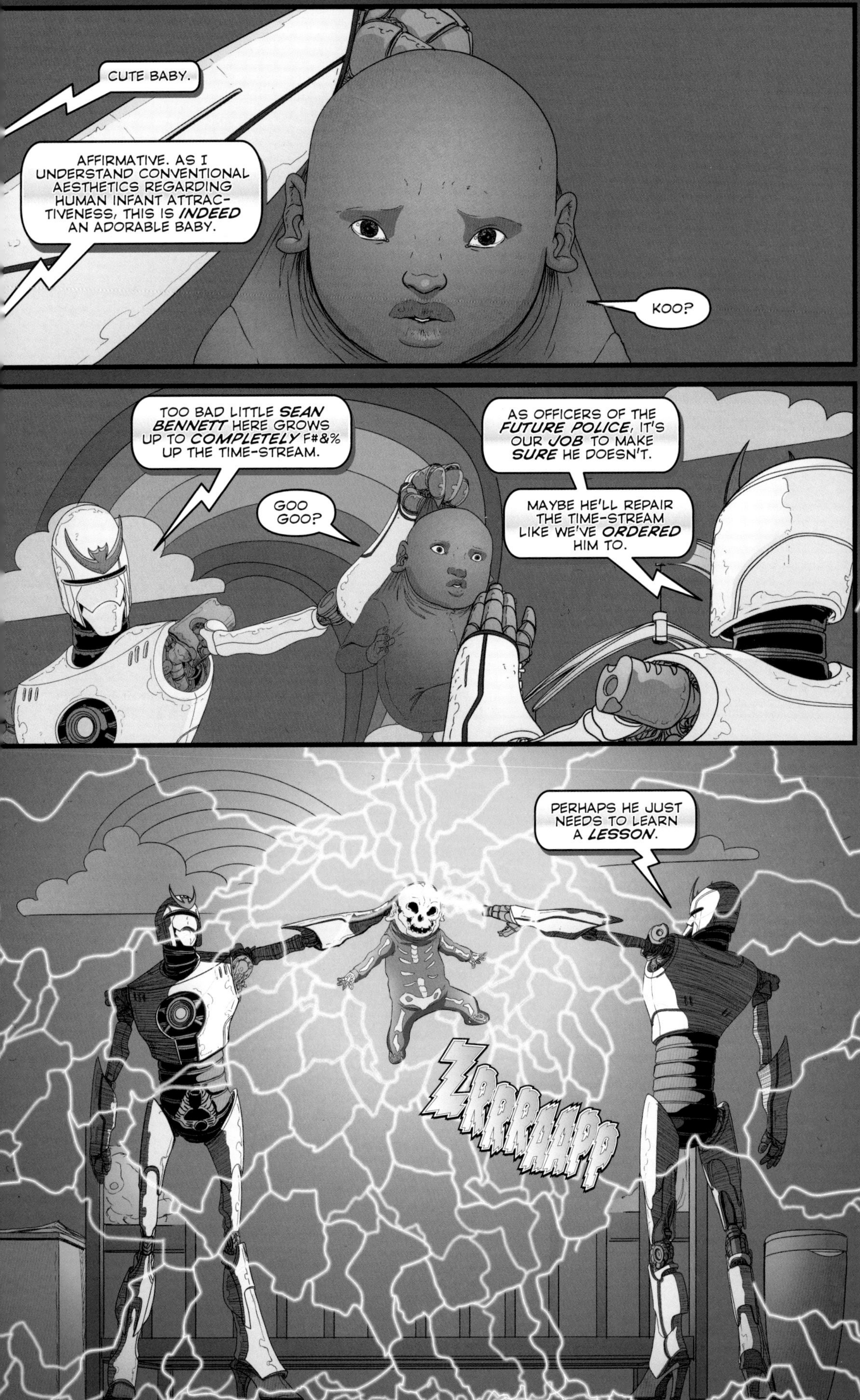
CUTE BABY.
AFFIRMATIVE. AS I UNDERSTAND CONVENTIONAL AESTHETICS REGARDING HUMAN INFANT ATTRACTIVENESS, THIS IS INDEED AN ADORABLE BABY.
KOO?
TOO BAD LITTLE SEAN BENNETT HERE GROWS UP TO COMPLETELY F#&% UP THE TIME-STREAM.
GOO GOO?
AS OFFICERS OF THE FUTURE POLICE, IT'S OUR JOB TO MAKE SURE HE DOESN'T.
MAYBE HE'LL REPAIR THE TIME-STREAM LIKE WE'VE ORDERED HIM TO.
PERHAPS HE JUST NEEDS TO LEARN A LESSON.
ZRRRAAAPP

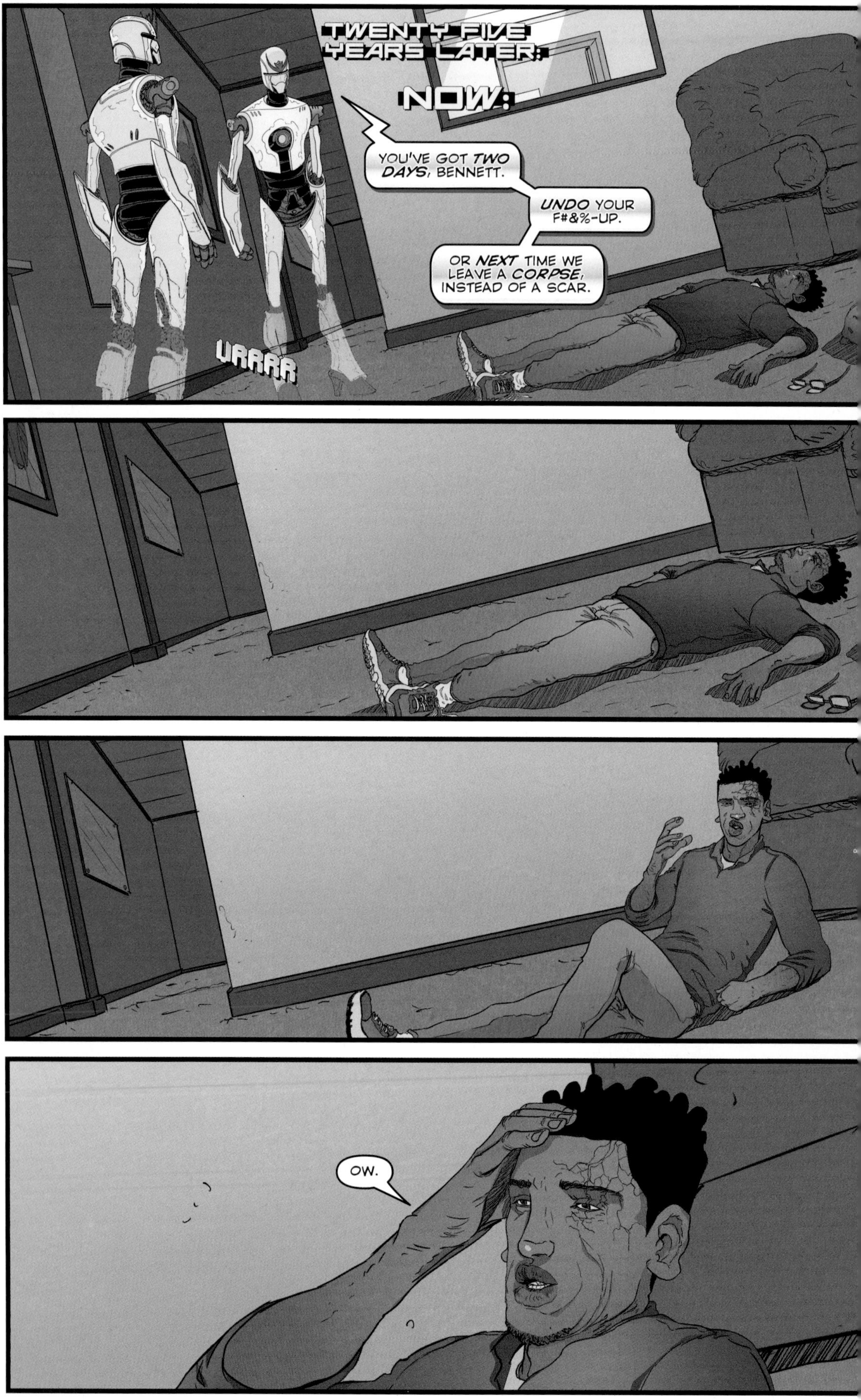
TWENTY FIVE YEARS LATER:
NOW:
YOU'VE GOT TWO DAYS, BENNETT.
UNDO YOUR F#&%-UP.
OR NEXT TIME WE LEAVE A CORPSE, INSTEAD OF A SCAR.
URRRR
OW.

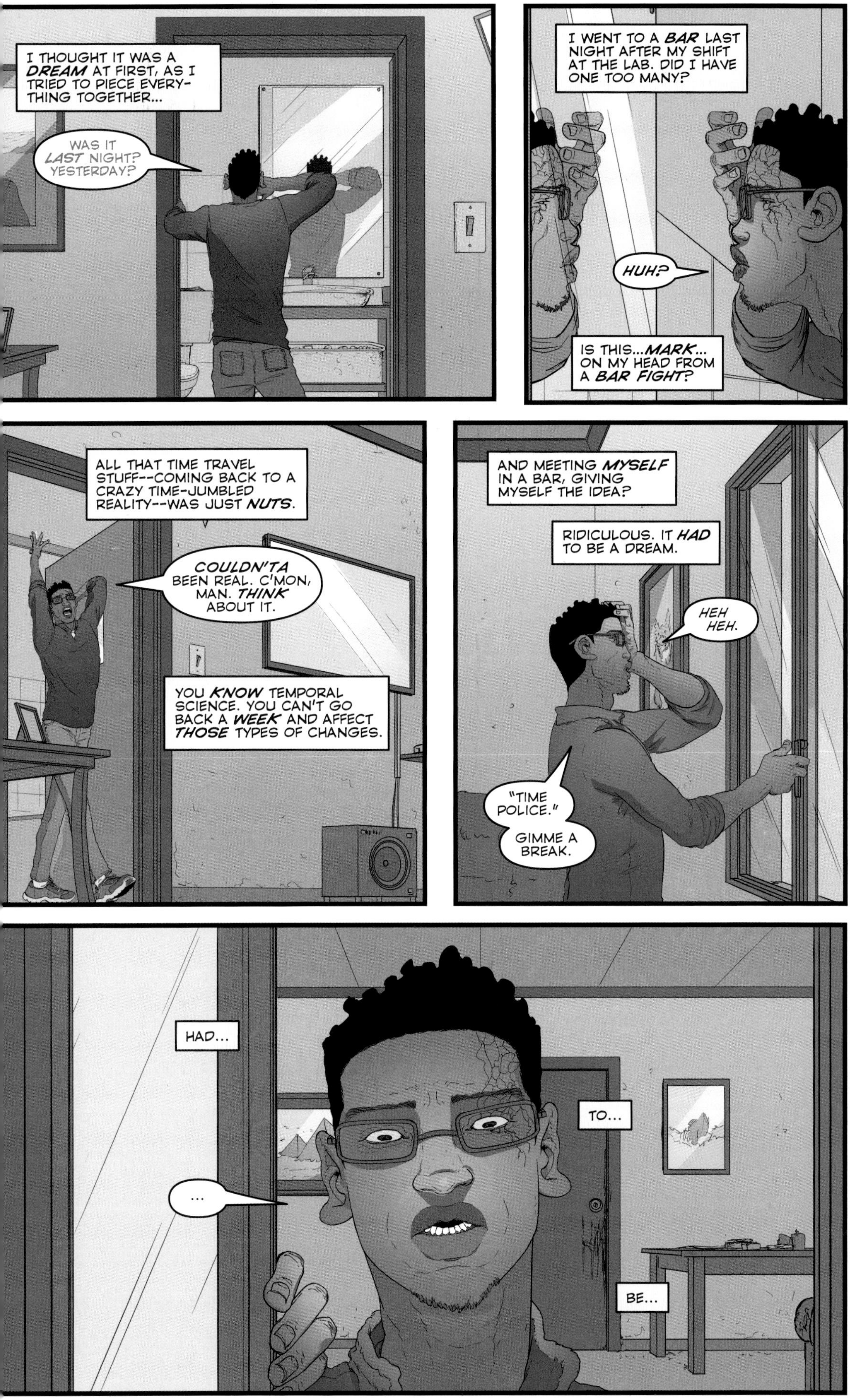

I THOUGHT IT WAS A DREAM AT FIRST, AS I TRIED TO PIECE EVERY-THING TOGETHER...
WAS IT LAST NIGHT? YESTERDAY?
I WENT TO A BAR LAST NIGHT AFTER MY SHIFT AT THE LAB. DID I HAVE ONE TOO MANY?
HUH?
IS THIS...MARK... ON MY HEAD FROM A BAR FIGHT?
ALL THAT TIME TRAVEL STUFF--COMING BACK TO A CRAZY TIME-JUMBLED REALITY--WAS JUST NUTS.
COULDN'TA BEEN REAL. C'MON, MAN. THINK ABOUT IT.
YOU KNOW TEMPORAL SCIENCE. YOU CAN'T GO BACK A WEEK AND AFFECT THOSE TYPES OF CHANGES.
AND MEETING MYSELF IN A BAR, GIVING MYSELF THE IDEA?
RIDICULOUS. IT HAD TO BE A DREAM.
HEH HEH.
"TIME POLICE."
GIMME A BREAK.
HAD...
TO...
...
BE...

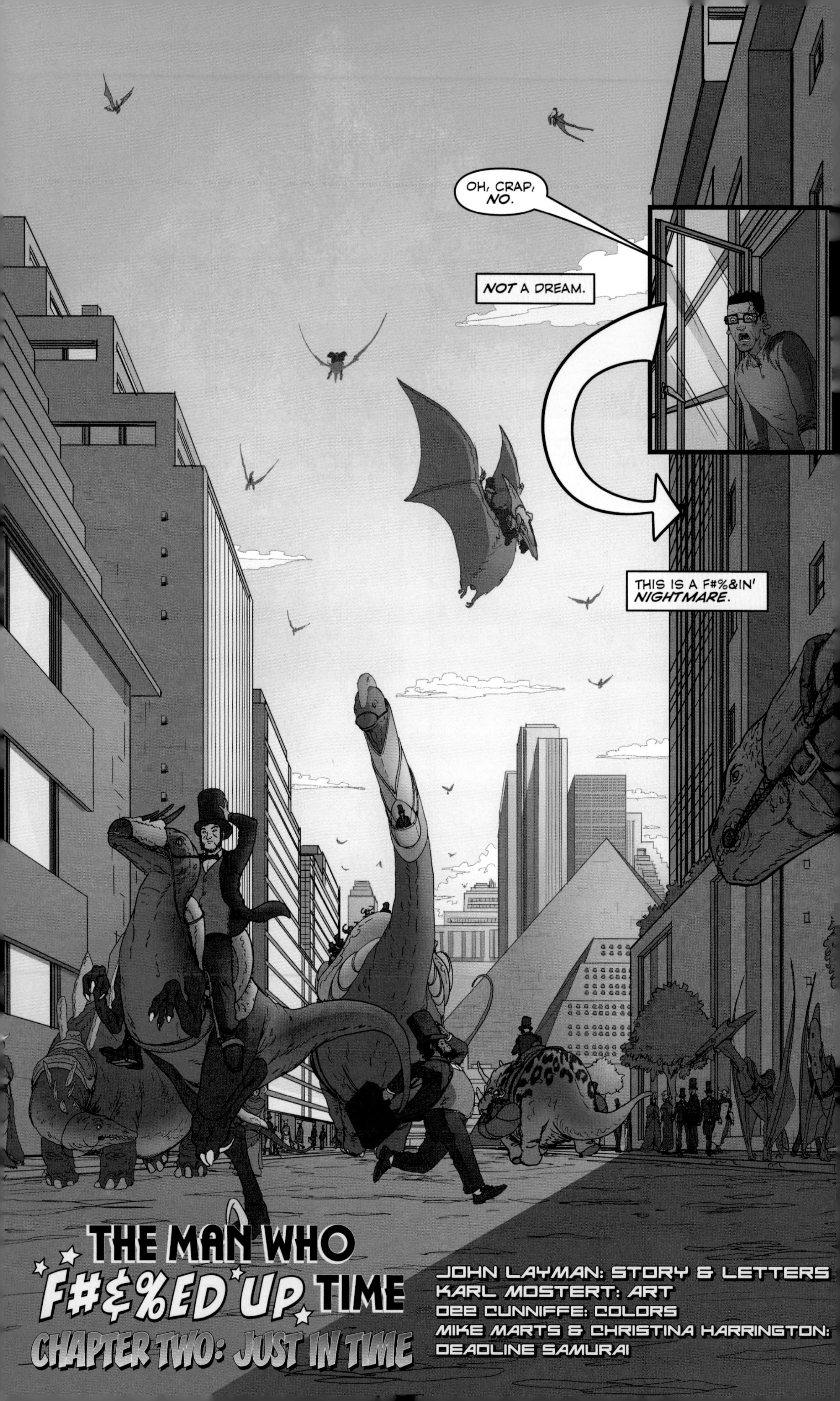
OH, CRAP, NO.
NOT A DREAM.
THIS IS A F#%&IN' NIGHTMARE.
THE MAN WHO F#&%ED UP TIME
CHAPTER TWO: JUST IN TIME
JOHN LAYMAN: STORY & LETTERS
KARL MOSTERT: ART
DEE CUNNIFFE: COLORS
MIKE MARTS & CHRISTINA HARRINGTON: DEADLINE SAMURAI

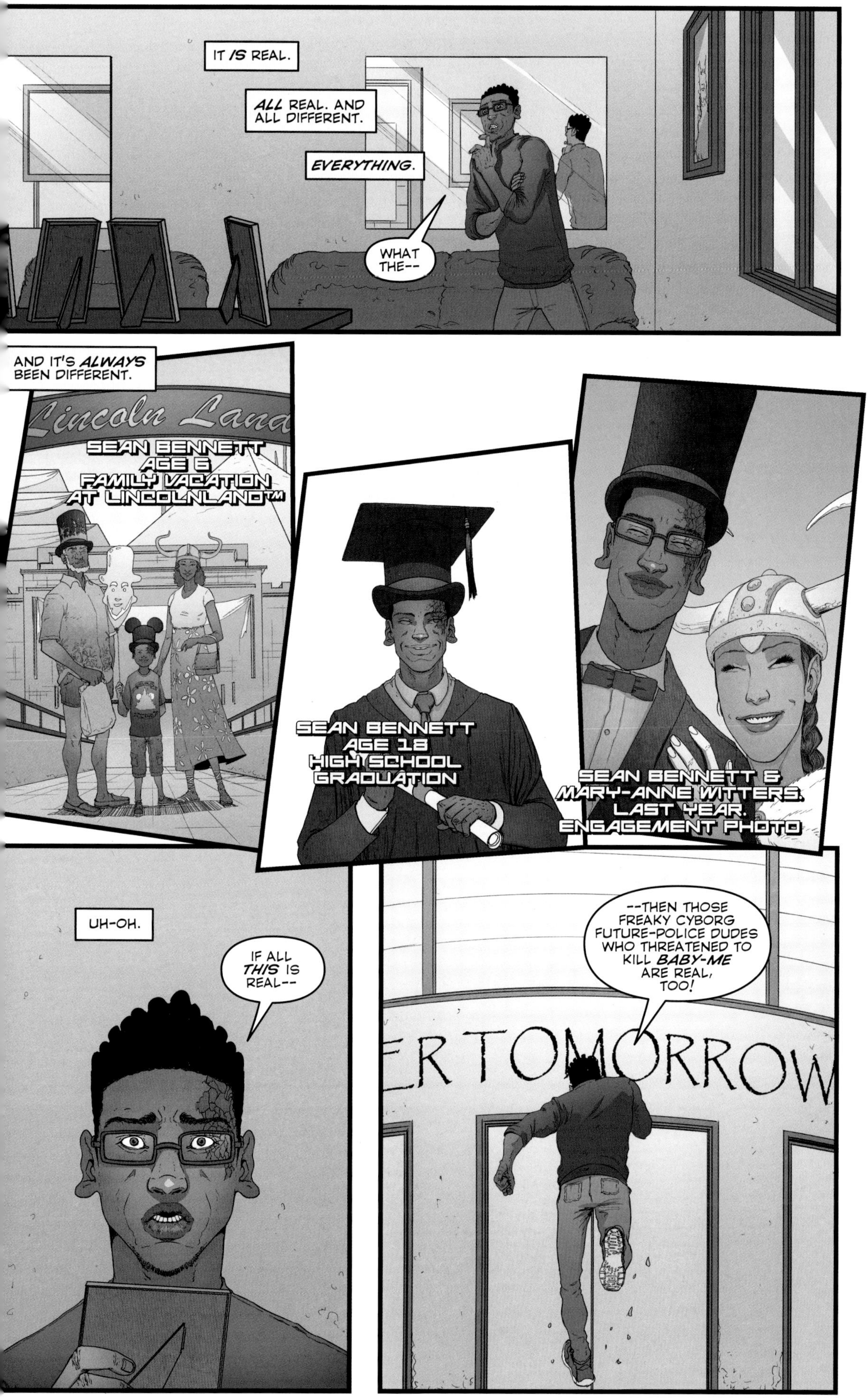

IT IS REAL.
ALL REAL. AND ALL DIFFERENT.
EVERYTHING.
WHAT THE--
AND IT'S ALWAYS BEEN DIFFERENT.
Lincoln Land
SEAN BENNETT AGE 6 FAMILY VACATION AT LINCOLNLAND™
SEAN BENNETT AGE 18 HIGH SCHOOL GRADUATION
SEAN BENNETT & MARY-ANNE WITTERS. LAST YEAR. ENGAGEMENT PHOTO
UH-OH.
IF ALL THIS IS REAL--
--THEN THOSE FREAKY CYBORG FUTURE-POLICE DUDES WHO THREATENED TO KILL BABY-ME ARE REAL, TOO!
ERTOMORROW

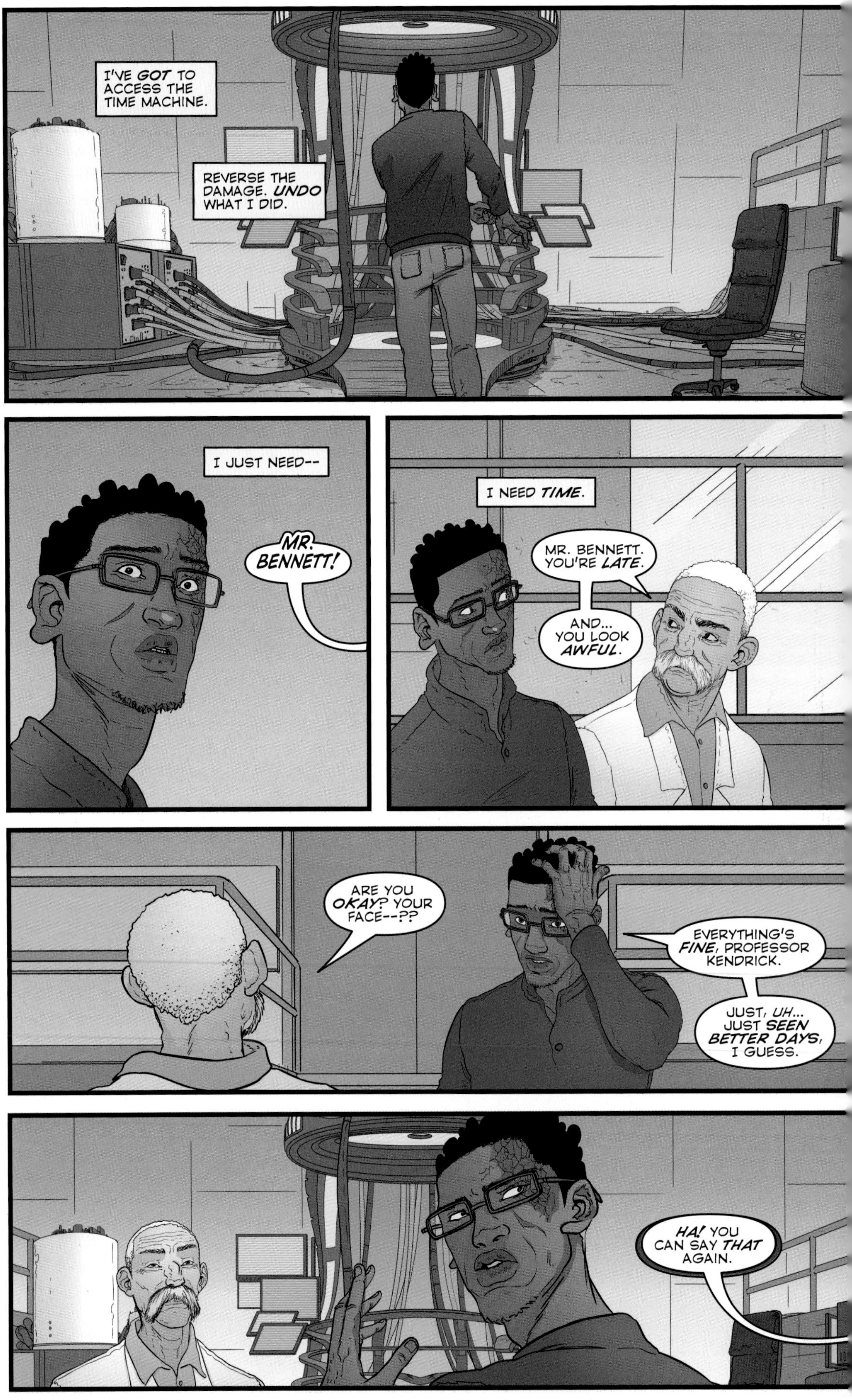

I'VE GOT TO ACCESS THE TIME MACHINE.
REVERSE THE DAMAGE. UNDO WHAT I DID.
I JUST NEED--
MR. BENNETT!
I NEED TIME.
MR. BENNETT. YOU'RE LATE.
AND... YOU LOOK AWFUL.
ARE YOU OKAY? YOUR FACE--??
EVERYTHING'S FINE, PROFESSOR KENDRICK.
JUST, UH... JUST SEEN BETTER DAYS, I GUESS.
HA! YOU CAN SAY THAT AGAIN.

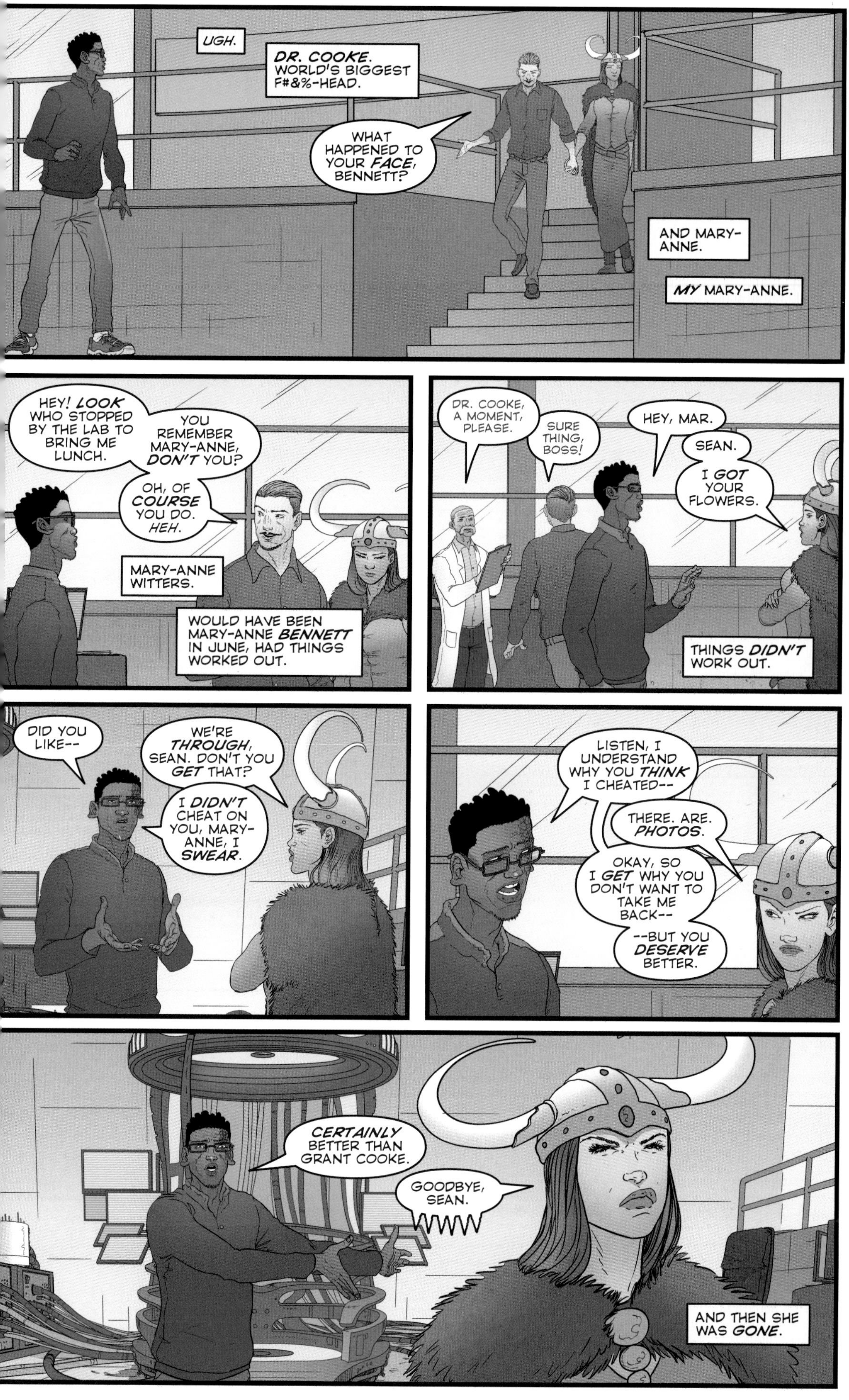

UGH.
DR. COOKE. WORLD'S BIGGEST F#&%-HEAD.
WHAT HAPPENED TO YOUR FACE, BENNETT?
AND MARY-ANNE.
MY MARY-ANNE.
HEY! LOOK WHO STOPPED BY THE LAB TO BRING ME LUNCH.
YOU REMEMBER MARY-ANNE, DON'T YOU?
OH, OF COURSE YOU DO. HEH.
MARY-ANNE WITTERS.
WOULD HAVE BEEN MARY-ANNE BENNETT IN JUNE, HAD THINGS WORKED OUT.
DR. COOKE, A MOMENT, PLEASE.
SURE THING, BOSS!
HEY, MAR.
SEAN.
I GOT YOUR FLOWERS.
THINGS DIDN'T WORK OUT.
DID YOU LIKE--
WE'RE THROUGH, SEAN. DON'T YOU GET THAT?
I DIDN'T CHEAT ON YOU, MARY-ANNE, I SWEAR.
LISTEN, I UNDERSTAND WHY YOU THINK I CHEATED--
THERE. ARE. PHOTOS.
OKAY, SO I GET WHY YOU DON'T WANT TO TAKE ME BACK--
--BUT YOU DESERVE BETTER.
CERTAINLY BETTER THAN GRANT COOKE.
GOODBYE, SEAN.
AND THEN SHE WAS GONE.

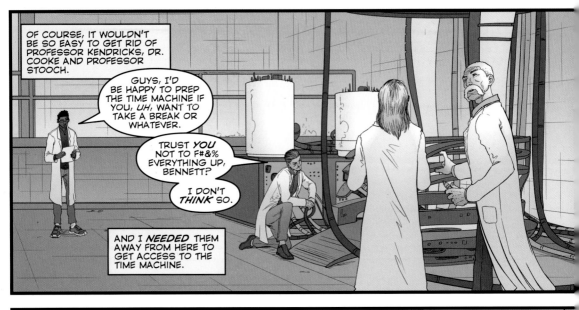

OF COURSE, IT WOULDN'T BE SO EASY TO GET RID OF PROFESSOR KENDRICKS, DR. COOKE AND PROFESSOR STOOCH.

GUYS, I'D BE HAPPY TO PREP THE TIME MACHINE IF YOU, *UH*, WANT TO TAKE A BREAK OR WHATEVER.

TRUST *YOU* NOT TO F#&% EVERYTHING UP, BENNETT?

I DON'T *THINK* SO.

AND I *NEEDED* THEM AWAY FROM HERE TO GET ACCESS TO THE TIME MACHINE.

GETTING RID OF THEM WAS GOING TO BE *IMPOSSIBLE*.

OF COURSE, SOME PEOPLE WOULD SAY A *TIME MACHINE* IS IMPOSSIBLE AS WELL.

HMM.

ENTER *THE FINER TOMORROW INC.* BOARD OF DIRECTORS.

ARE YOU PEOPLE CRAZY?!?!

WHAT THE F#&% ARE YOU THINKING?

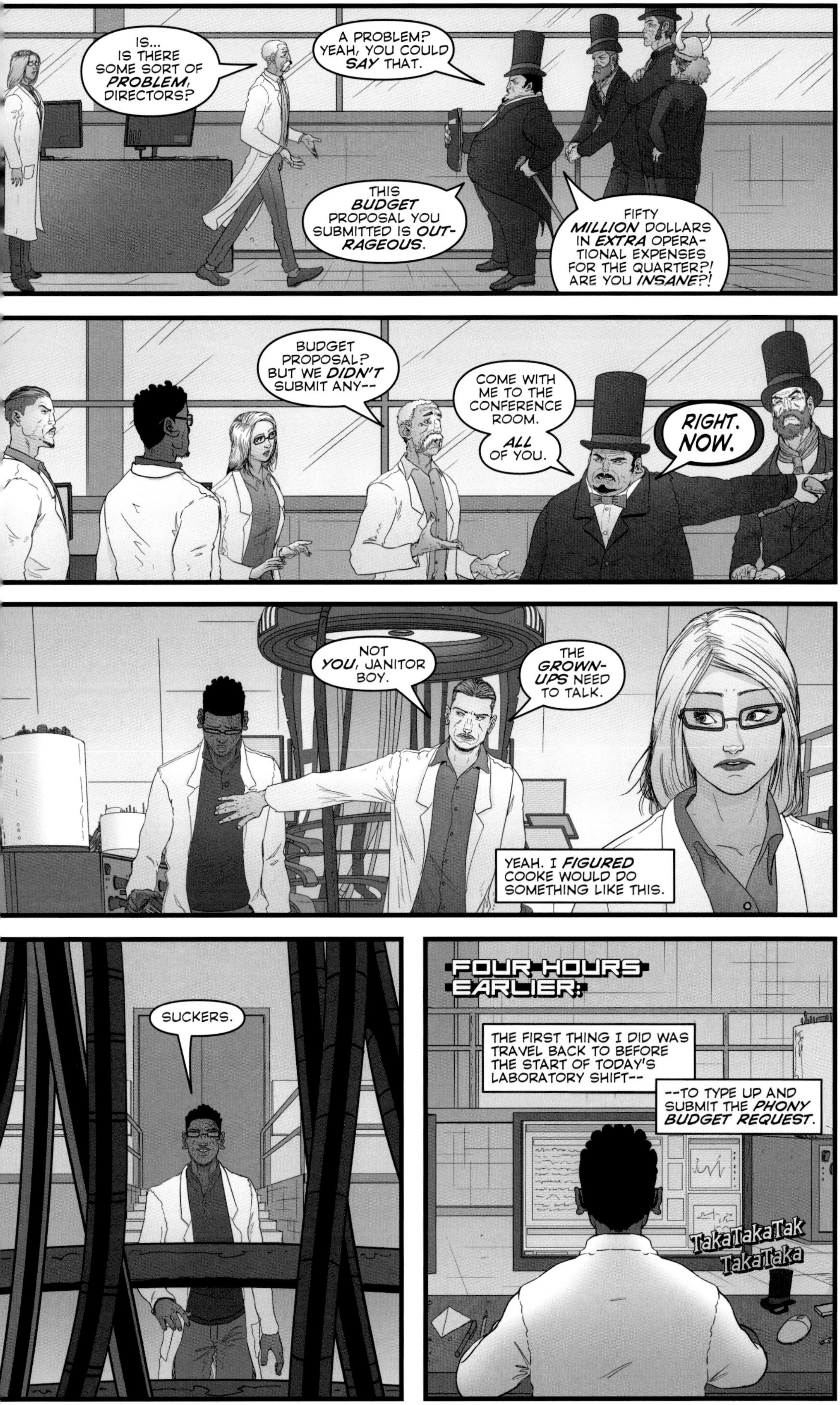
IS... IS THERE SOME SORT OF *PROBLEM*, DIRECTORS?
A PROBLEM? YEAH, YOU COULD *SAY* THAT.
THIS *BUDGET* PROPOSAL YOU SUBMITTED IS *OUT-RAGEOUS*.
FIFTY *MILLION* DOLLARS IN *EXTRA* OPERA-TIONAL EXPENSES FOR THE QUARTER?! ARE YOU *INSANE*?!
BUDGET PROPOSAL? BUT WE *DIDN'T* SUBMIT ANY--
COME WITH ME TO THE CONFERENCE ROOM.
ALL OF YOU.
RIGHT. NOW.
NOT *YOU*, JANITOR BOY.
THE *GROWN-UPS* NEED TO TALK.
YEAH. I *FIGURED* COOKE WOULD DO SOMETHING LIKE THIS.
SUCKERS.
FOUR HOURS EARLIER:
THE FIRST THING I DID WAS TRAVEL BACK TO BEFORE THE START OF TODAY'S LABORATORY SHIFT--
--TO TYPE UP AND SUBMIT THE *PHONY BUDGET REQUEST*.
TakaTakaTak
TakaTaka

AND THEN:

ONE WEEK EARLIER:

(AGAIN.)

THIS SHOULDN'T BE *TOO* DIFFICULT.

URRRRRRRRRRR

RETRIEVE THE TIME MACHINE UPGRADE SCHEMATIC I'D LEFT AT THE LAB THE *LAST* TIME I TRAVELED BACK.

I EVEN *SHREDDED* THEM FOR GOOD MEASURE.

GOOD RIDDANCE.

SKRAKACH

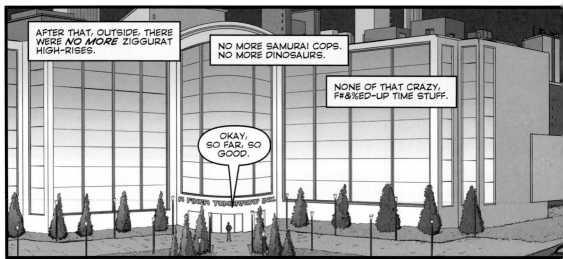

AFTER THAT, OUTSIDE, THERE WERE *NO MORE* ZIGGURAT HIGH-RISES.

NO MORE SAMURAI COPS. NO MORE DINOSAURS.

NONE OF THAT CRAZY, F#&%ED-UP TIME STUFF.

OKAY, SO FAR, SO GOOD.

A FINER TOMORROW INC.

BUT *NOT* DONE YET, THOUGH.

STILL GOT THE *CHILDHOOD SCAR* FROM THOSE TIME POLICE CYBORGS, SO I *HAVEN'T* TAKEN CARE OF EVERYTHING.

AND I *DID* SAY I'D UNDO *EVERY-THING*.

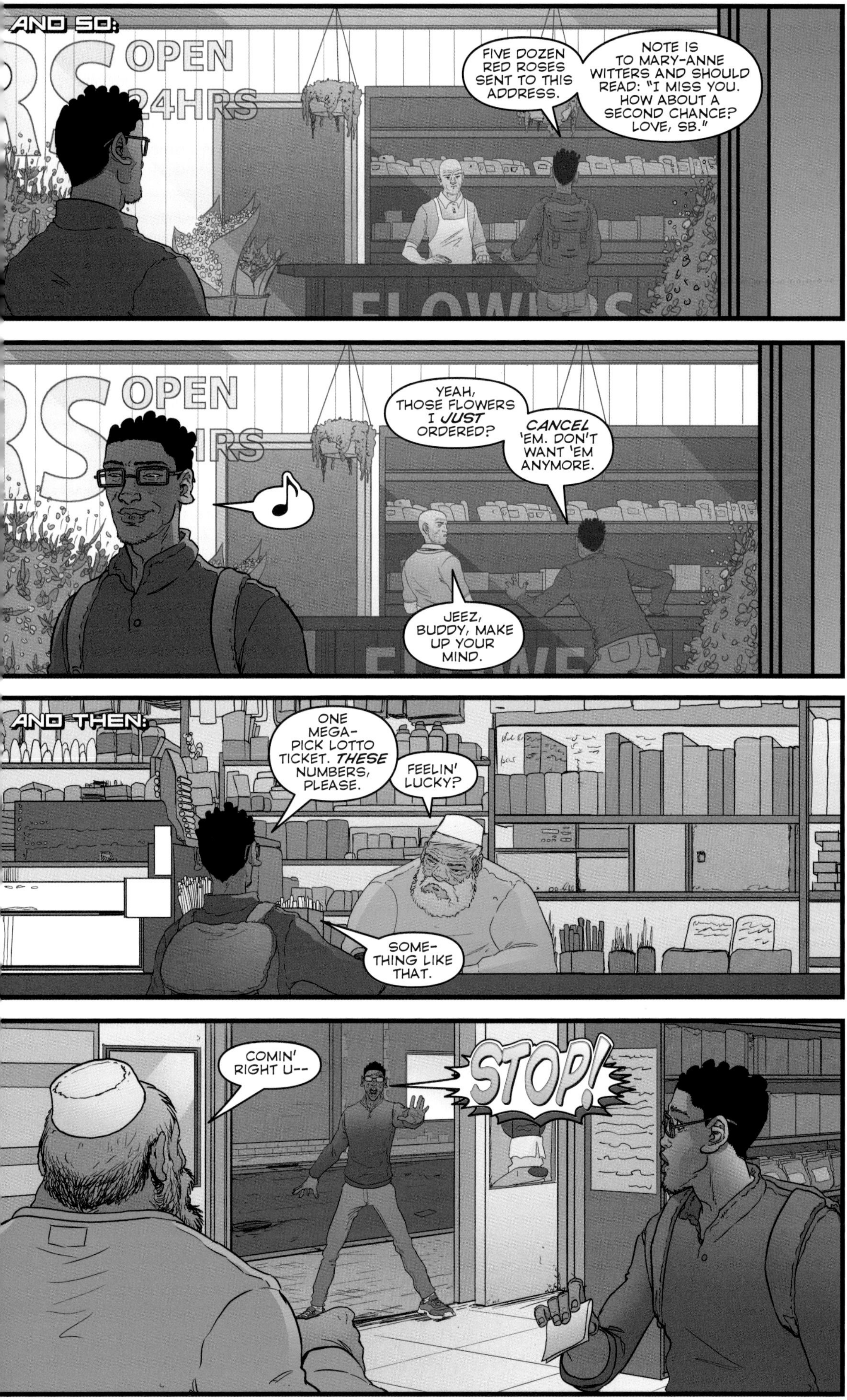
AND SO:
FIVE DOZEN RED ROSES SENT TO THIS ADDRESS.
NOTE IS TO MARY-ANNE WITTERS AND SHOULD READ: "I MISS YOU. HOW ABOUT A SECOND CHANCE? LOVE, SB."
OPEN 24HRS
FLOWERS
YEAH, THOSE FLOWERS I *JUST* ORDERED?
CANCEL 'EM. DON'T WANT 'EM ANYMORE.
♪
JEEZ, BUDDY, MAKE UP YOUR MIND.
AND THEN:
ONE MEGA-PICK LOTTO TICKET. *THESE* NUMBERS, PLEASE.
FEELIN' LUCKY?
SOME-THING LIKE THAT.
COMIN' RIGHT U--
STOP!

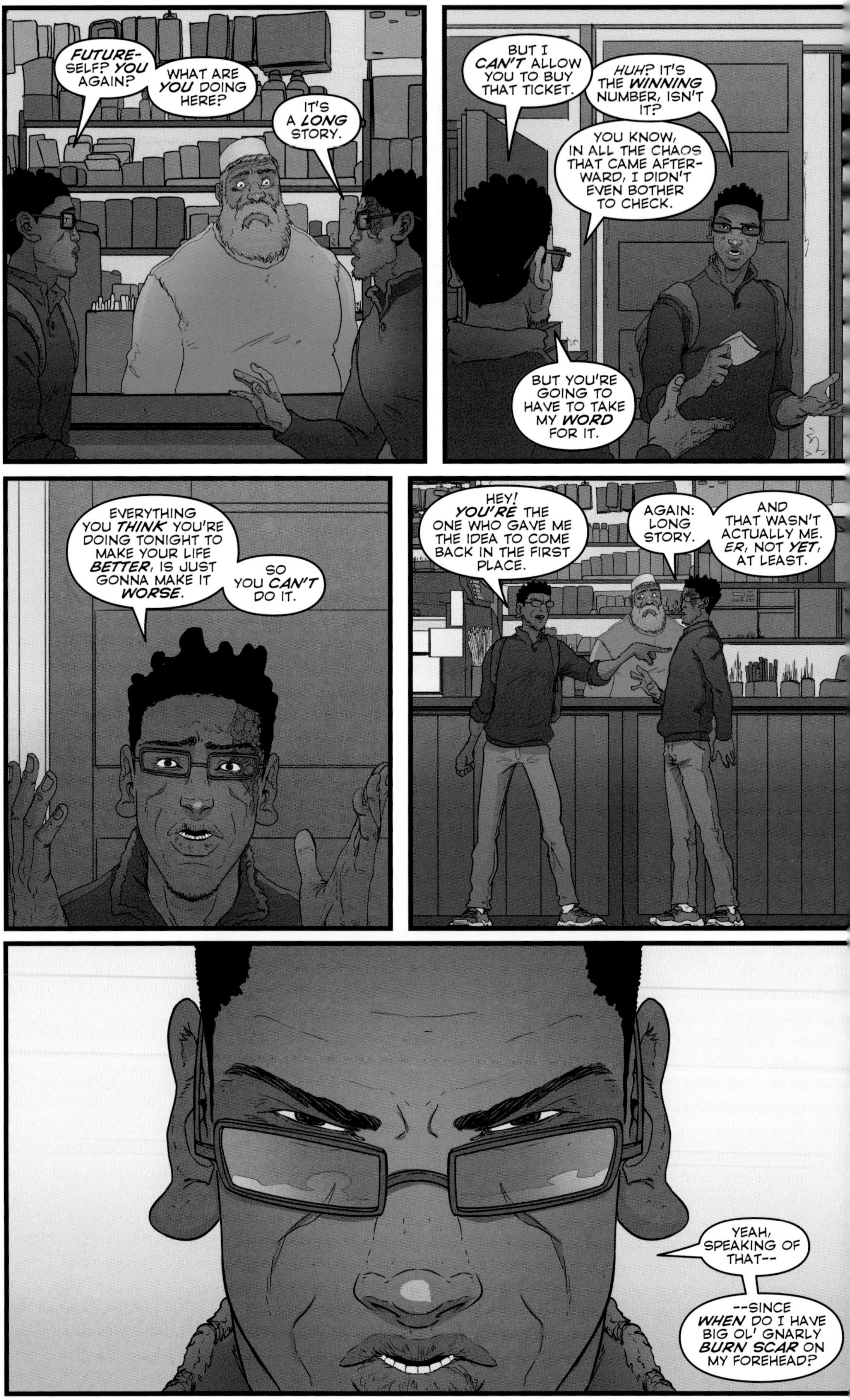
FUTURE-SELF? YOU AGAIN?
WHAT ARE YOU DOING HERE?
IT'S A LONG STORY.
BUT I CAN'T ALLOW YOU TO BUY THAT TICKET.
HUH? IT'S THE WINNING NUMBER, ISN'T IT?
YOU KNOW, IN ALL THE CHAOS THAT CAME AFTER-WARD, I DIDN'T EVEN BOTHER TO CHECK.
BUT YOU'RE GOING TO HAVE TO TAKE MY WORD FOR IT.
EVERYTHING YOU THINK YOU'RE DOING TONIGHT TO MAKE YOUR LIFE BETTER, IS JUST GONNA MAKE IT WORSE.
SO YOU CAN'T DO IT.
HEY! YOU'RE THE ONE WHO GAVE ME THE IDEA TO COME BACK IN THE FIRST PLACE.
AGAIN: LONG STORY.
AND THAT WASN'T ACTUALLY ME. ER, NOT YET, AT LEAST.
YEAH, SPEAKING OF THAT--
--SINCE WHEN DO I HAVE BIG OL' GNARLY BURN SCAR ON MY FOREHEAD?

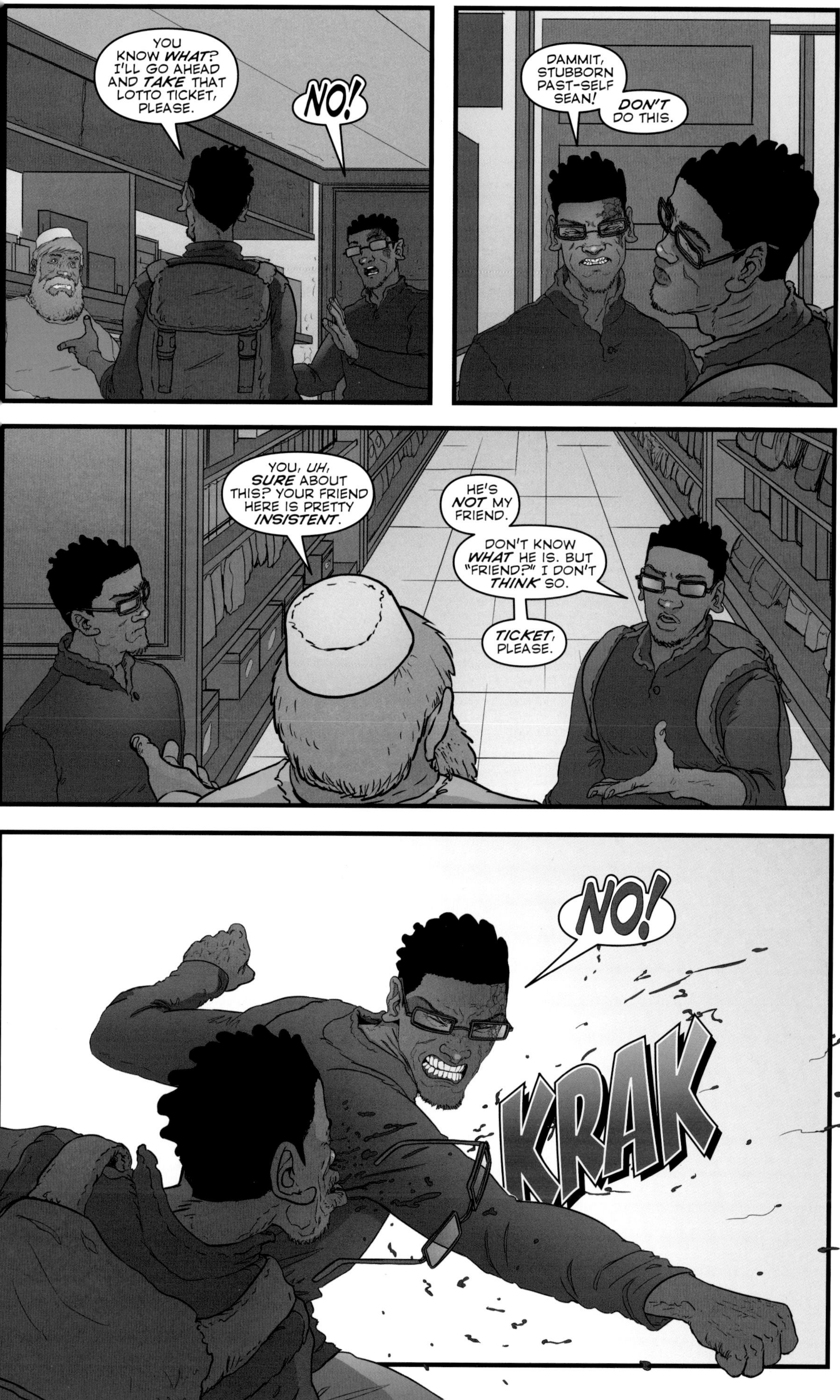
YOU KNOW *WHAT*? I'LL GO AHEAD AND *TAKE* THAT LOTTO TICKET, PLEASE.
NO!
DAMMIT, STUBBORN PAST-SELF SEAN!
DON'T DO THIS.
YOU, *UH*, *SURE* ABOUT THIS? YOUR FRIEND HERE IS PRETTY *INSISTENT*.
HE'S *NOT* MY FRIEND.
DON'T KNOW *WHAT* HE IS. BUT "FRIEND?" I DON'T *THINK* SO.
TICKET, PLEASE.
NO!
KRAK

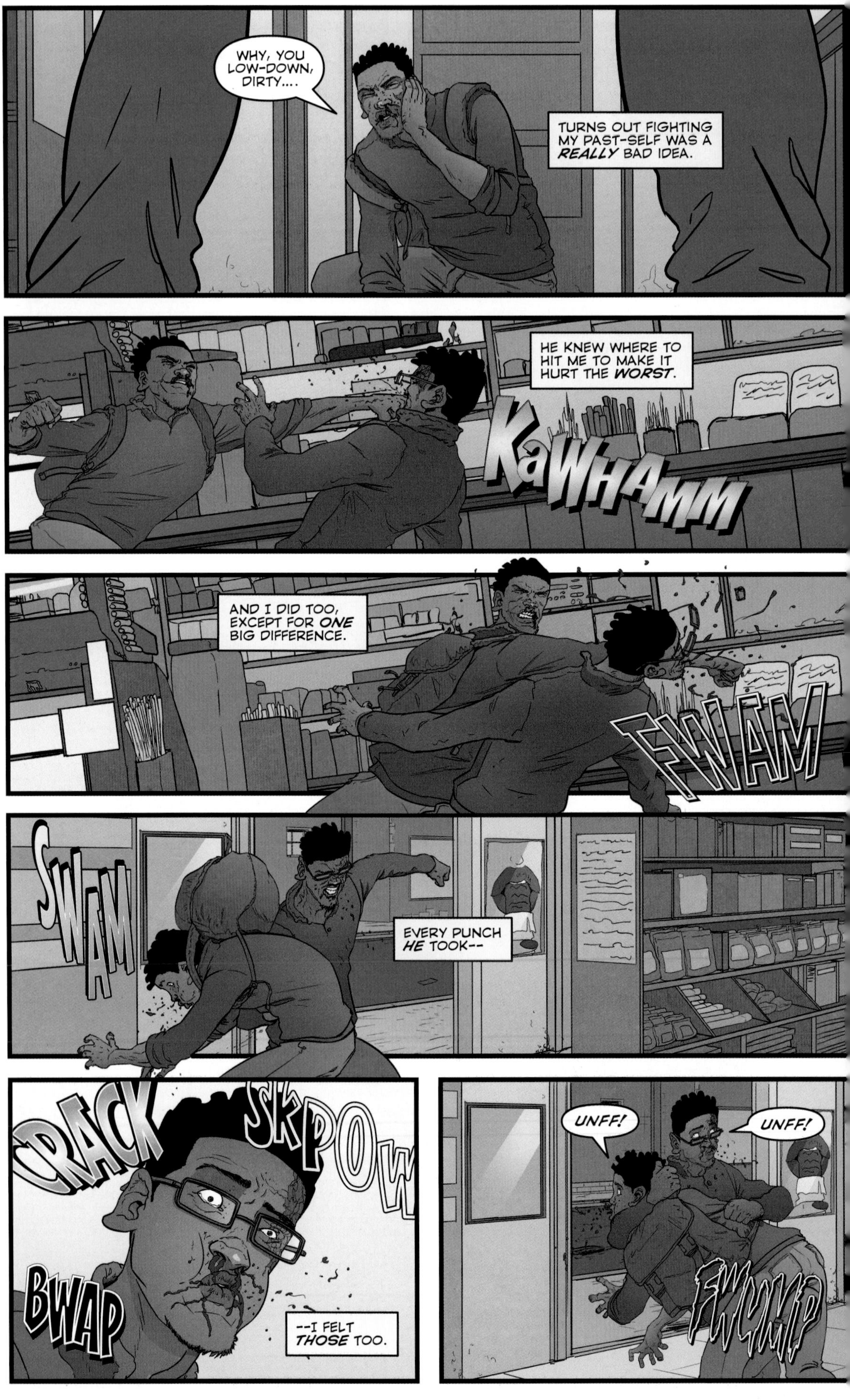
WHY, YOU LOW-DOWN, DIRTY....
TURNS OUT FIGHTING MY PAST-SELF WAS A REALLY BAD IDEA.
HE KNEW WHERE TO HIT ME TO MAKE IT HURT THE WORST.
KaWHAMM
AND I DID TOO, EXCEPT FOR ONE BIG DIFFERENCE.
FWAM
SWAM
EVERY PUNCH HE TOOK--
CRACK
SKPOW
BWAP
--I FELT THOSE TOO.
UNFF!
UNFF!
FWUMP

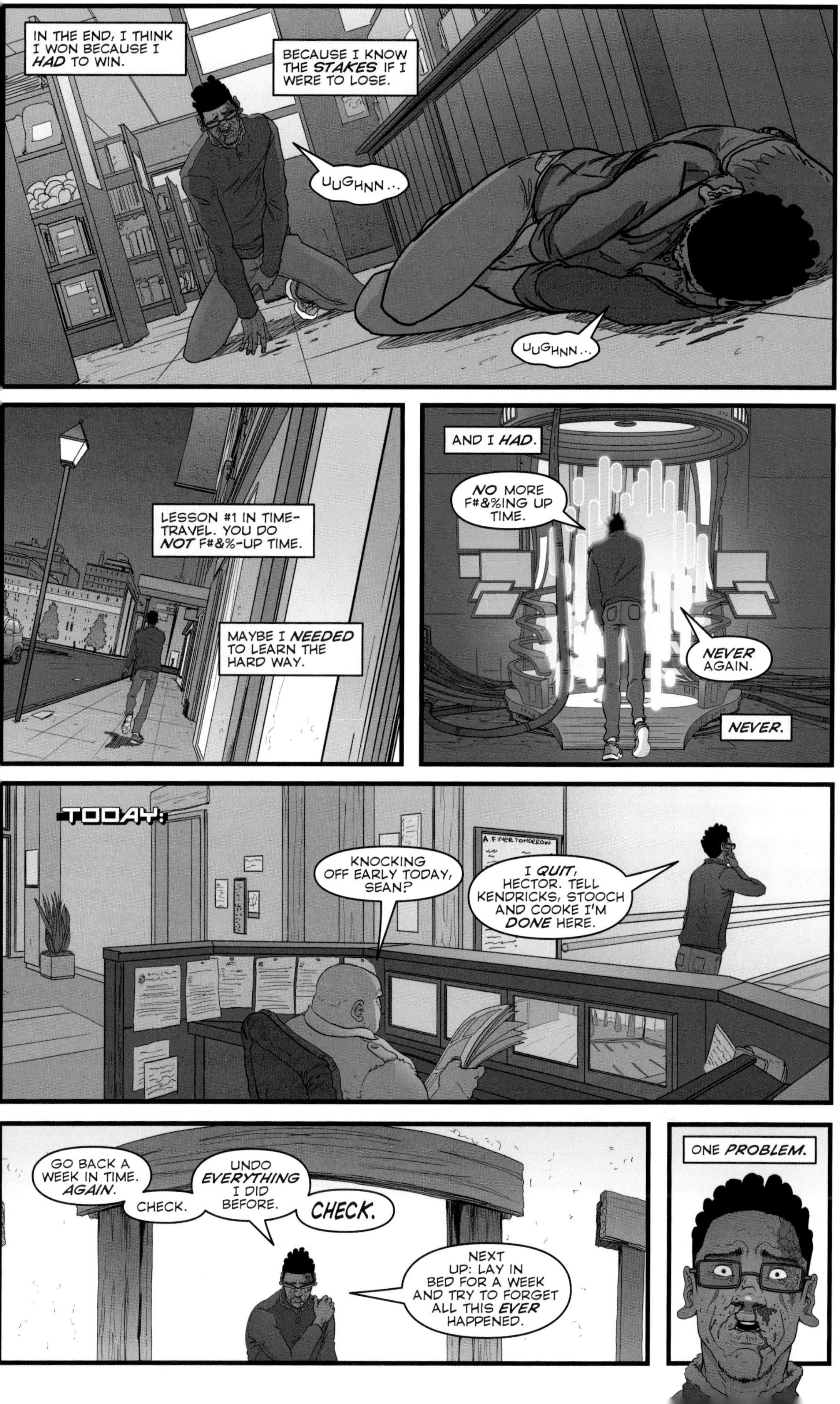
IN THE END, I THINK I WON BECAUSE I HAD TO WIN.
BECAUSE I KNOW THE STAKES IF I WERE TO LOSE.
UUGHNN...
UUGHNN...
LESSON #1 IN TIME-TRAVEL. YOU DO NOT F#&%-UP TIME.
MAYBE I NEEDED TO LEARN THE HARD WAY.
AND I HAD.
NO MORE F#&%ING UP TIME.
NEVER AGAIN.
NEVER.
TODAY:
A FINER TOMORROW
KNOCKING OFF EARLY TODAY, SEAN?
I QUIT, HECTOR. TELL KENDRICKS, STOOCH AND COOKE I'M DONE HERE.
GO BACK A WEEK IN TIME. AGAIN.
CHECK.
UNDO EVERYTHING I DID BEFORE.
CHECK.
NEXT UP: LAY IN BED FOR A WEEK AND TRY TO FORGET ALL THIS EVER HAPPENED.
ONE PROBLEM.

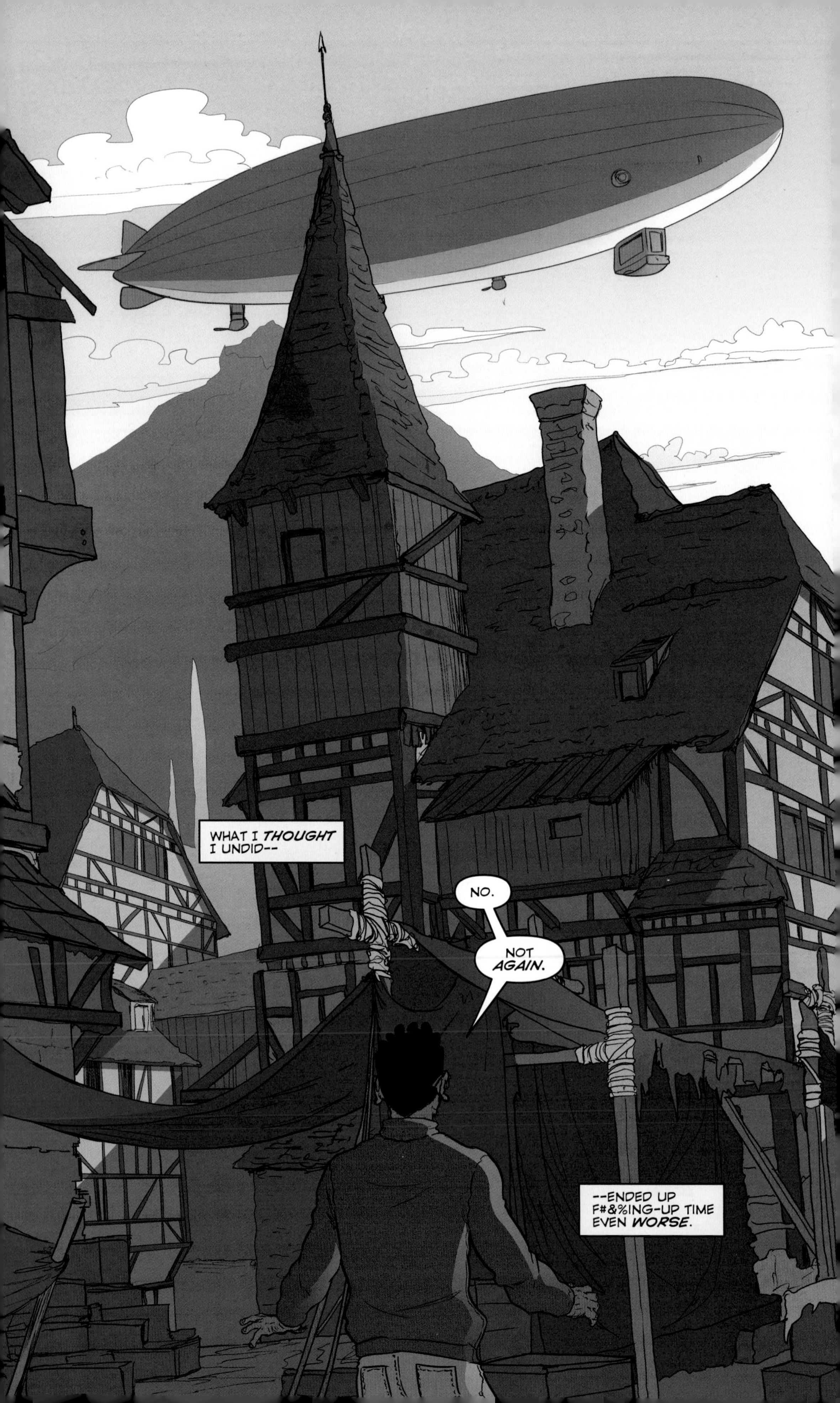
WHAT I *THOUGHT* I UNDID--
NO.
NOT *AGAIN*.
--ENDED UP F#&%ING-UP TIME EVEN *WORSE*.

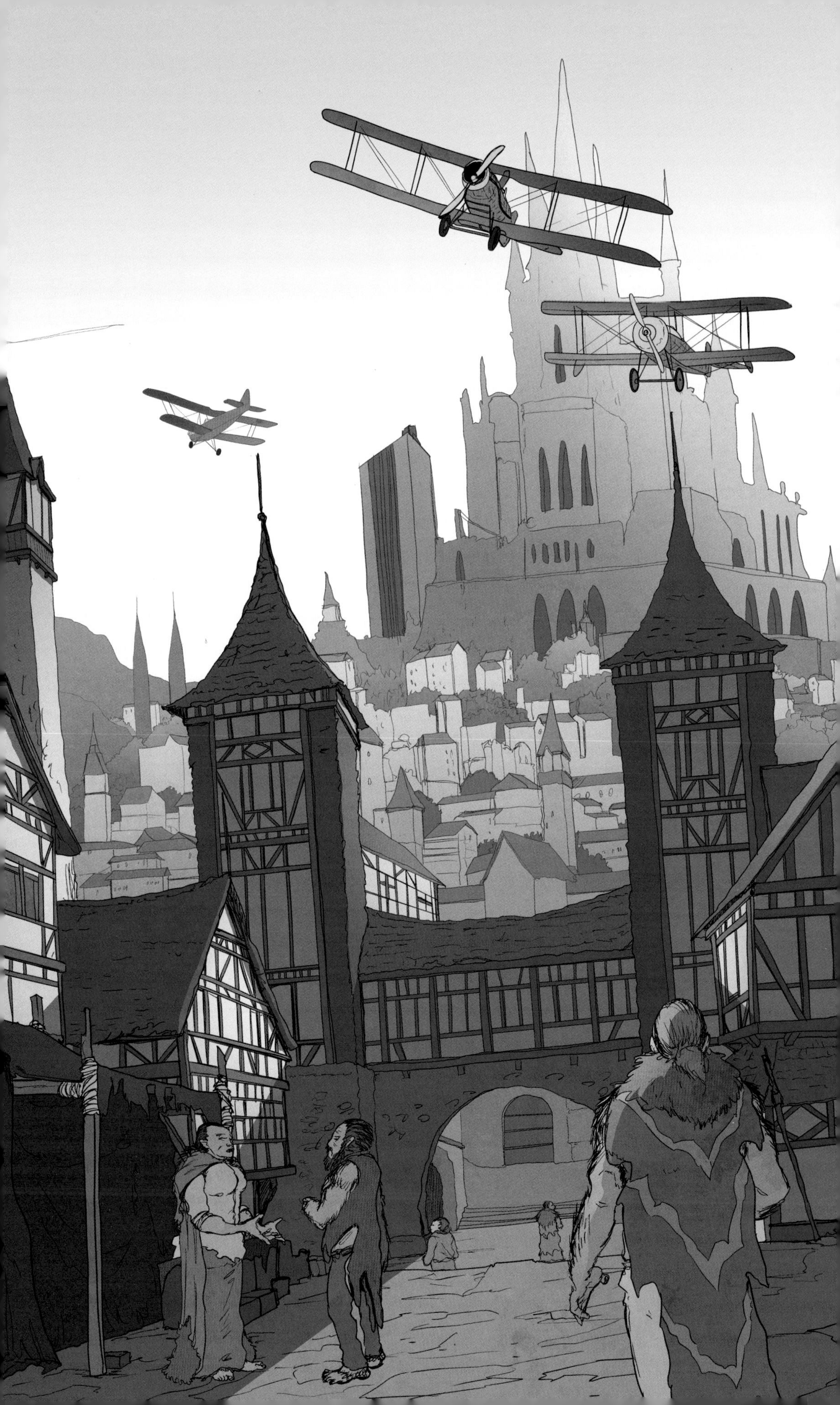

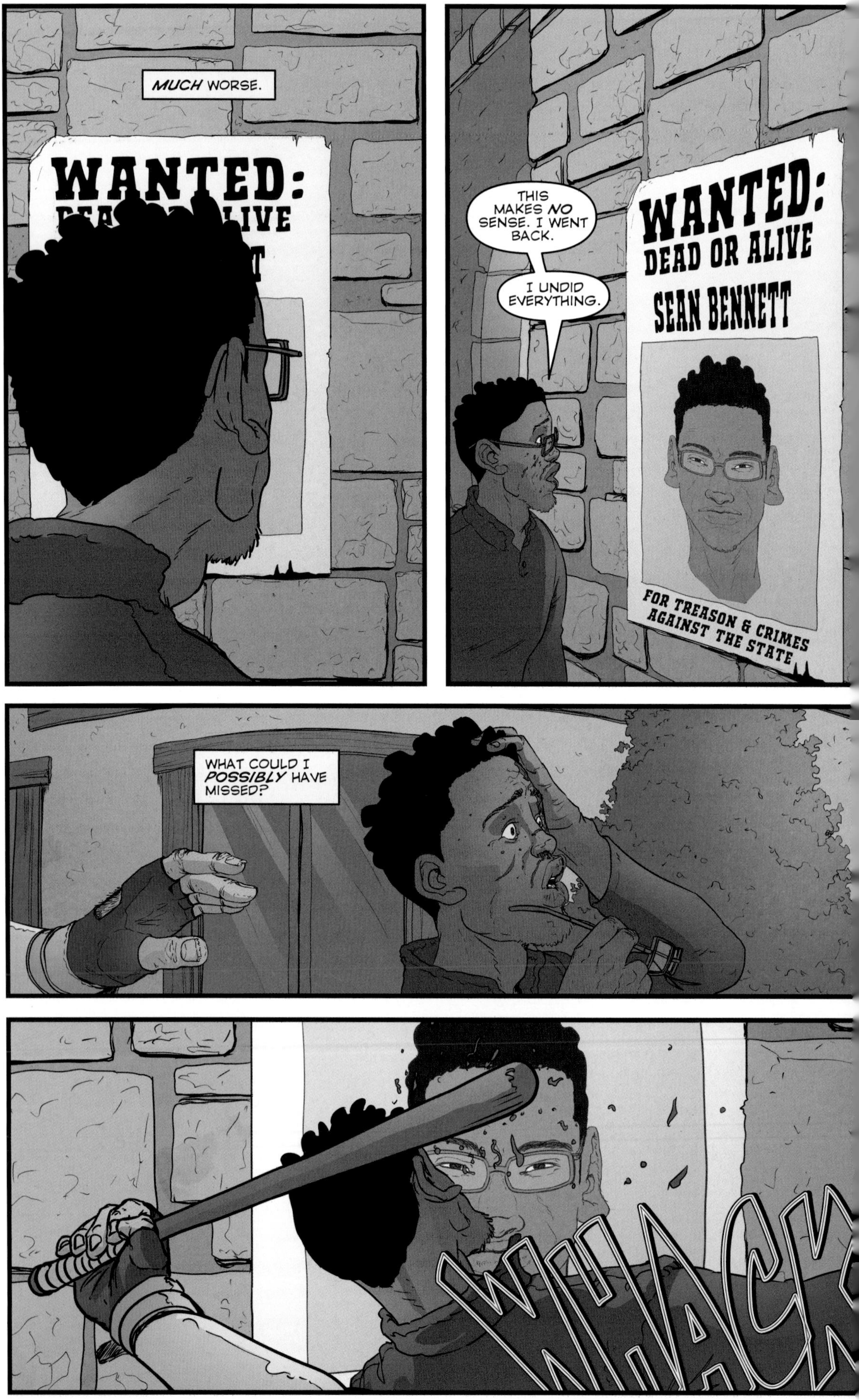
MUCH WORSE.
WANTED:
THIS MAKES NO SENSE. I WENT BACK.
I UNDID EVERYTHING.
WANTED: DEAD OR ALIVE
SEAN BENNETT
FOR TREASON & CRIMES AGAINST THE STATE
WHAT COULD I POSSIBLY HAVE MISSED?
WHACK

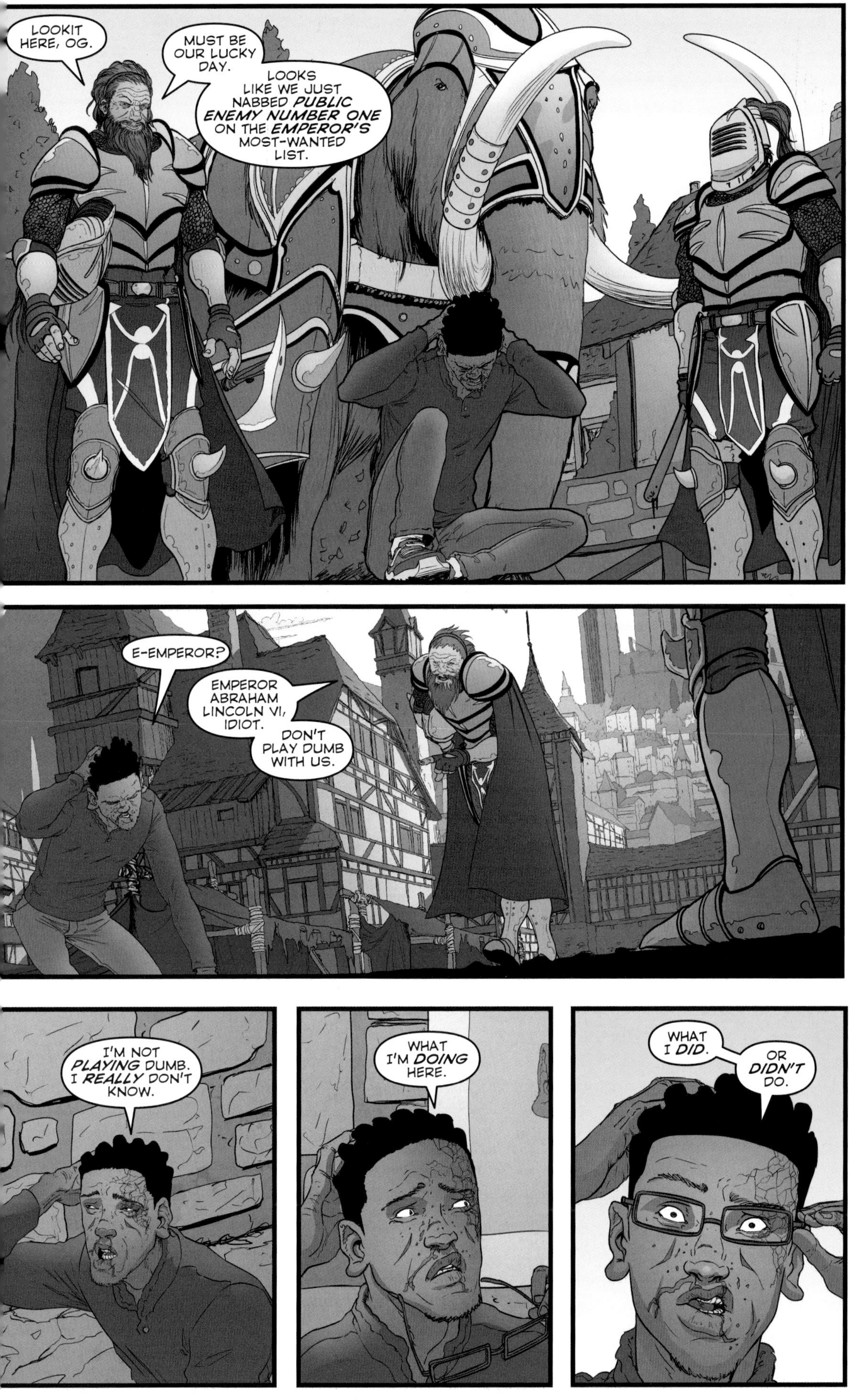
LOOKIT HERE, OG.
MUST BE OUR LUCKY DAY.
LOOKS LIKE WE JUST NABBED *PUBLIC ENEMY NUMBER ONE* ON THE *EMPEROR'S* MOST-WANTED LIST.
E-EMPEROR?
EMPEROR ABRAHAM LINCOLN VI, IDIOT.
DON'T PLAY DUMB WITH US.
I'M NOT *PLAYING* DUMB. I *REALLY* DON'T KNOW.
WHAT I'M *DOING* HERE.
WHAT I *DID*.
OR *DIDN'T* DO.

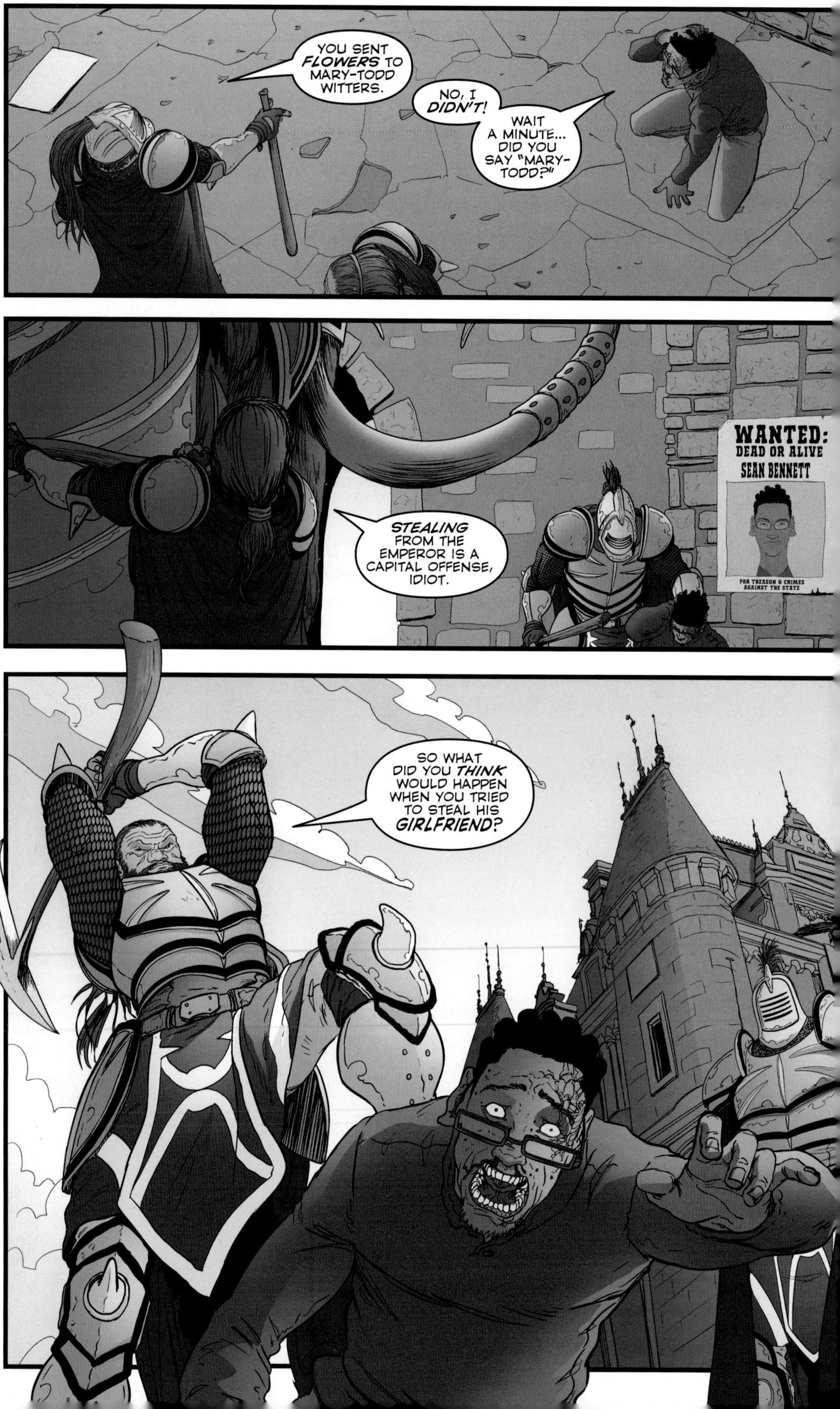
YOU SENT FLOWERS TO MARY-TODD WITTERS.
NO, I DIDN'T!
WAIT A MINUTE... DID YOU SAY "MARY-TODD?"
STEALING FROM THE EMPEROR IS A CAPITAL OFFENSE, IDIOT.
WANTED: DEAD OR ALIVE
SEAN BENNETT
FOR TREASON & CRIMES AGAINST THE STATE
SO WHAT DID YOU THINK WOULD HAPPEN WHEN YOU TRIED TO STEAL HIS GIRLFRIEND?

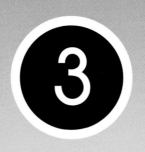

3

RACE AGAINST TIME

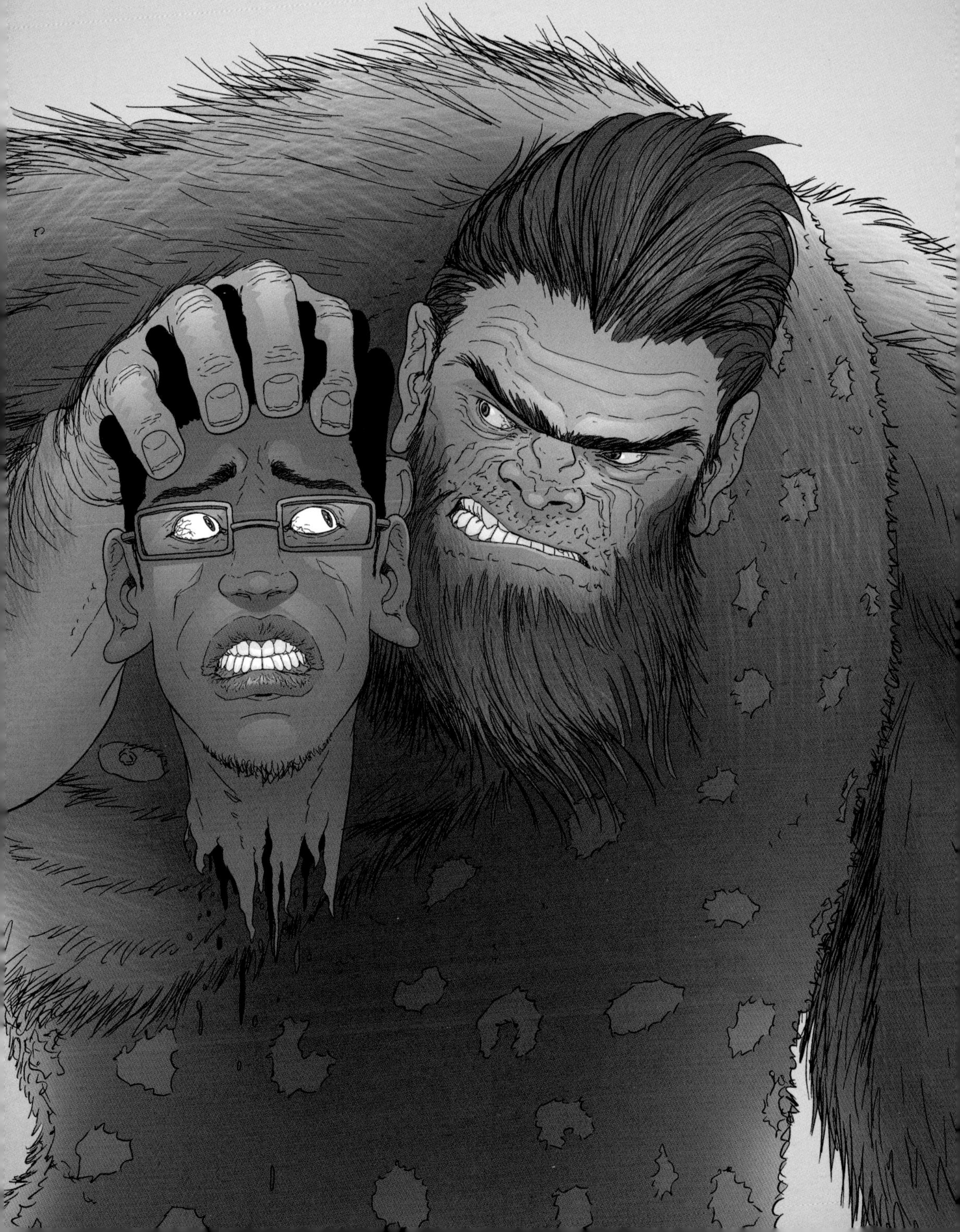

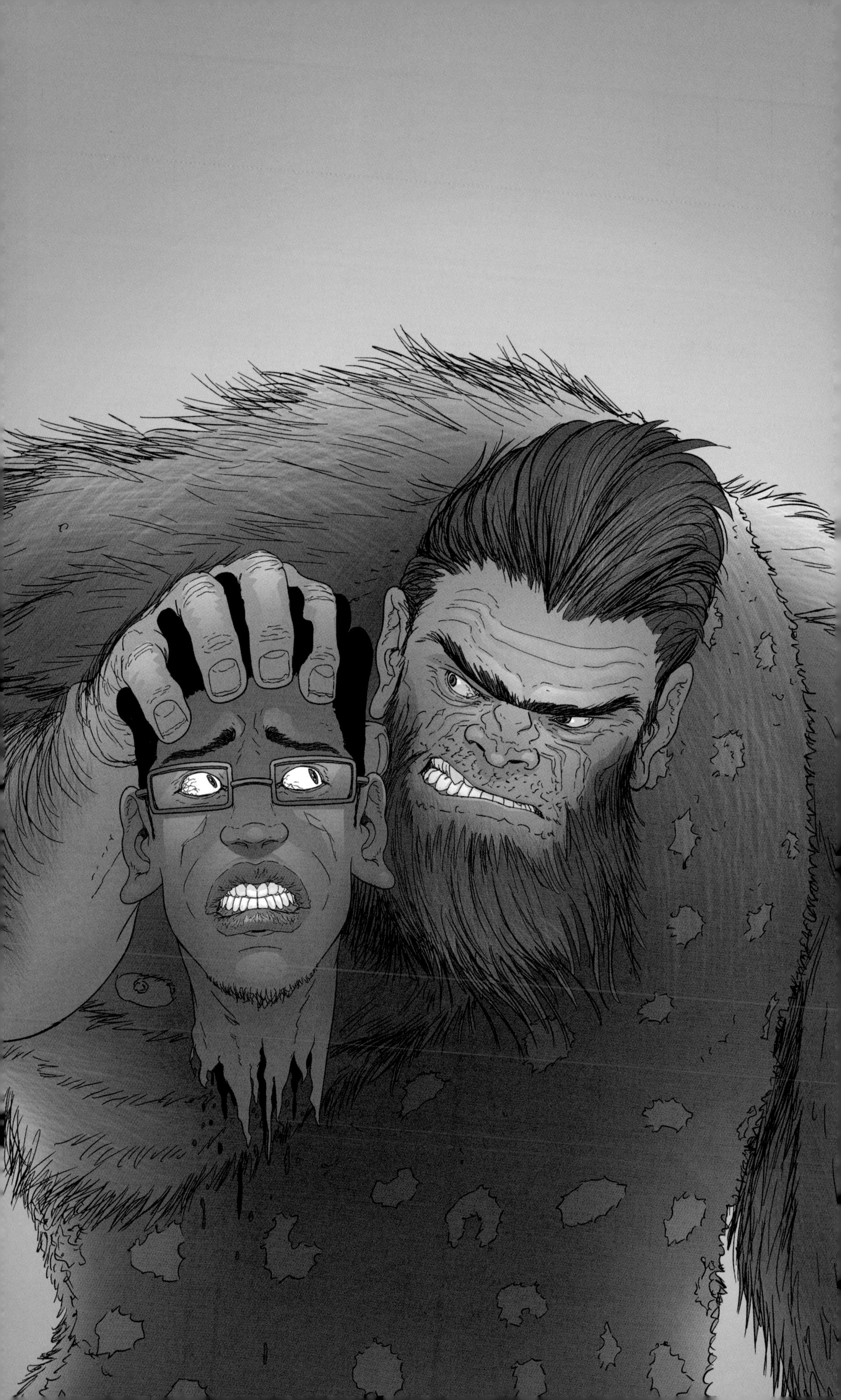

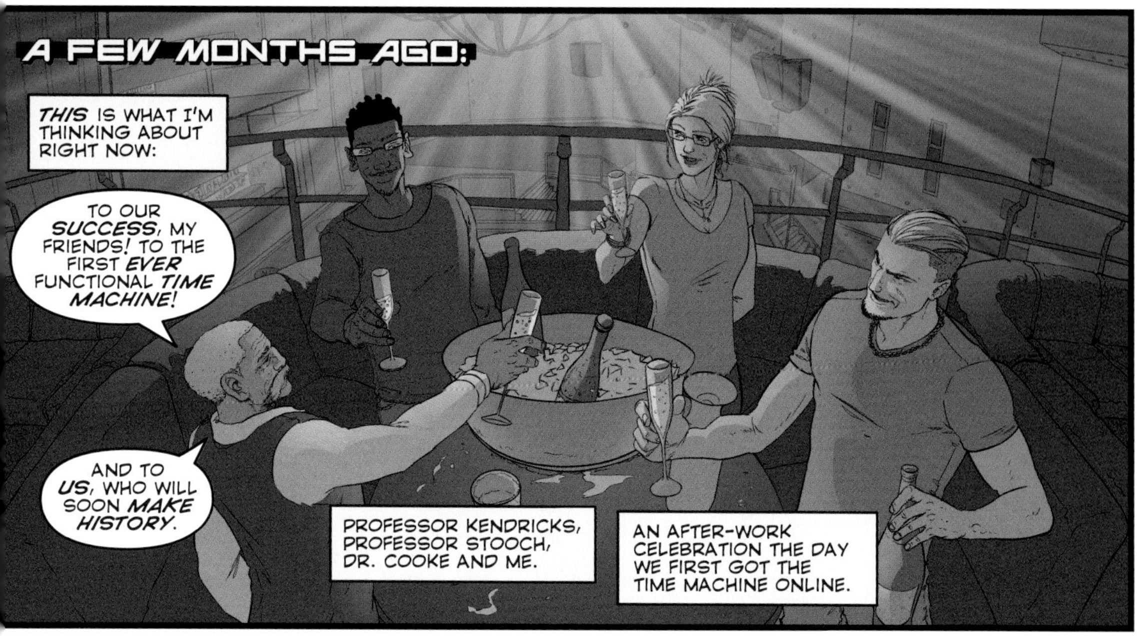
A FEW MONTHS AGO:
THIS IS WHAT I'M THINKING ABOUT RIGHT NOW:
TO OUR SUCCESS, MY FRIENDS! TO THE FIRST EVER FUNCTIONAL TIME MACHINE!
AND TO US, WHO WILL SOON MAKE HISTORY.
PROFESSOR KENDRICKS, PROFESSOR STOOCH, DR. COOKE AND ME.
AN AFTER-WORK CELEBRATION THE DAY WE FIRST GOT THE TIME MACHINE ONLINE.
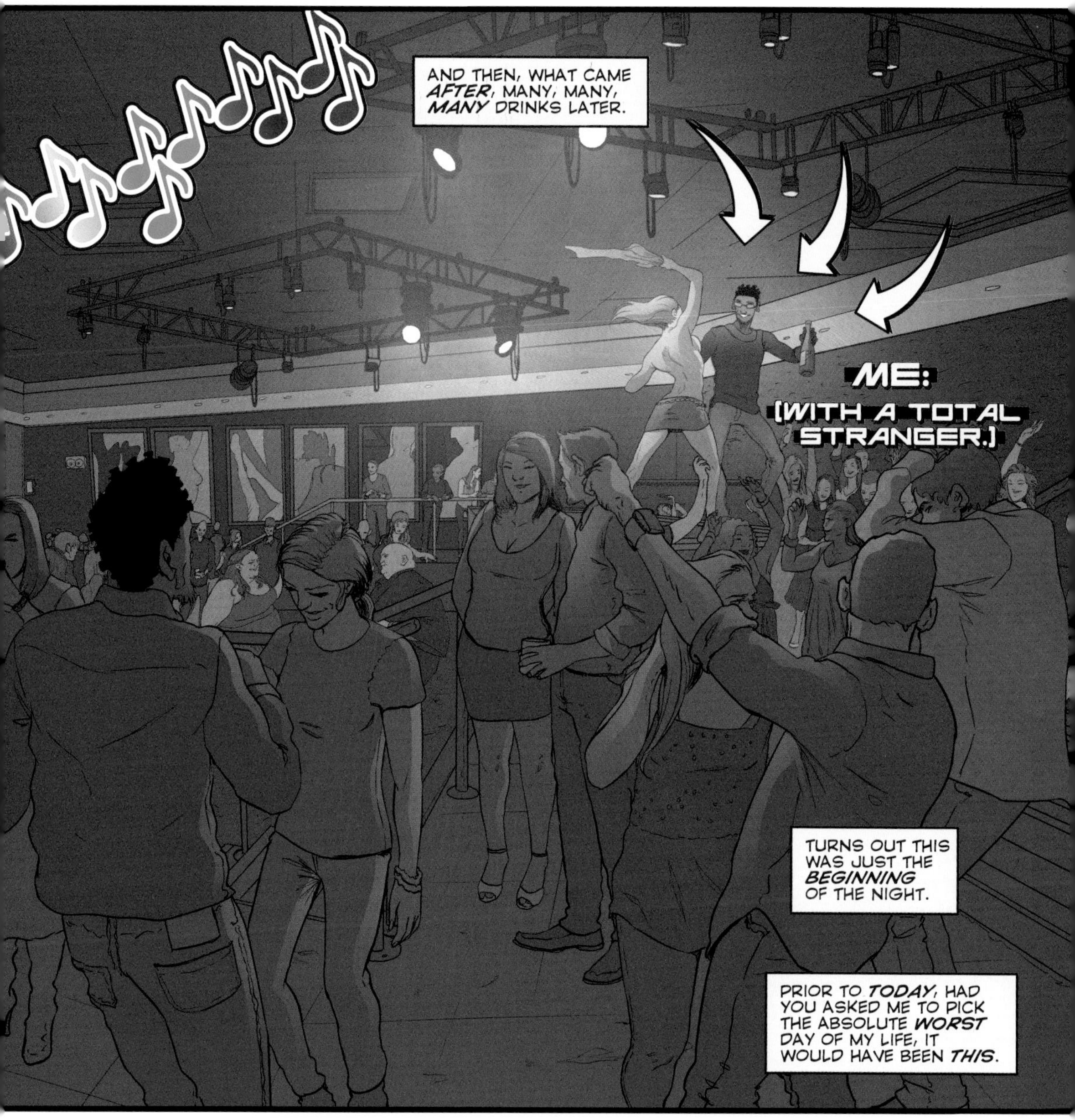
AND THEN, WHAT CAME AFTER, MANY, MANY, MANY DRINKS LATER.
ME:
[WITH A TOTAL STRANGER.]
TURNS OUT THIS WAS JUST THE BEGINNING OF THE NIGHT.
PRIOR TO TODAY, HAD YOU ASKED ME TO PICK THE ABSOLUTE WORST DAY OF MY LIFE, IT WOULD HAVE BEEN THIS.

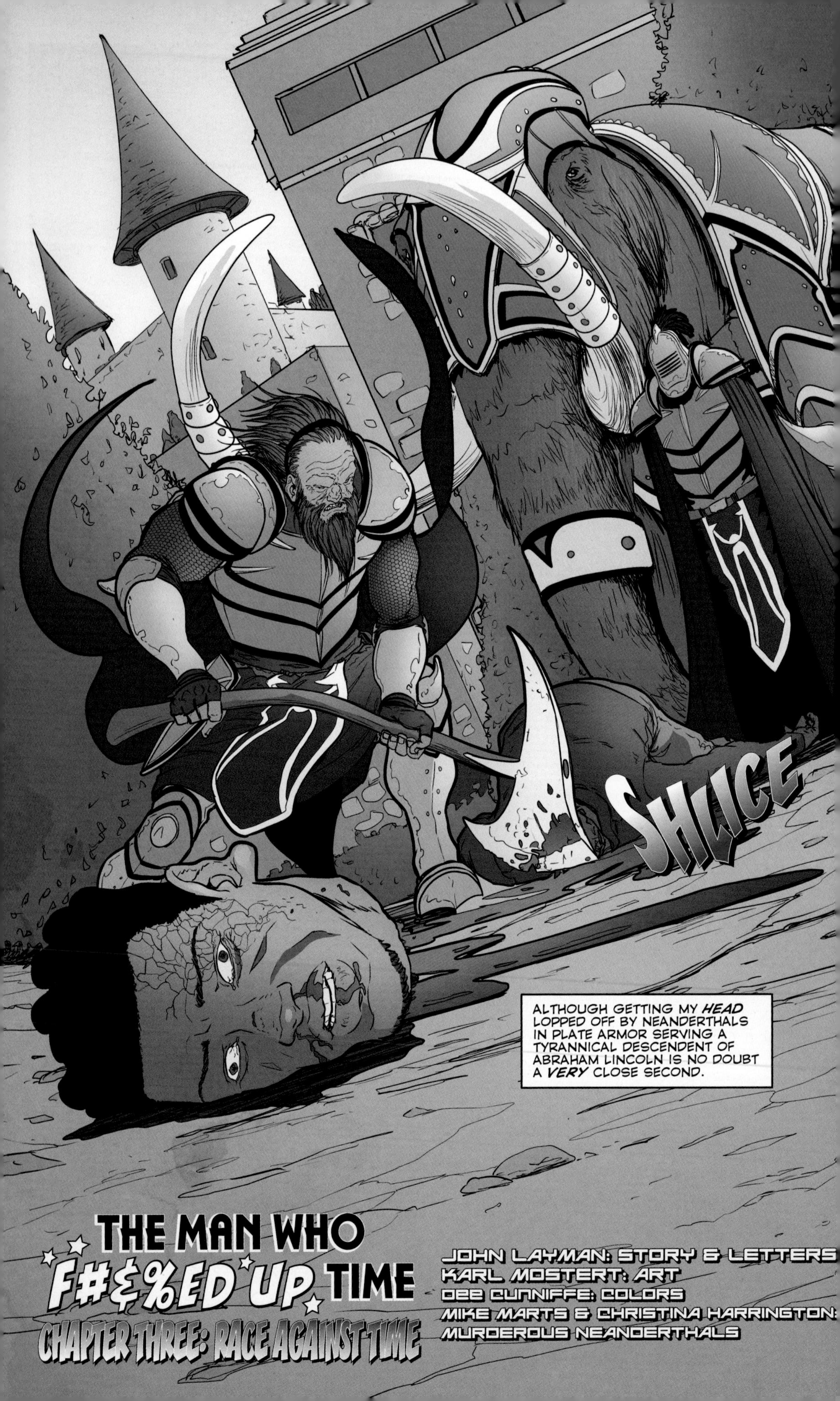
SHLICE
ALTHOUGH GETTING MY HEAD LOPPED OFF BY NEANDERTHALS IN PLATE ARMOR SERVING A TYRANNICAL DESCENDENT OF ABRAHAM LINCOLN IS NO DOUBT A VERY CLOSE SECOND.
THE MAN WHO F#&%ED UP TIME
CHAPTER THREE: RACE AGAINST TIME
JOHN LAYMAN: STORY & LETTERS
KARL MOSTERT: ART
DEE CUNNIFFE: COLORS
MIKE MARTS & CHRISTINA HARRINGTON: MURDEROUS NEANDERTHALS

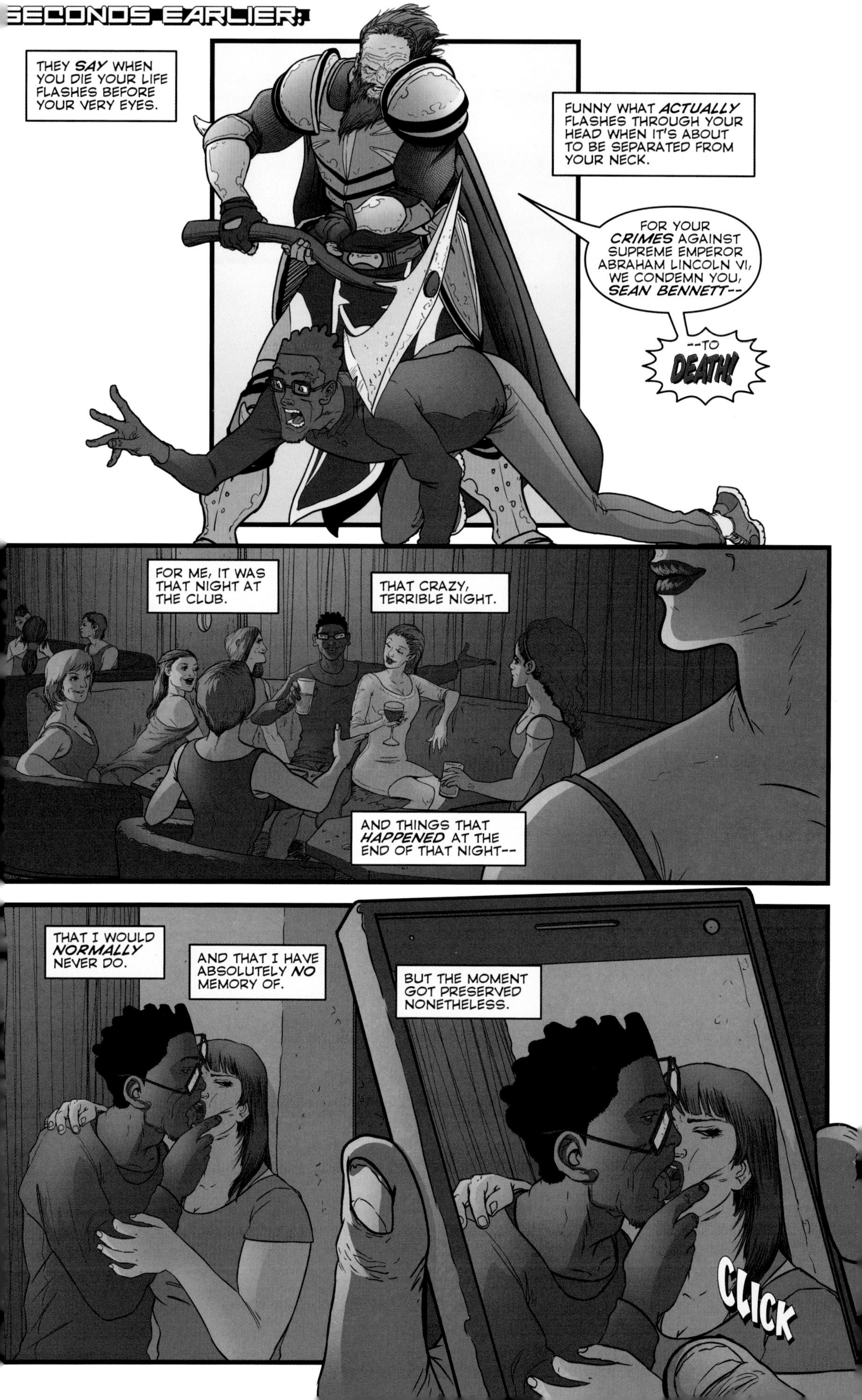
SECONDS EARLIER:
THEY SAY WHEN YOU DIE YOUR LIFE FLASHES BEFORE YOUR VERY EYES.
FUNNY WHAT ACTUALLY FLASHES THROUGH YOUR HEAD WHEN IT'S ABOUT TO BE SEPARATED FROM YOUR NECK.
FOR YOUR CRIMES AGAINST SUPREME EMPEROR ABRAHAM LINCOLN VI, WE CONDEMN YOU, SEAN BENNETT--
--TO DEATH!
FOR ME, IT WAS THAT NIGHT AT THE CLUB.
THAT CRAZY, TERRIBLE NIGHT.
AND THINGS THAT HAPPENED AT THE END OF THAT NIGHT--
THAT I WOULD NORMALLY NEVER DO.
AND THAT I HAVE ABSOLUTELY NO MEMORY OF.
BUT THE MOMENT GOT PRESERVED NONETHELESS.
CLICK

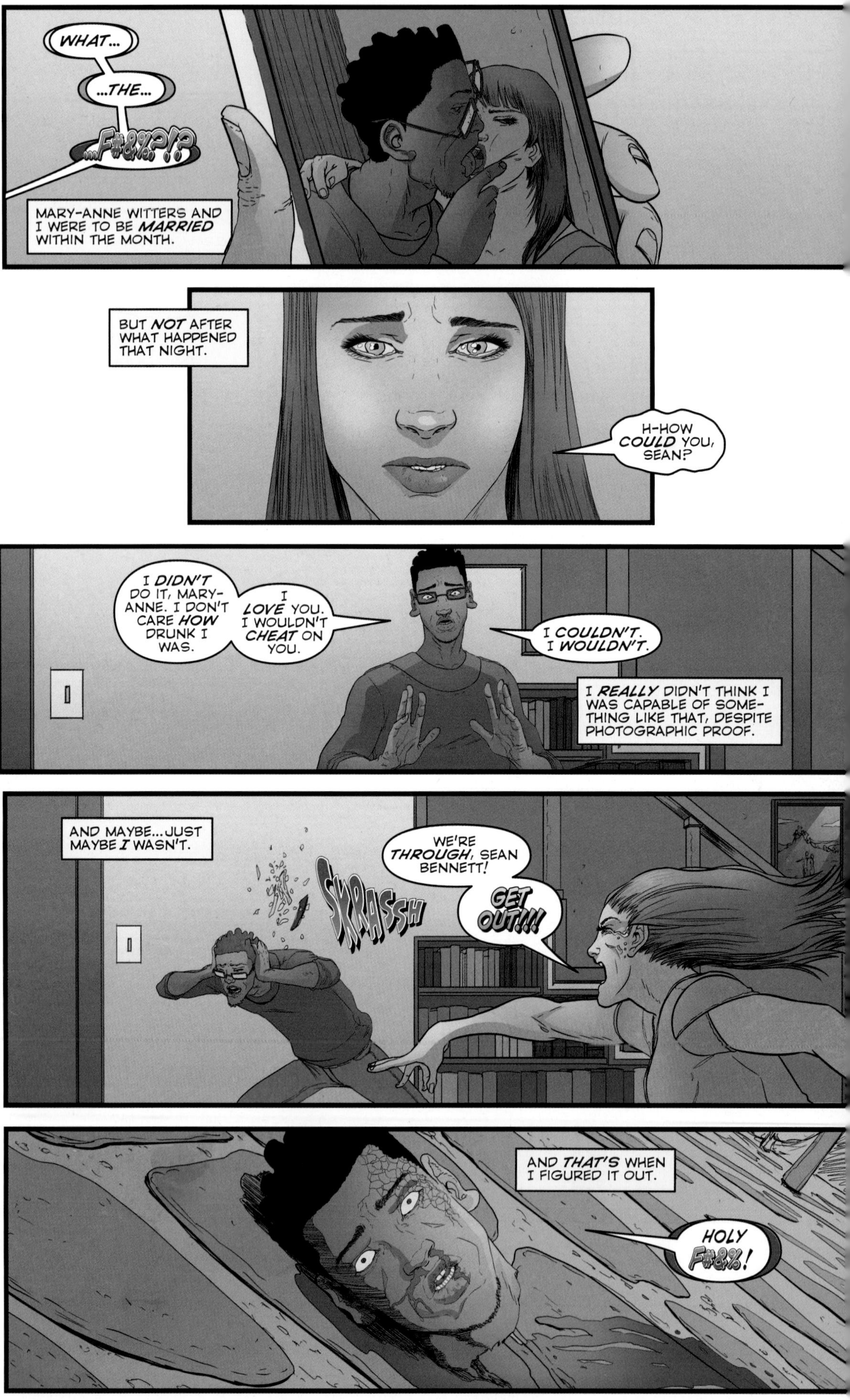
WHAT...
...THE...
...F#&%?!?
MARY-ANNE WITTERS AND I WERE TO BE MARRIED WITHIN THE MONTH.
BUT NOT AFTER WHAT HAPPENED THAT NIGHT.
H-HOW COULD YOU, SEAN?
I DIDN'T DO IT, MARY-ANNE. I DON'T CARE HOW DRUNK I WAS.
I LOVE YOU. I WOULDN'T CHEAT ON YOU.
I COULDN'T. I WOULDN'T.
I REALLY DIDN'T THINK I WAS CAPABLE OF SOMETHING LIKE THAT, DESPITE PHOTOGRAPHIC PROOF.
AND MAYBE...JUST MAYBE I WASN'T.
SKRASSH
WE'RE THROUGH, SEAN BENNETT!
GET OUT!!!
AND THAT'S WHEN I FIGURED IT OUT.
HOLY F#&%!

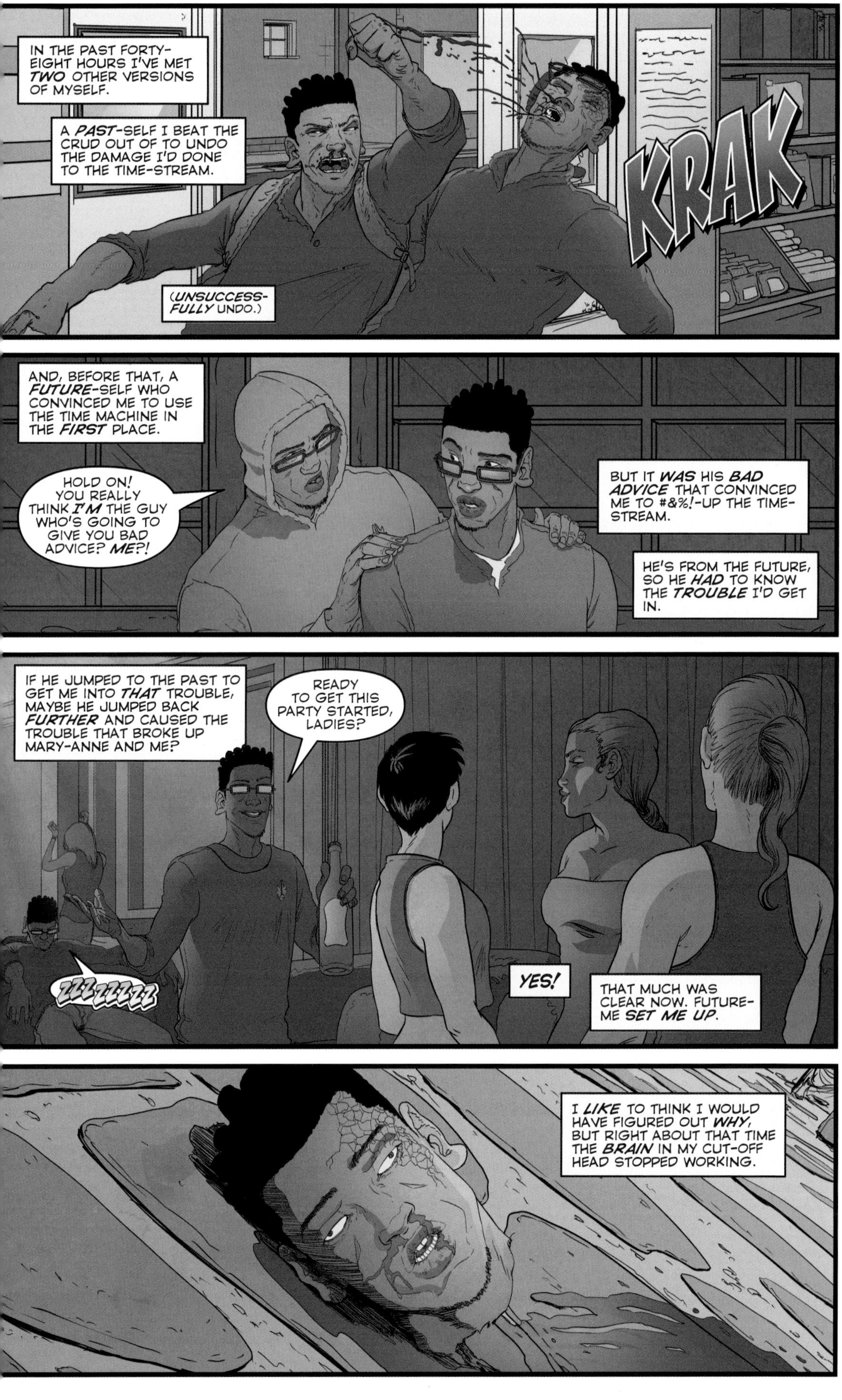
IN THE PAST FORTY-EIGHT HOURS I'VE MET TWO OTHER VERSIONS OF MYSELF.
A PAST-SELF I BEAT THE CRUD OUT OF TO UNDO THE DAMAGE I'D DONE TO THE TIME-STREAM.
KRAK
(UNSUCCESSFULLY UNDO.)
AND, BEFORE THAT, A FUTURE-SELF WHO CONVINCED ME TO USE THE TIME MACHINE IN THE FIRST PLACE.
HOLD ON! YOU REALLY THINK I'M THE GUY WHO'S GOING TO GIVE YOU BAD ADVICE? ME?!
BUT IT WAS HIS BAD ADVICE THAT CONVINCED ME TO #&%!-UP THE TIME-STREAM.
HE'S FROM THE FUTURE, SO HE HAD TO KNOW THE TROUBLE I'D GET IN.
IF HE JUMPED TO THE PAST TO GET ME INTO THAT TROUBLE, MAYBE HE JUMPED BACK FURTHER AND CAUSED THE TROUBLE THAT BROKE UP MARY-ANNE AND ME?
READY TO GET THIS PARTY STARTED, LADIES?
ZZZZZZZZ
YES!
THAT MUCH WAS CLEAR NOW. FUTURE-ME SET ME UP.
I LIKE TO THINK I WOULD HAVE FIGURED OUT WHY, BUT RIGHT ABOUT THAT TIME THE BRAIN IN MY CUT-OFF HEAD STOPPED WORKING.

AND JUST A FEW
SECONDS LATER...

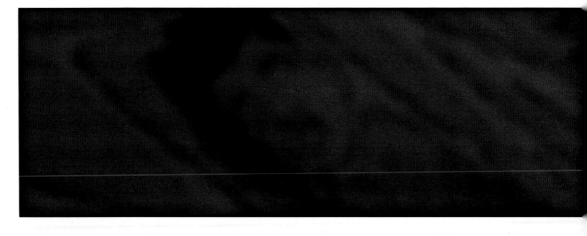

I DIED.

[redacted]

[redacted]

[redacted]

[redacted]

A FEW SECONDS EARLIER:

[AGAIN.]

FOR YOUR *CRIMES* AGAINST SUPREME EMPEROR ABRAHAM LINCOLN VI, WE CONDEMN YOU, *SEAN BENNETT*--

--TO *HUH?!?*

URRRRRRRRR

APOLOGIES, BUT WE *CAN'T* ALLOW THIS EXECUTION TO HAPPEN.

ZRRRAAPI

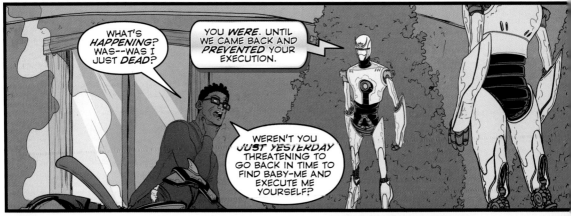

WHAT'S *HAPPENING*? WAS--WAS I JUST *DEAD*?

YOU *WERE*. UNTIL WE CAME BACK AND *PREVENTED* YOUR EXECUTION.

WEREN'T YOU *JUST YESTERDAY* THREATENING TO GO BACK IN TIME TO FIND BABY-ME AND EXECUTE ME YOURSELF?

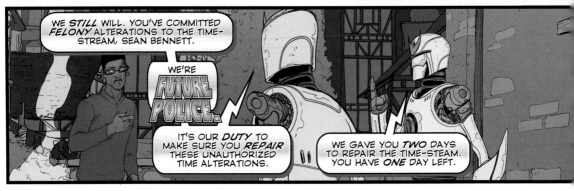

WE *STILL* WILL. YOU'VE COMMITTED *FELONY* ALTERATIONS TO THE TIME-STREAM, SEAN BENNETT.

WE'RE **FUTURE POLICE.**

IT'S OUR *DUTY* TO MAKE SURE YOU *REPAIR* THESE UNAUTHORIZED TIME ALTERATIONS.

WE GAVE YOU *TWO* DAYS TO REPAIR THE TIME-STEAM. YOU HAVE *ONE* DAY LEFT.

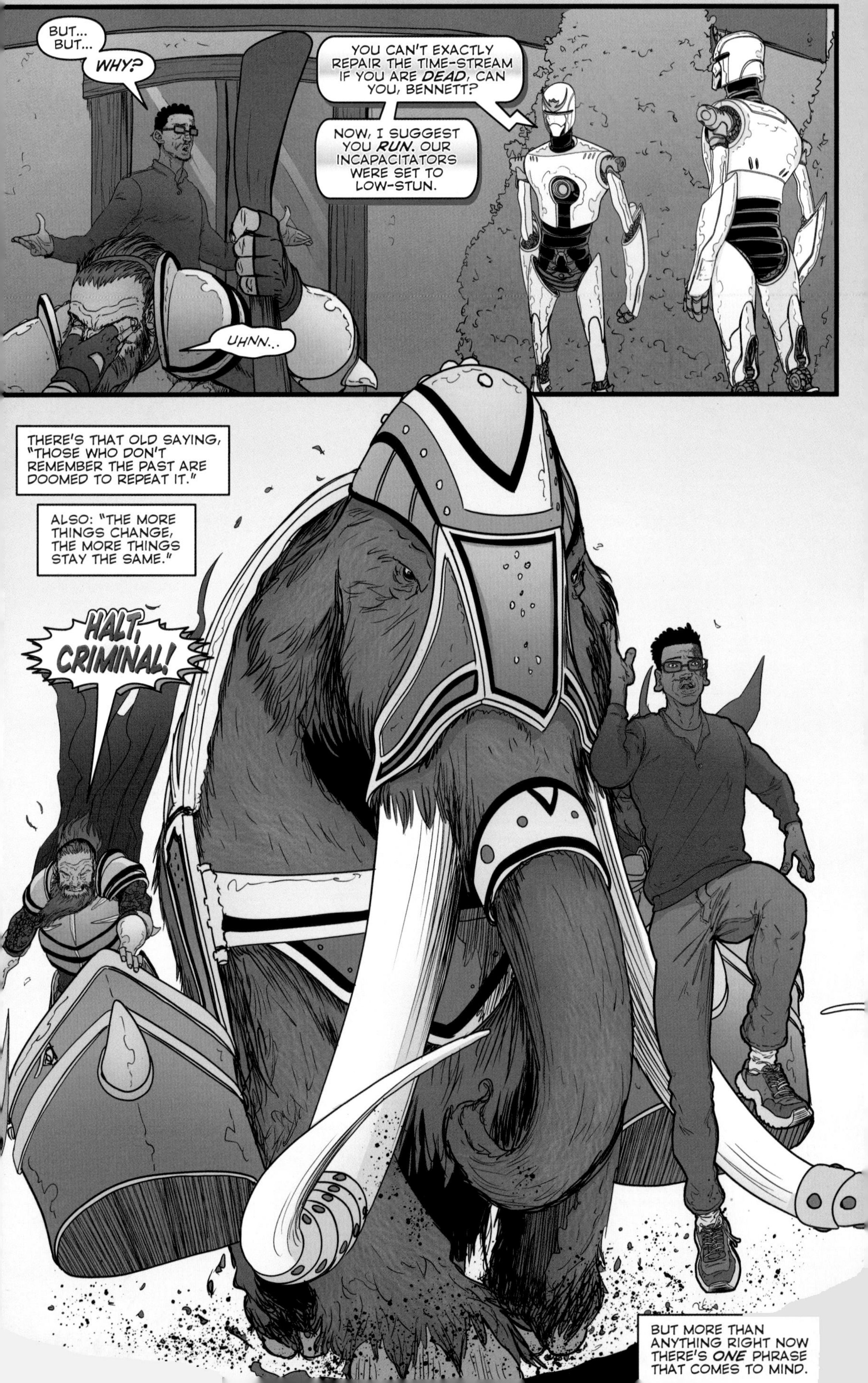
BUT... BUT... WHY?
YOU CAN'T EXACTLY REPAIR THE TIME-STREAM IF YOU ARE DEAD, CAN YOU, BENNETT?
NOW, I SUGGEST YOU RUN. OUR INCAPACITATORS WERE SET TO LOW-STUN.
UHNN...
THERE'S THAT OLD SAYING, "THOSE WHO DON'T REMEMBER THE PAST ARE DOOMED TO REPEAT IT."
ALSO: "THE MORE THINGS CHANGE, THE MORE THINGS STAY THE SAME."
HALT, CRIMINAL!
BUT MORE THAN ANYTHING RIGHT NOW THERE'S ONE PHRASE THAT COMES TO MIND.

"F#&% IT!"

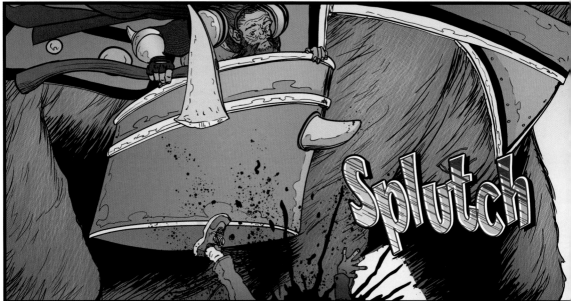

Splutch

AFTER ALL I'D JUST BEEN
THROUGH, I *REALLY* WASN'T
IN THE MOOD TO TRY TO
OUTRUN A MASTODON.

DEAD AGAIN.

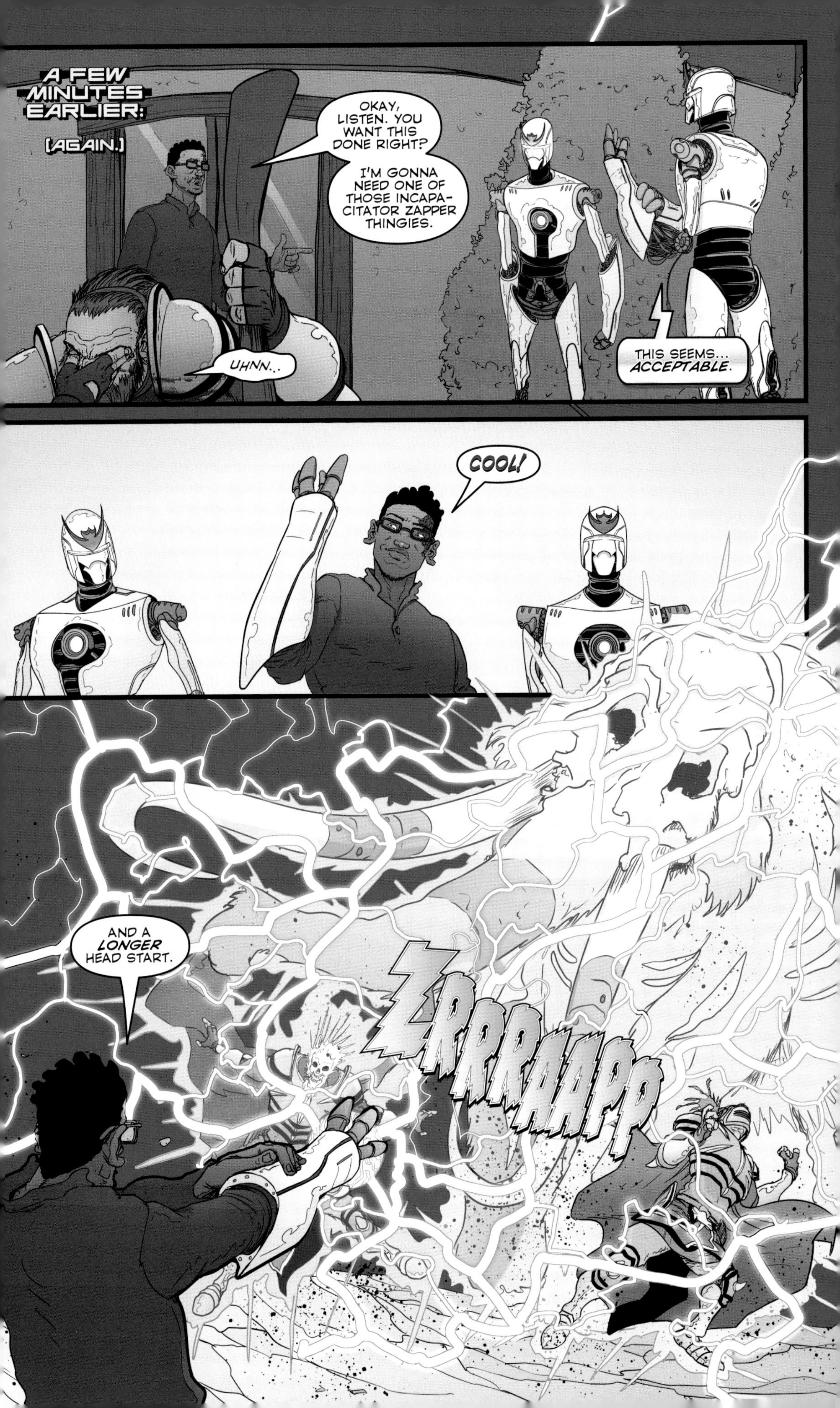
A FEW MINUTES EARLIER:
[AGAIN.]
OKAY, LISTEN. YOU WANT THIS DONE RIGHT?
I'M GONNA NEED ONE OF THOSE INCAPACITATOR ZAPPER THINGIES.
UHNN...
THIS SEEMS... ACCEPTABLE.
COOL!
AND A LONGER HEAD START.
ZRRRAAPP

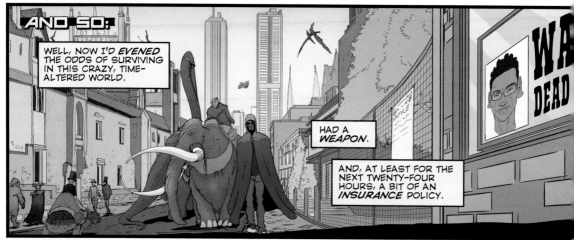

AND SO:

WELL, NOW I'D *EVENED* THE ODDS OF SURVIVING IN THIS CRAZY, TIME-ALTERED WORLD.

HAD A *WEAPON*.

AND, AT LEAST FOR THE NEXT TWENTY-FOUR HOURS, A BIT OF AN *INSURANCE* POLICY.

WHAT I *DIDN'T* HAVE WAS A CLUE OF HOW TO *UNDO* ALL THIS.

AND WHEN I USE THE TIME MACHINE I ONLY MAKE THINGS *WORSE*.

EXTREE, EXTREE! BELOVED EMPEROR SETS DATE FOR WEDDING OF THE CENTURY!

READ ALL ABOUT IT!

WHAT THE F#&% HAVE I *DONE*?

AND HOW DO I FIX--

HEY, YOU! OUTTA THE WAY!

CLOMP CLOMP CLOMP
CLOMP CLOMP CLOMP
CLOMP CLOMP CLOMP
CLOMP CLOMP CLOMP
CLOMP CLOMP

HUH?

OKAY, *THAT'S* NEW.

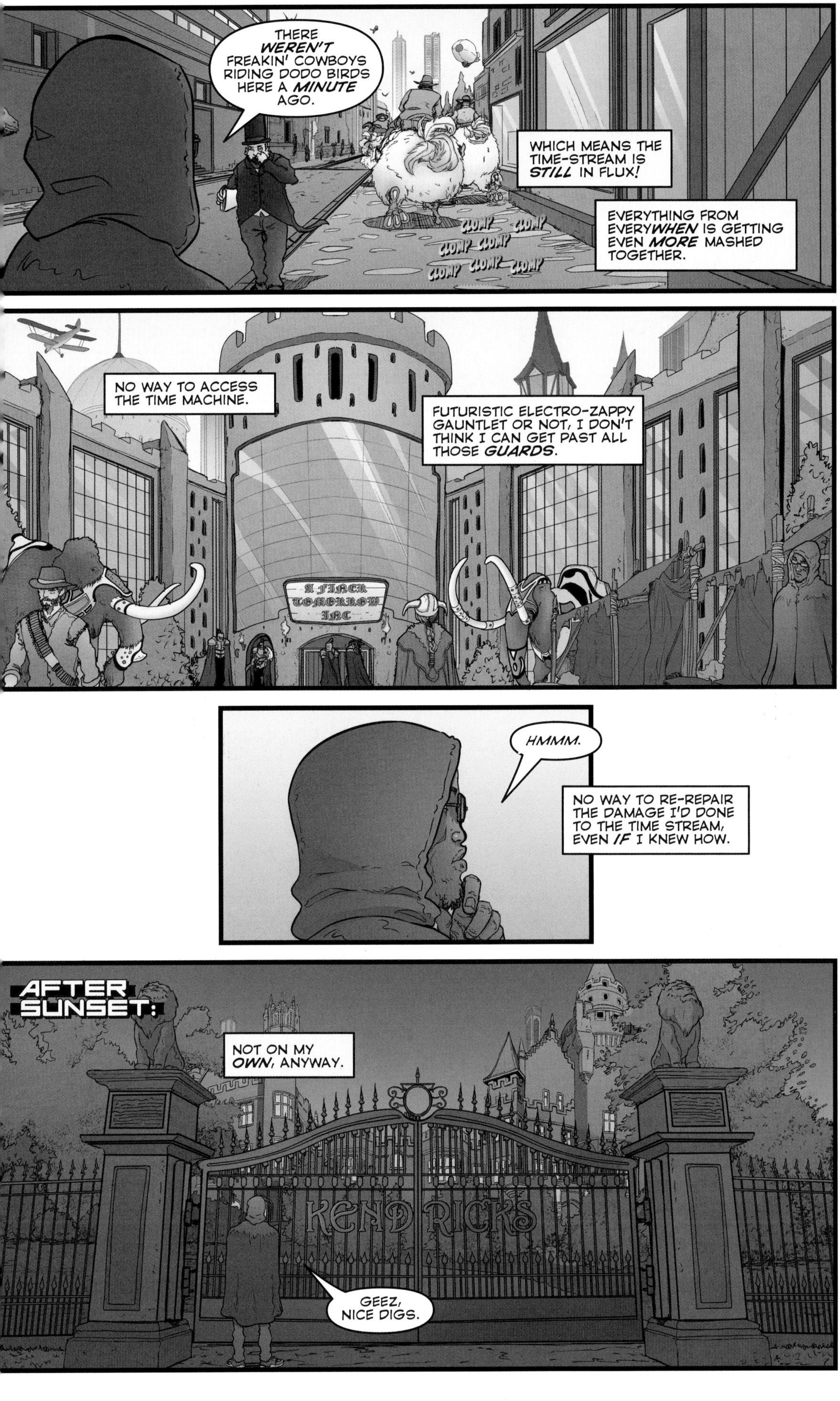
THERE WEREN'T FREAKIN' COWBOYS RIDING DODO BIRDS HERE A MINUTE AGO.
WHICH MEANS THE TIME-STREAM IS STILL IN FLUX!
EVERYTHING FROM EVERYWHEN IS GETTING EVEN MORE MASHED TOGETHER.
CLOMP CLOMP CLOMP CLOMP CLOMP CLOMP CLOMP CLOMP
NO WAY TO ACCESS THE TIME MACHINE.
FUTURISTIC ELECTRO-ZAPPY GAUNTLET OR NOT, I DON'T THINK I CAN GET PAST ALL THOSE GUARDS.
A FINER TOMORROW INC
HMMM.
NO WAY TO RE-REPAIR THE DAMAGE I'D DONE TO THE TIME STREAM, EVEN IF I KNEW HOW.
AFTER SUNSET:
NOT ON MY OWN, ANYWAY.
KENDRICKS
GEEZ, NICE DIGS.

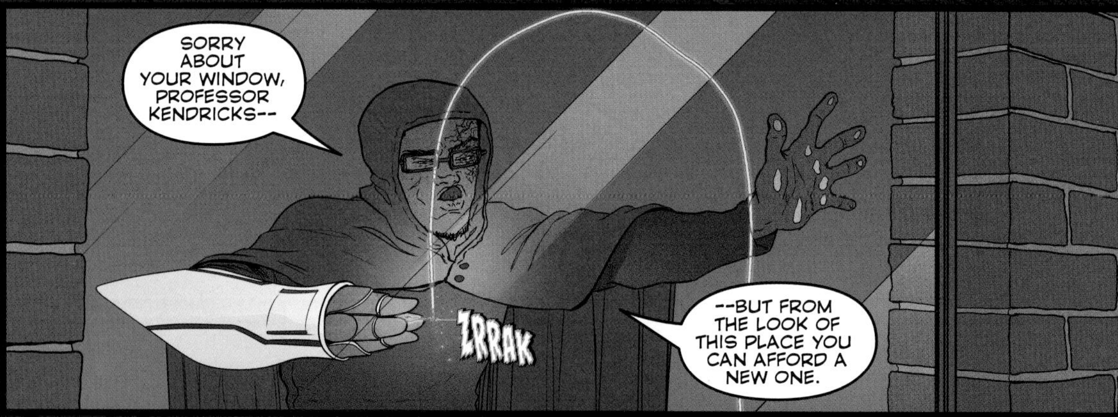
SORRY ABOUT YOUR WINDOW, PROFESSOR KENDRICKS--
ZRRAK
--BUT FROM THE LOOK OF THIS PLACE YOU CAN AFFORD A NEW ONE.

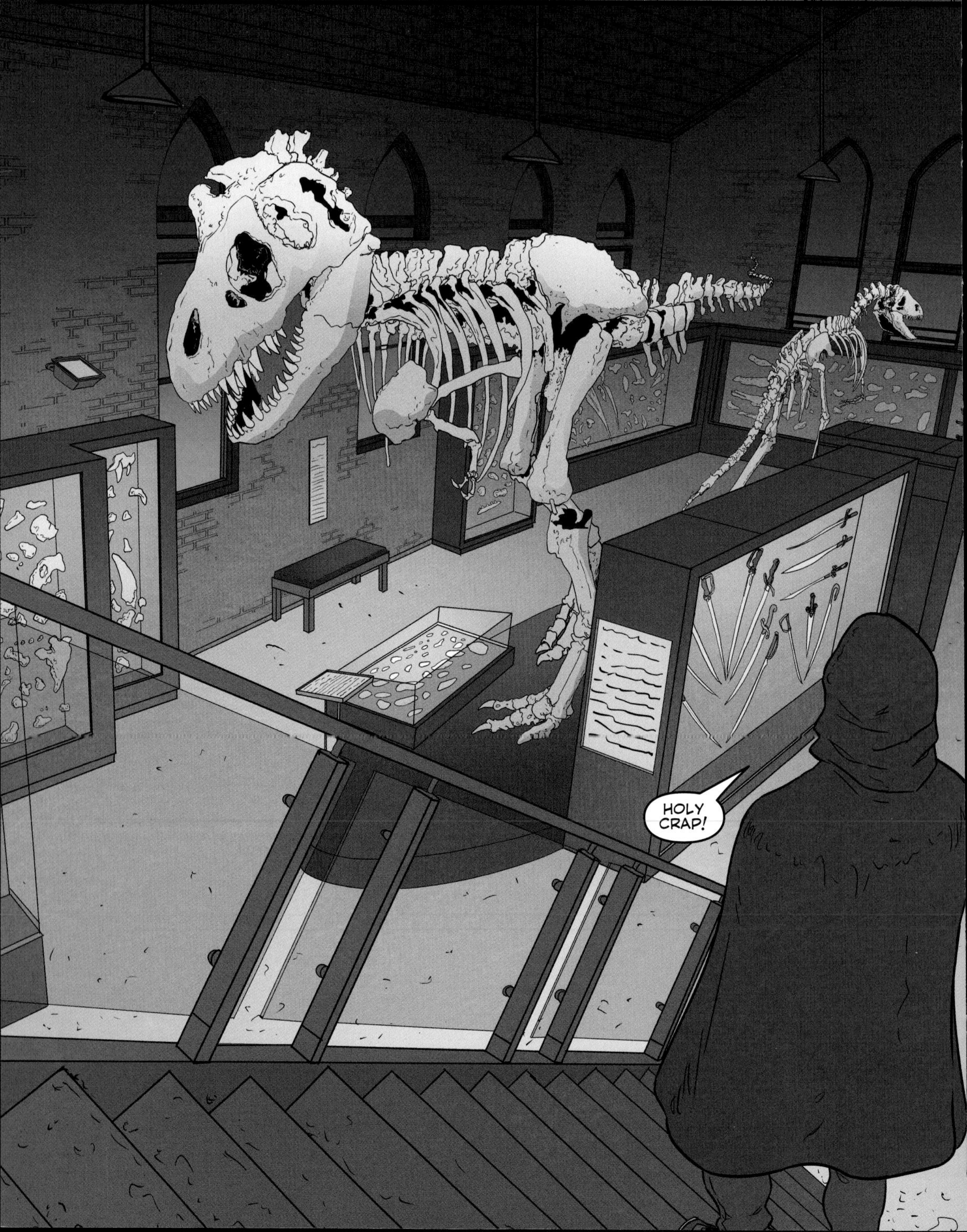
HOLY CRAP!

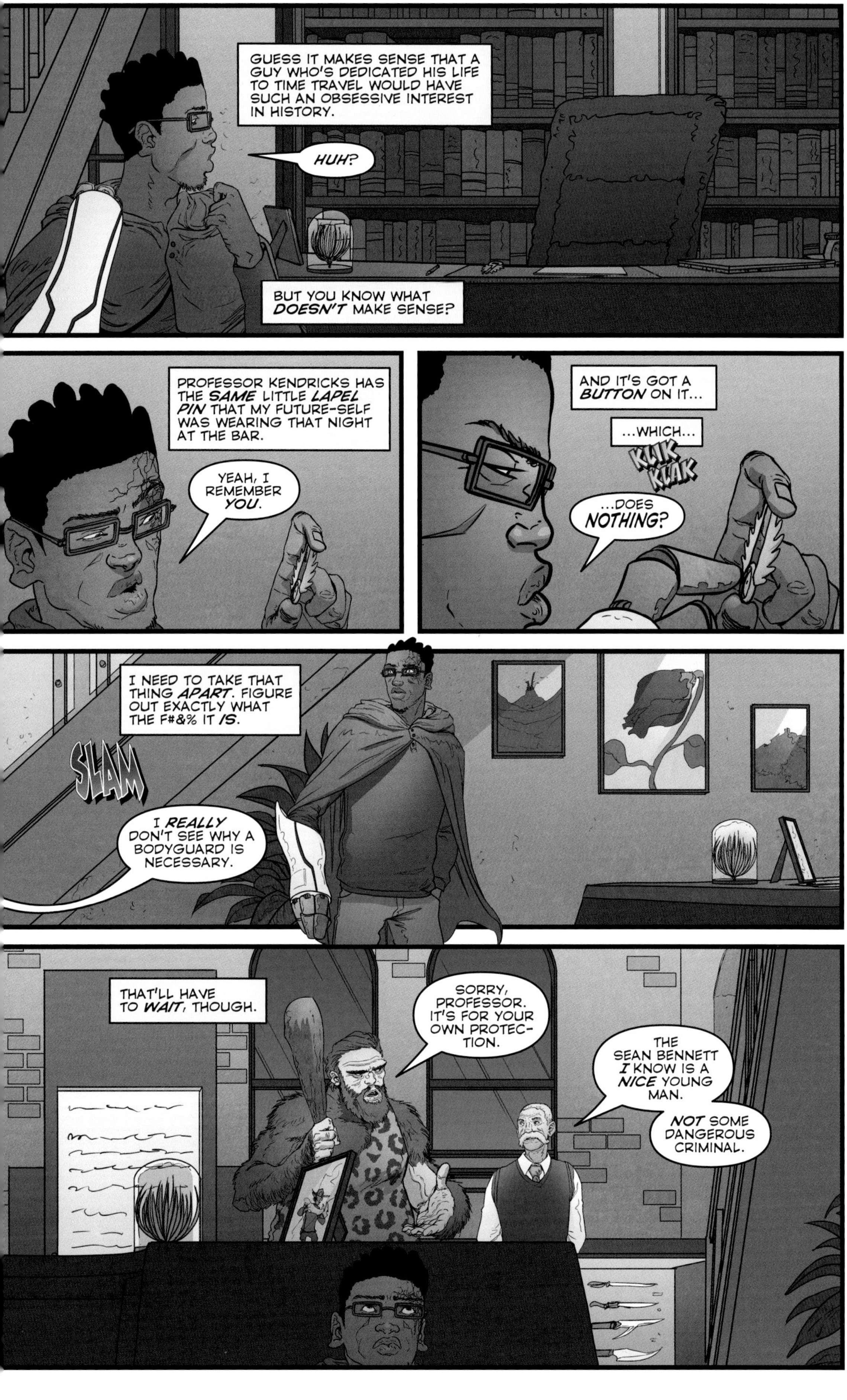
GUESS IT MAKES SENSE THAT A GUY WHO'S DEDICATED HIS LIFE TO TIME TRAVEL WOULD HAVE SUCH AN OBSESSIVE INTEREST IN HISTORY.
HUH?
BUT YOU KNOW WHAT DOESN'T MAKE SENSE?
PROFESSOR KENDRICKS HAS THE SAME LITTLE LAPEL PIN THAT MY FUTURE-SELF WAS WEARING THAT NIGHT AT THE BAR.
YEAH, I REMEMBER YOU.
AND IT'S GOT A BUTTON ON IT...
...WHICH...
KLIK KLAK
...DOES NOTHING?
I NEED TO TAKE THAT THING APART. FIGURE OUT EXACTLY WHAT THE F#&% IT IS.
SLAM
I REALLY DON'T SEE WHY A BODYGUARD IS NECESSARY.
THAT'LL HAVE TO WAIT, THOUGH.
SORRY, PROFESSOR. IT'S FOR YOUR OWN PROTEC-TION.
THE SEAN BENNETT I KNOW IS A NICE YOUNG MAN.
NOT SOME DANGEROUS CRIMINAL.

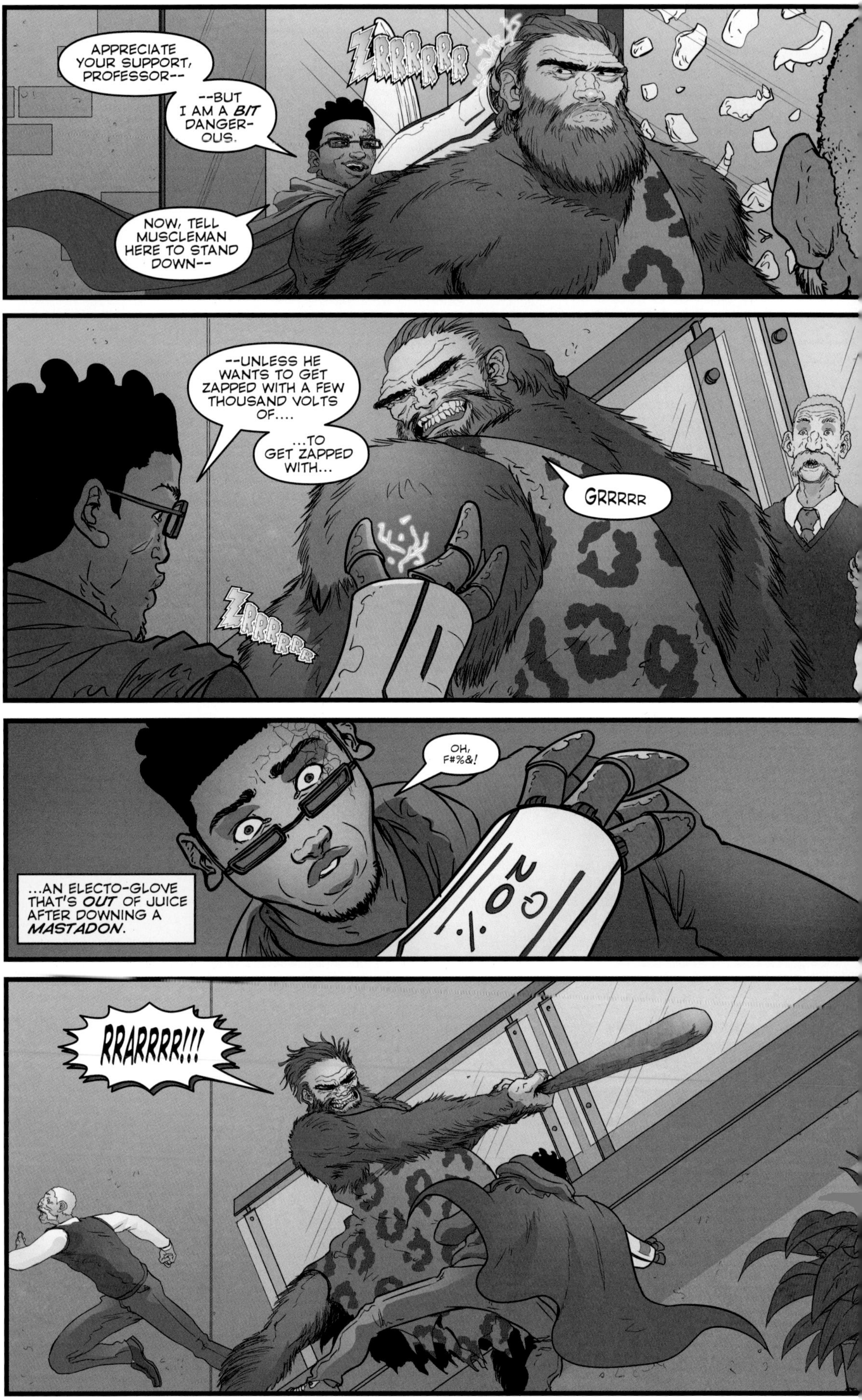
APPRECIATE YOUR SUPPORT, PROFESSOR--
ZRRRRRR
--BUT I AM A *BIT* DANGEROUS.
NOW, TELL MUSCLEMAN HERE TO STAND DOWN--
--UNLESS HE WANTS TO GET ZAPPED WITH A FEW THOUSAND VOLTS OF....
...TO GET ZAPPED WITH...
GRRRRR
ZRRRRRRR
OH, F#%&!
...AN ELECTO-GLOVE THAT'S *OUT* OF JUICE AFTER DOWNING A *MASTADON*.
0%
RRARRRR!!!

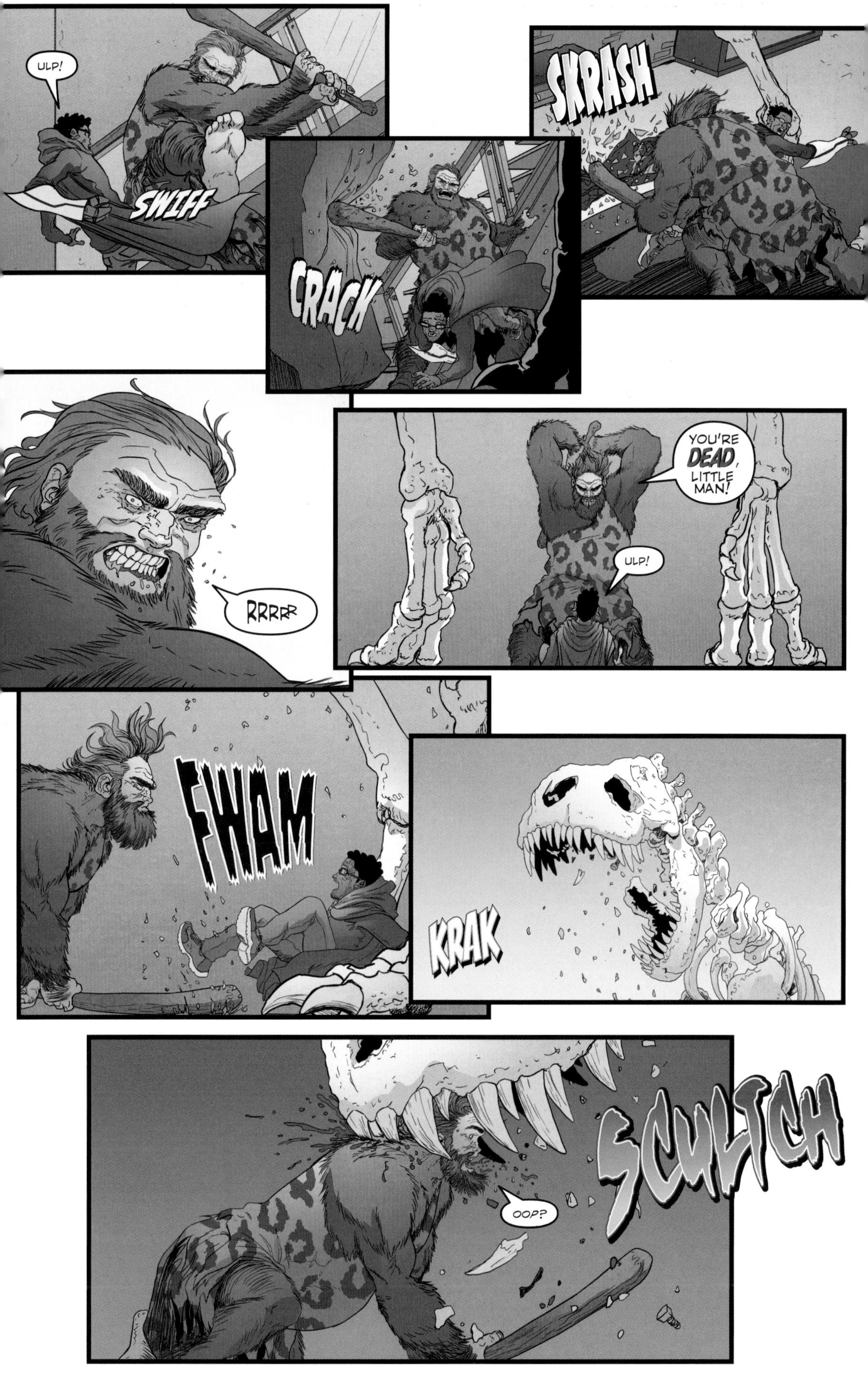
ULP!
SWIFF
CRACK
SKRASH
RRRRR
YOU'RE DEAD, LITTLE MAN!
ULP!
FWAM
KRAK
SCULTCH
OOP?

YOU...YOU *KILLED* HIM, SEAN.

NOT ON *PURPOSE.*

AND IF ALL GOES LIKE IT *SHOULD,* I'M GOING TO *UNDO* THIS.

FIND SOME WAY TO GO BACK IN TIME, AND MAKE SURE THIS *NEVER* HAPPENS.

HAPPENED.

WHATEVER.

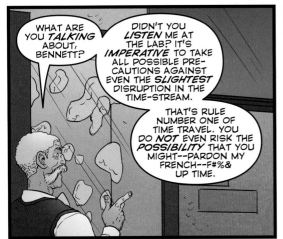

WHAT ARE YOU *TALKING* ABOUT, BENNETT?

DIDN'T YOU *LISTEN* ME AT THE LAB? IT'S *IMPERATIVE* TO TAKE ALL POSSIBLE PRE-CAUTIONS AGAINST EVEN THE *SLIGHTEST* DISRUPTION IN THE TIME-STREAM.

THAT'S RULE NUMBER ONE OF TIME TRAVEL. YOU DO *NOT* EVEN RISK THE *POSSIBILITY* THAT YOU MIGHT--PARDON MY FRENCH--F#%& UP TIME.

THAT'S THE *PROBLEM,* PROFESSOR. *THAT'S* WHY I NEED YOUR *HELP!*

I *ALREADY* F#%&ED UP TIME!

MY FUTURE-SELF CONVINCED ME TO GO BACK IN TIME--*ONLY* A WEEK--AND MAKE A FEW *TINY* CHANGES.

NOW EVERYTHING IS *COMPLETELY* SCREWY.

DINOSAURS *SHOULDN'T* WALK THE EARTH. OR MAMMOTHS. OR DODO BIRDS.

AND ABE LINCOLN WAS ASSASSINATED BEFORE HE COULD BECOME SOME SORT OF TYRANT DICTATOR, AND SPAWN A *LINE* OF TYRANT DICTATORS.

ABRAHAM LINCOLN?

ASSASSINATED?!?

YOU KNOW, I DO RECALL FROM THE HISTORY BOOKS, AN *ATTEMPTED* ASSASSINATION.

AND IT'S SAID THAT LINCOLN WAS NEVER THE SAME AFTER THE ATTEMPT.

AT THE FORD THEATRE. 1865.

BUT THE ASSASSINATION WAS *THWARTED*.

YES, *HERE* IT IS.

THEY TOOK A DAGUERREOTYPE PHOTO OF THE MAN WHO *PREVENTED* THE MURDER, BUT I'M NOT SURE THEY EVER GOT THAT HERO'S *NAME*.

...

OH, MY!

SAV

I'M SORRY, BENNETT. BUT I *WARNED* YOU ABOUT THE DANGERS OF *RECKLESS* TIME TRAVEL, AND I *WON'T* HELP YOU.

THIS IS *YOUR* PROBLEM, AND IT'S UP TO *YOU* TO SOLVE IT.

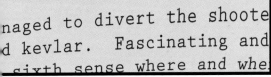

naged to divert the shoote
d kevlar. Fascinating and
sixth sense where and whe

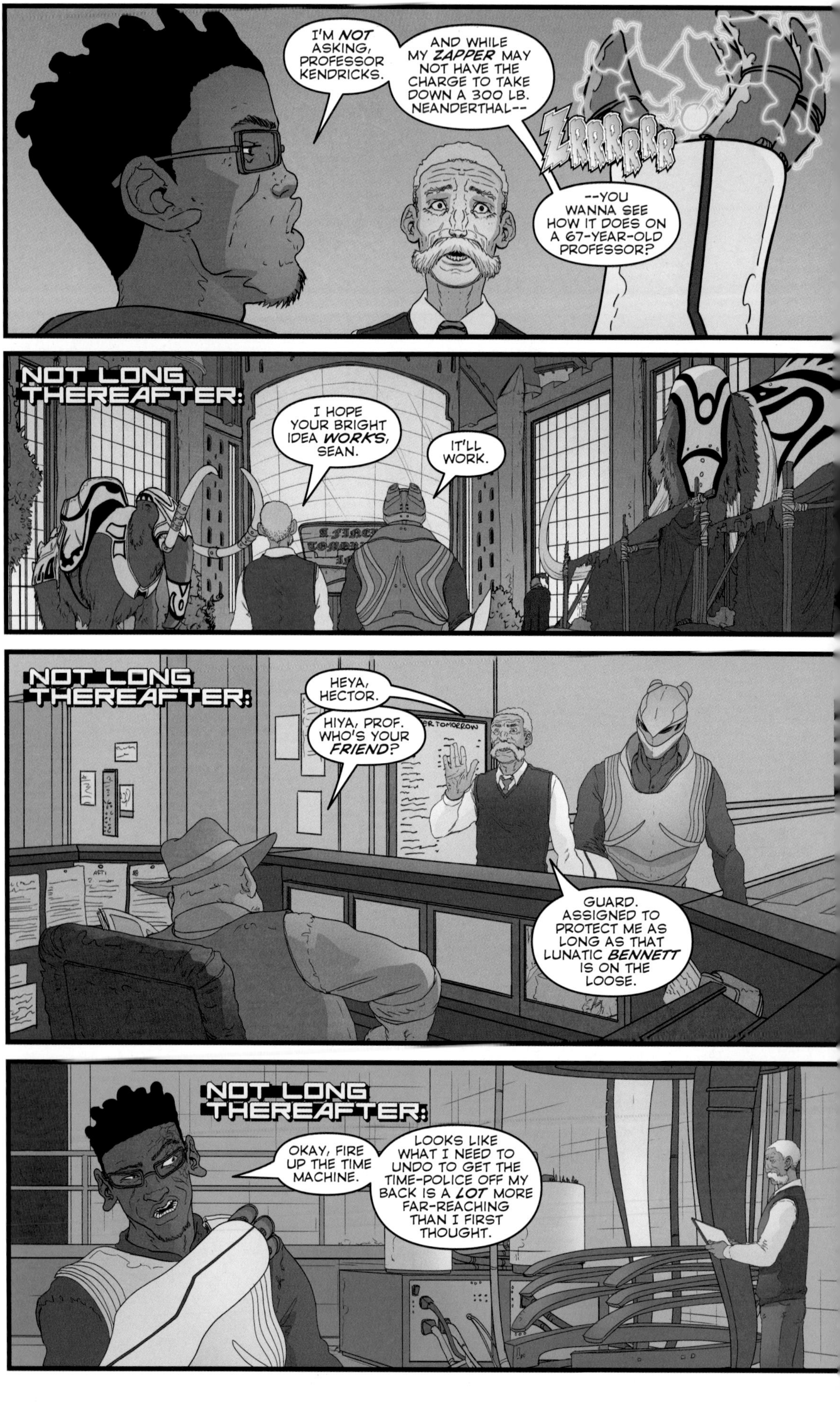
I'M NOT ASKING, PROFESSOR KENDRICKS.
AND WHILE MY ZAPPER MAY NOT HAVE THE CHARGE TO TAKE DOWN A 300 LB. NEANDERTHAL--
ZRRRRRR
--YOU WANNA SEE HOW IT DOES ON A 67-YEAR-OLD PROFESSOR?
NOT LONG THEREAFTER:
I HOPE YOUR BRIGHT IDEA WORKS, SEAN.
IT'LL WORK.
NOT LONG THEREAFTER:
HEYA, HECTOR.
HIYA, PROF. WHO'S YOUR FRIEND?
GUARD. ASSIGNED TO PROTECT ME AS LONG AS THAT LUNATIC BENNETT IS ON THE LOOSE.
NOT LONG THEREAFTER:
OKAY, FIRE UP THE TIME MACHINE.
LOOKS LIKE WHAT I NEED TO UNDO TO GET THE TIME-POLICE OFF MY BACK IS A LOT MORE FAR-REACHING THAN I FIRST THOUGHT.

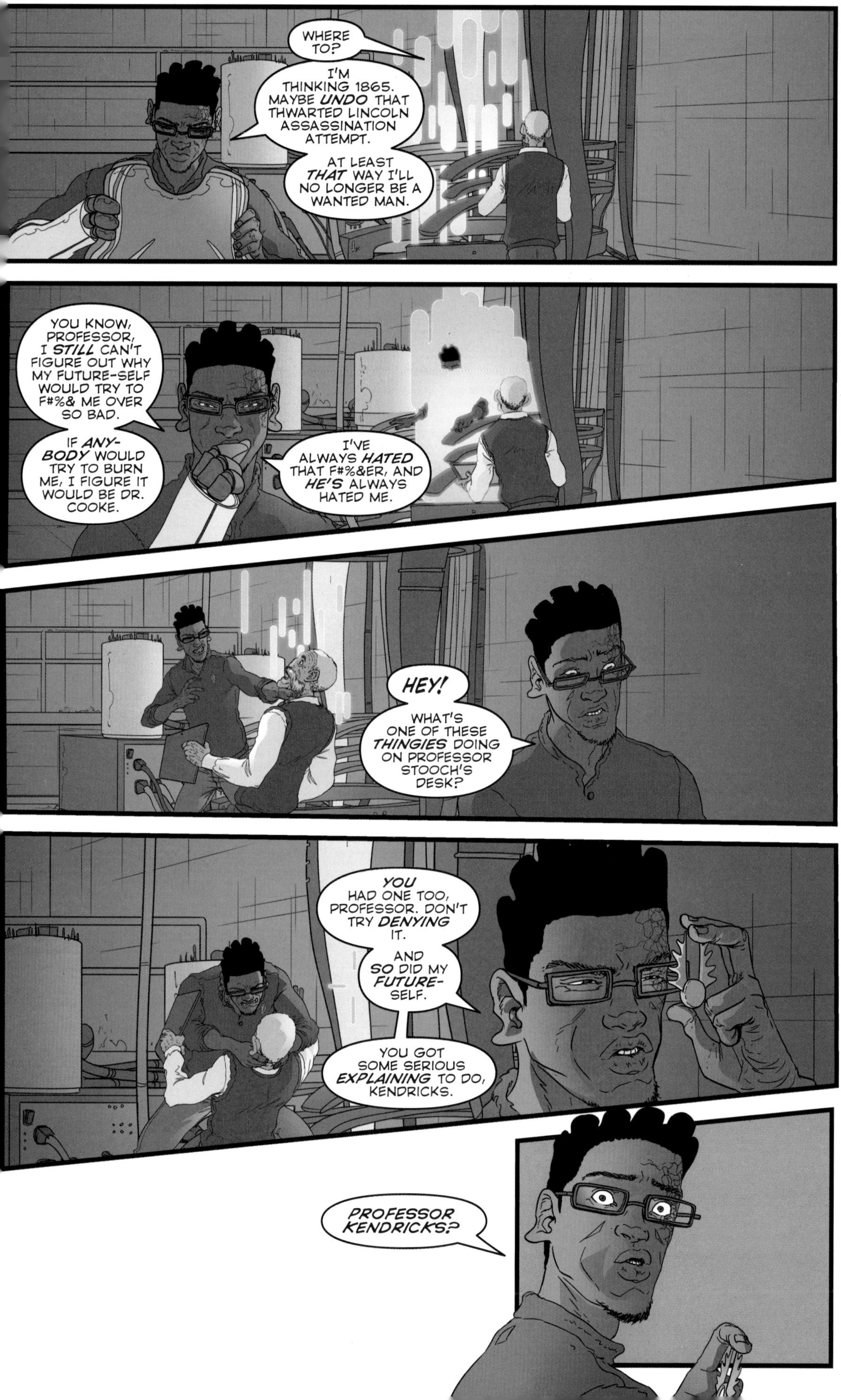
WHERE TO?
I'M THINKING 1865. MAYBE UNDO THAT THWARTED LINCOLN ASSASSINATION ATTEMPT.
AT LEAST THAT WAY I'LL NO LONGER BE A WANTED MAN.
YOU KNOW, PROFESSOR, I STILL CAN'T FIGURE OUT WHY MY FUTURE-SELF WOULD TRY TO F#%& ME OVER SO BAD.
IF ANY-BODY WOULD TRY TO BURN ME, I FIGURE IT WOULD BE DR. COOKE.
I'VE ALWAYS HATED THAT F#%&ER, AND HE'S ALWAYS HATED ME.
HEY!
WHAT'S ONE OF THESE THINGIES DOING ON PROFESSOR STOOCH'S DESK?
YOU HAD ONE TOO, PROFESSOR. DON'T TRY DENYING IT.
AND SO DID MY FUTURE-SELF.
YOU GOT SOME SERIOUS EXPLAINING TO DO, KENDRICKS.
PROFESSOR KENDRICKS?

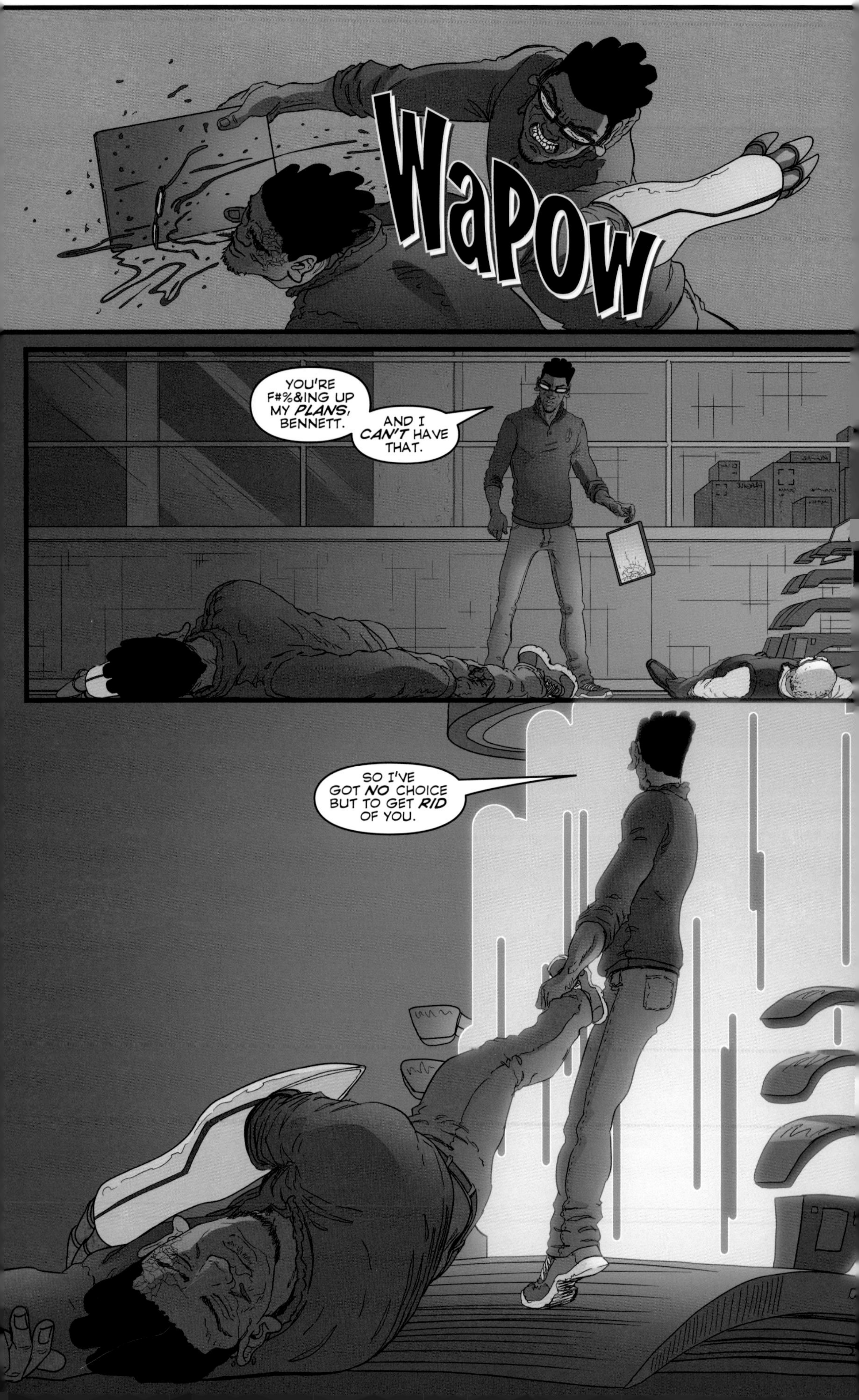
WAPOW
YOU'RE F#%&ING UP MY PLANS, BENNETT.
AND I CAN'T HAVE THAT.
SO I'VE GOT NO CHOICE BUT TO GET RID OF YOU.

4

SINS OF THE PAST

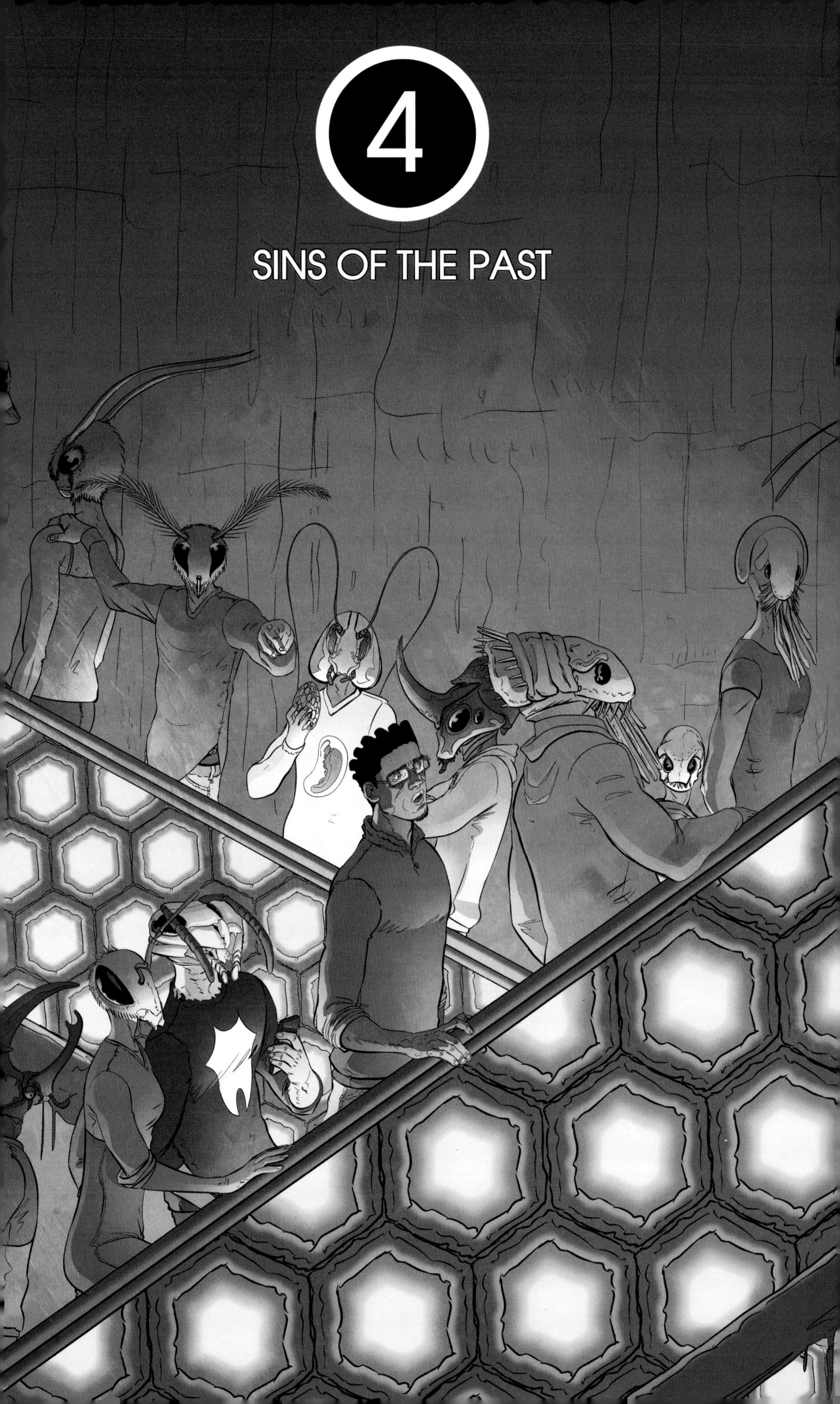

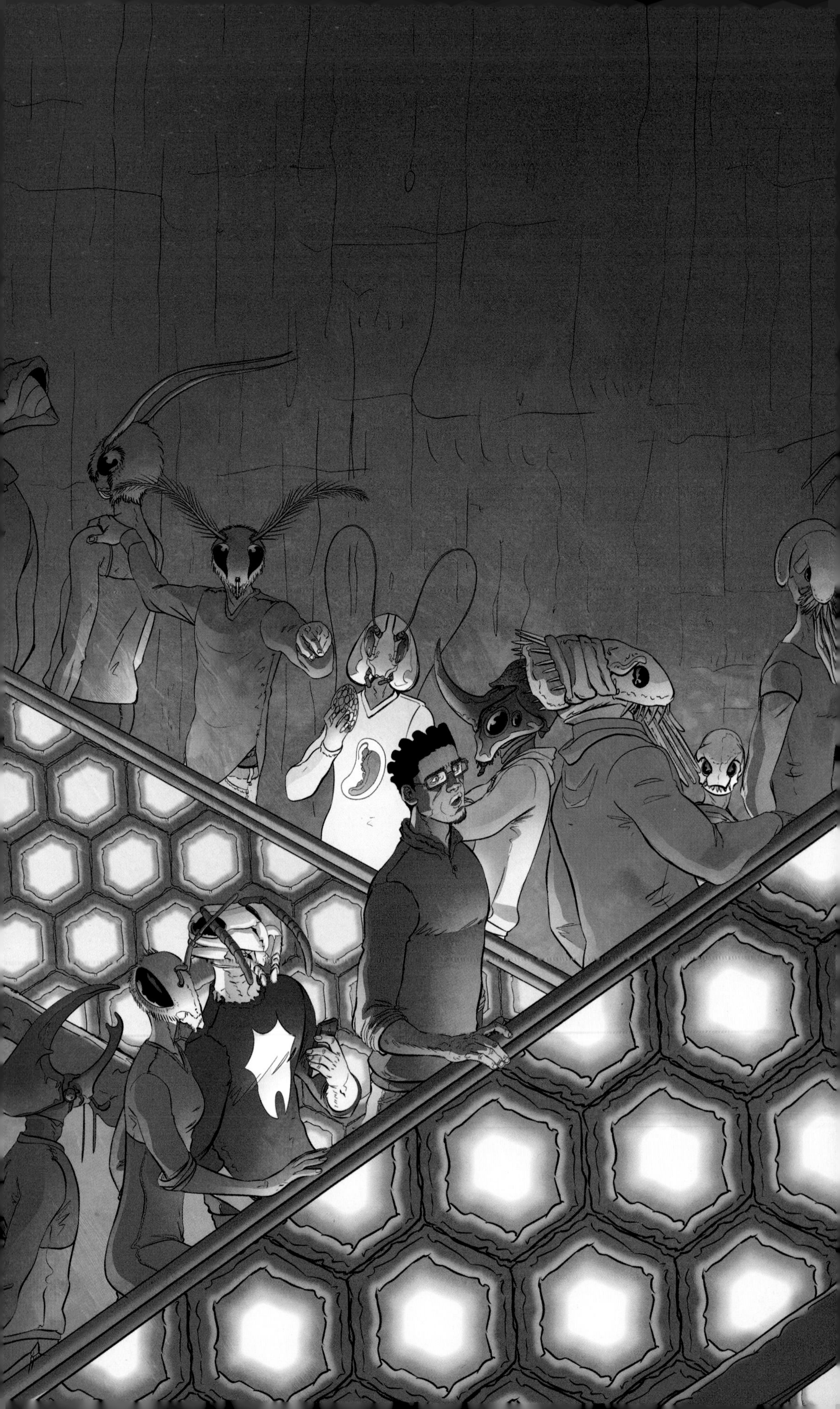

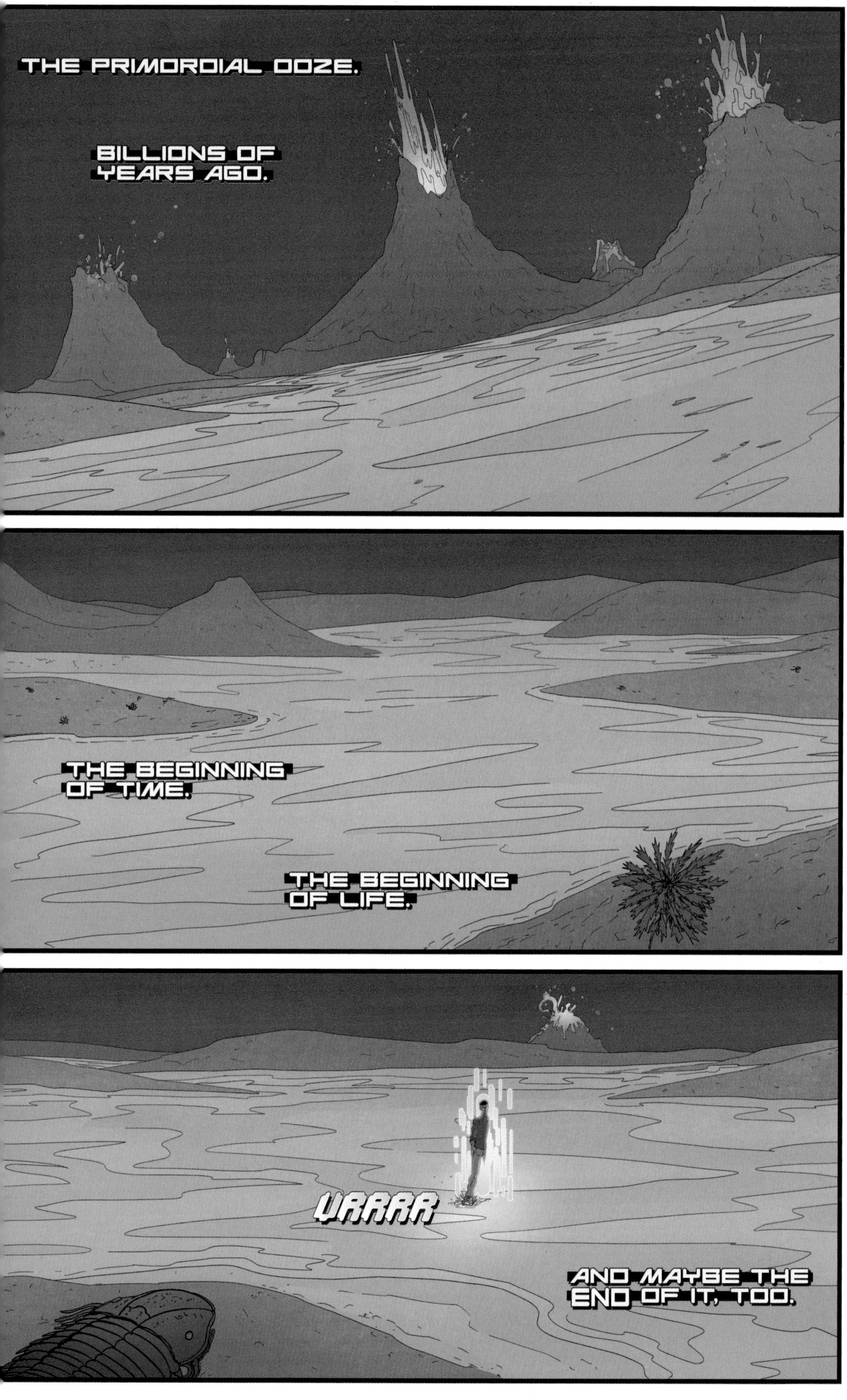
THE PRIMORDIAL OOZE.
BILLIONS OF YEARS AGO.
THE BEGINNING OF TIME.
THE BEGINNING OF LIFE.
URRRR
AND MAYBE THE END OF IT, TOO.

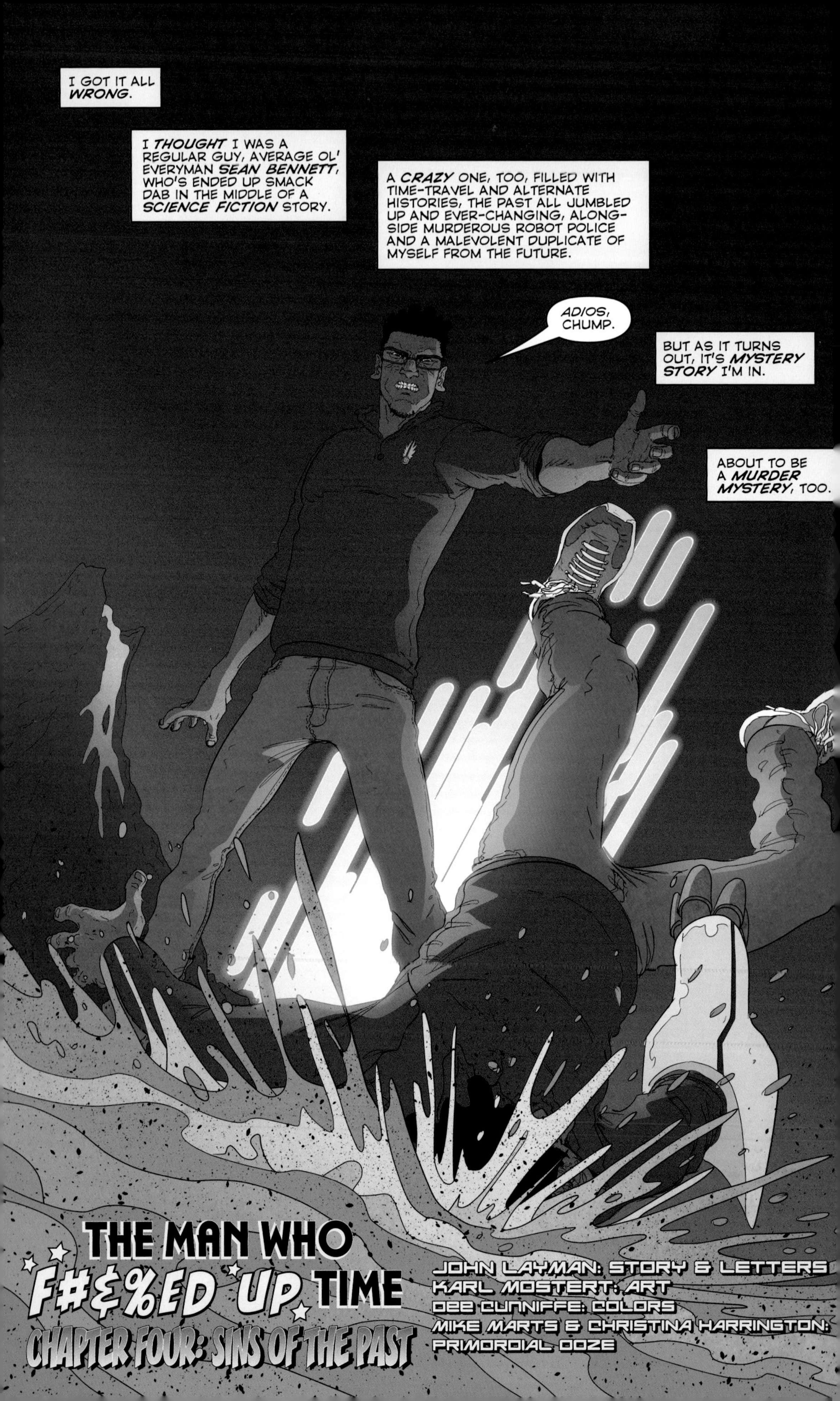
I GOT IT ALL WRONG.
I THOUGHT I WAS A REGULAR GUY, AVERAGE OL' EVERYMAN SEAN BENNETT, WHO'S ENDED UP SMACK DAB IN THE MIDDLE OF A SCIENCE FICTION STORY.
A CRAZY ONE, TOO, FILLED WITH TIME-TRAVEL AND ALTERNATE HISTORIES, THE PAST ALL JUMBLED UP AND EVER-CHANGING, ALONG-SIDE MURDEROUS ROBOT POLICE AND A MALEVOLENT DUPLICATE OF MYSELF FROM THE FUTURE.
ADIOS, CHUMP.
BUT AS IT TURNS OUT, IT'S MYSTERY STORY I'M IN.
ABOUT TO BE A MURDER MYSTERY, TOO.
THE MAN WHO F#&%ED UP TIME
CHAPTER FOUR: SINS OF THE PAST
JOHN LAYMAN: STORY & LETTERS
KARL MOSTERT: ART
DEE CUNNIFFE: COLORS
MIKE MARTS & CHRISTINA HARRINGTON: PRIMORDIAL OOZE

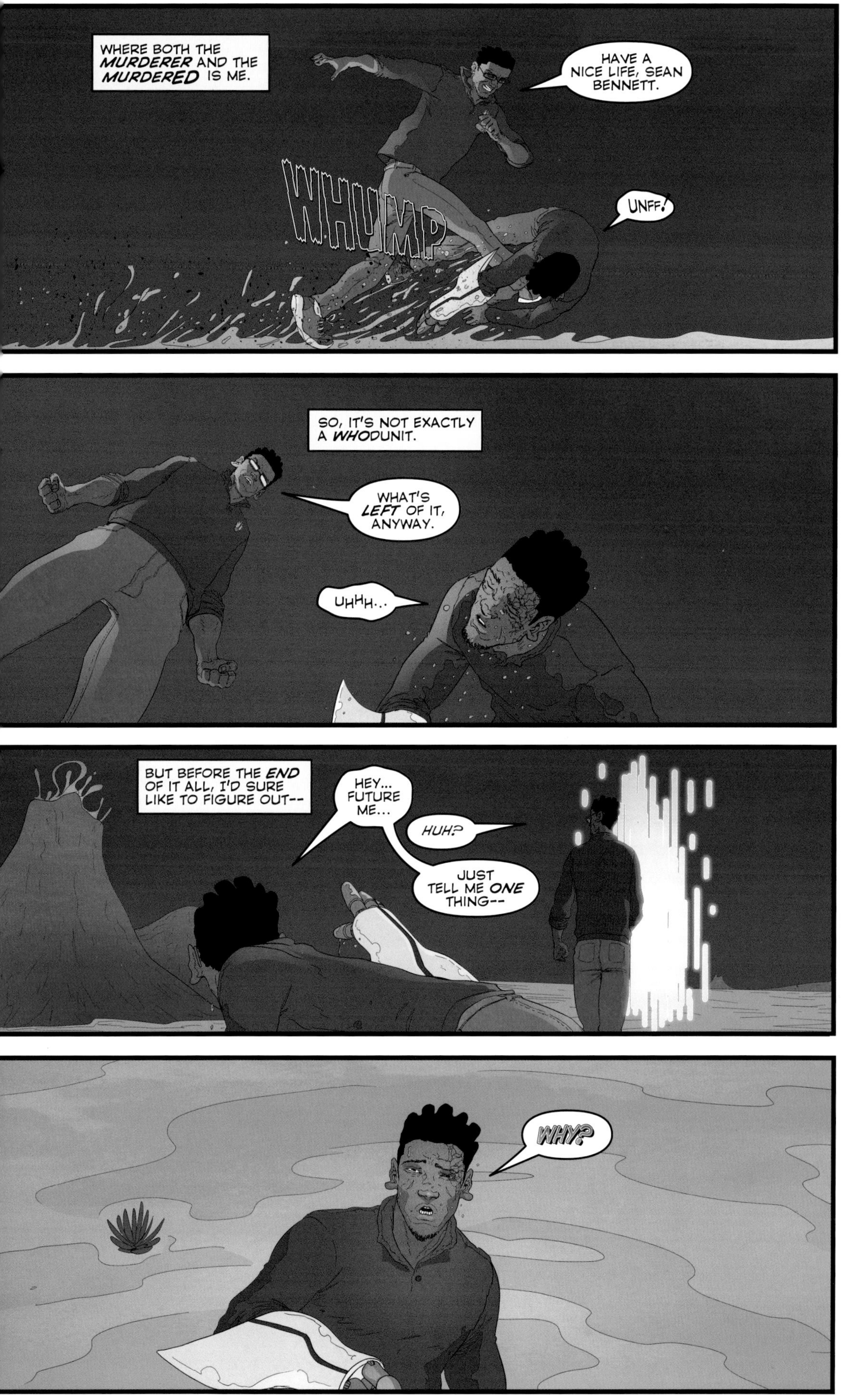
WHERE BOTH THE MURDERER AND THE MURDERED IS ME.
HAVE A NICE LIFE, SEAN BENNETT.
WHUMP
UNFF!
SO, IT'S NOT EXACTLY A WHODUNIT.
WHAT'S LEFT OF IT, ANYWAY.
UHHH...
BUT BEFORE THE END OF IT ALL, I'D SURE LIKE TO FIGURE OUT--
HEY... FUTURE ME...
HUH?
JUST TELL ME ONE THING--
WHY?

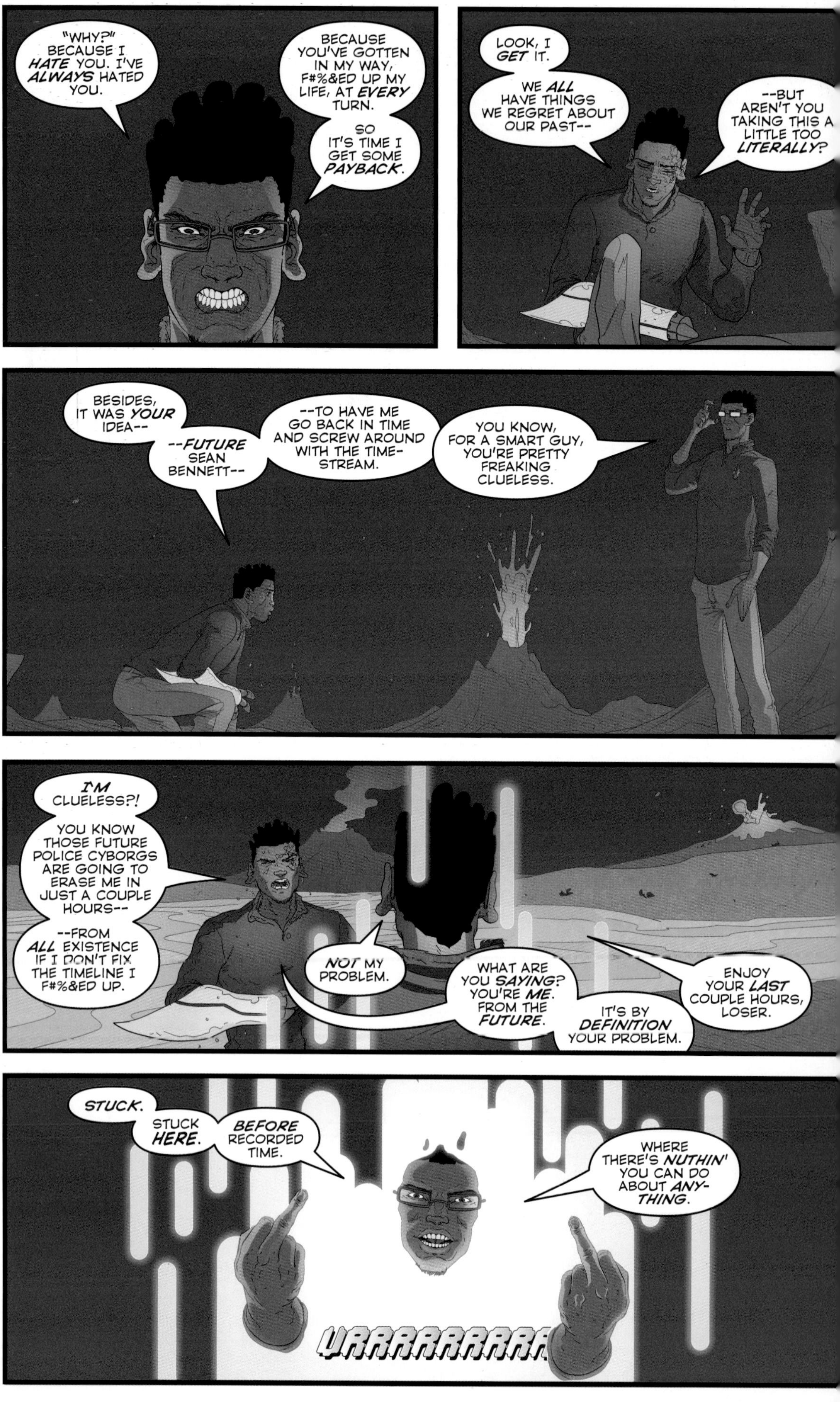

"WHY?" BECAUSE I HATE YOU. I'VE ALWAYS HATED YOU.
BECAUSE YOU'VE GOTTEN IN MY WAY, F#%&ED UP MY LIFE, AT EVERY TURN.
SO IT'S TIME I GET SOME PAYBACK.
LOOK, I GET IT.
WE ALL HAVE THINGS WE REGRET ABOUT OUR PAST--
--BUT AREN'T YOU TAKING THIS A LITTLE TOO LITERALLY?
BESIDES, IT WAS YOUR IDEA--
--FUTURE SEAN BENNETT--
--TO HAVE ME GO BACK IN TIME AND SCREW AROUND WITH THE TIME-STREAM.
YOU KNOW, FOR A SMART GUY, YOU'RE PRETTY FREAKING CLUELESS.
I'M CLUELESS?!
YOU KNOW THOSE FUTURE POLICE CYBORGS ARE GOING TO ERASE ME IN JUST A COUPLE HOURS--
--FROM ALL EXISTENCE IF I DON'T FIX THE TIMELINE I F#%&ED UP.
NOT MY PROBLEM.
WHAT ARE YOU SAYING? YOU'RE ME. FROM THE FUTURE.
IT'S BY DEFINITION YOUR PROBLEM.
ENJOY YOUR LAST COUPLE HOURS, LOSER.
STUCK.
STUCK HERE.
BEFORE RECORDED TIME.
WHERE THERE'S NUTHIN' YOU CAN DO ABOUT ANY-THING.
URRRRRRRRRR

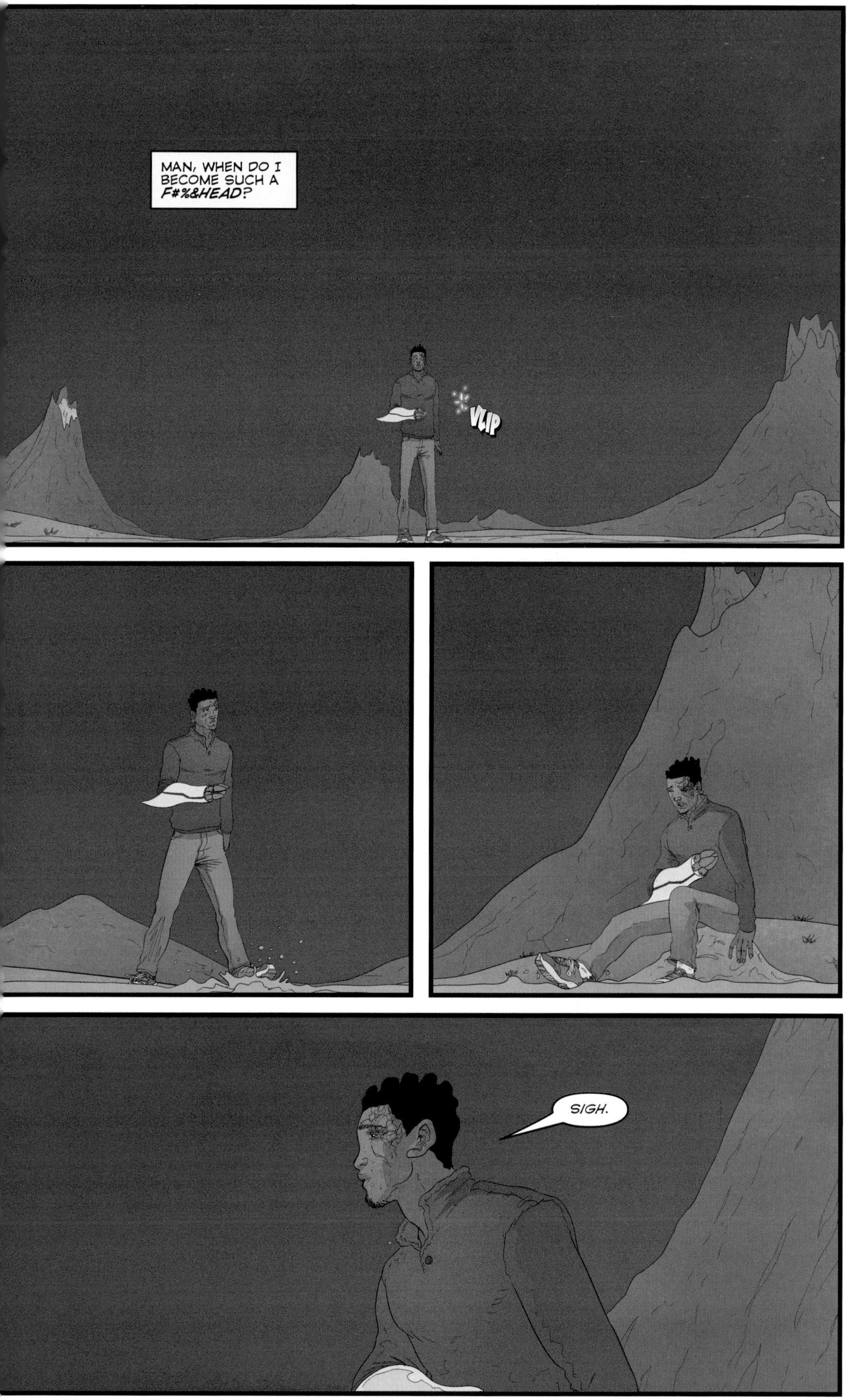
MAN, WHEN DO I BECOME SUCH A F#%&HEAD?
VLIP
SIGH.

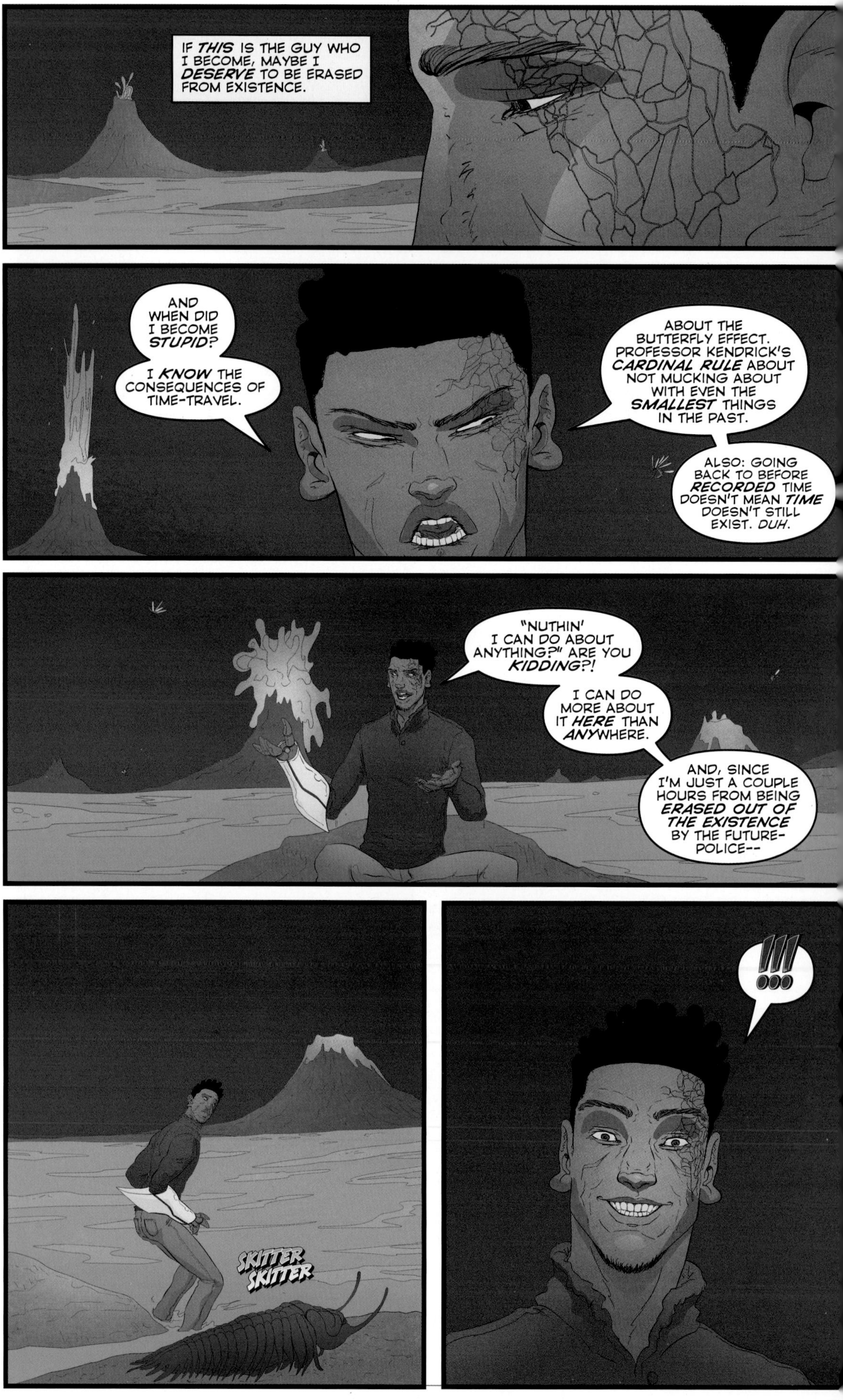
IF THIS IS THE GUY WHO I BECOME, MAYBE I DESERVE TO BE ERASED FROM EXISTENCE.
AND WHEN DID I BECOME STUPID?
I KNOW THE CONSEQUENCES OF TIME-TRAVEL.
ABOUT THE BUTTERFLY EFFECT. PROFESSOR KENDRICK'S CARDINAL RULE ABOUT NOT MUCKING ABOUT WITH EVEN THE SMALLEST THINGS IN THE PAST.
ALSO: GOING BACK TO BEFORE RECORDED TIME DOESN'T MEAN TIME DOESN'T STILL EXIST. DUH.
"NUTHIN' I CAN DO ABOUT ANYTHING?" ARE YOU KIDDING?!
I CAN DO MORE ABOUT IT HERE THAN ANYWHERE.
AND, SINCE I'M JUST A COUPLE HOURS FROM BEING ERASED OUT OF THE EXISTENCE BY THE FUTURE-POLICE--
SKITTER SKITTER
!!!

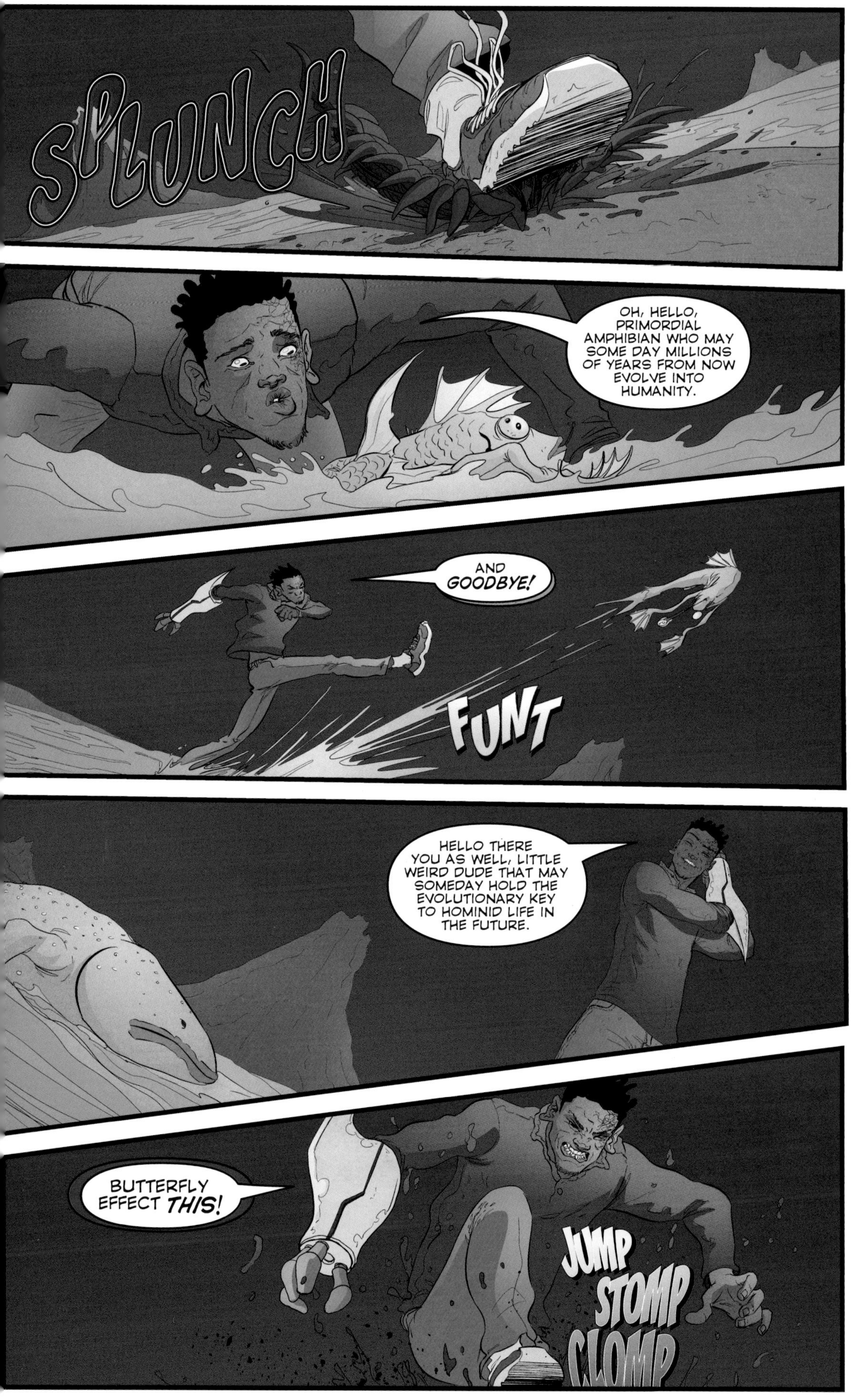
SPLUNCH
OH, HELLO, PRIMORDIAL AMPHIBIAN WHO MAY SOME DAY MILLIONS OF YEARS FROM NOW EVOLVE INTO HUMANITY.
AND GOODBYE!
FUNT
HELLO THERE YOU AS WELL, LITTLE WEIRD DUDE THAT MAY SOMEDAY HOLD THE EVOLUTIONARY KEY TO HOMINID LIFE IN THE FUTURE.
BUTTERFLY EFFECT THIS!
JUMP
STOMP
CLOMP

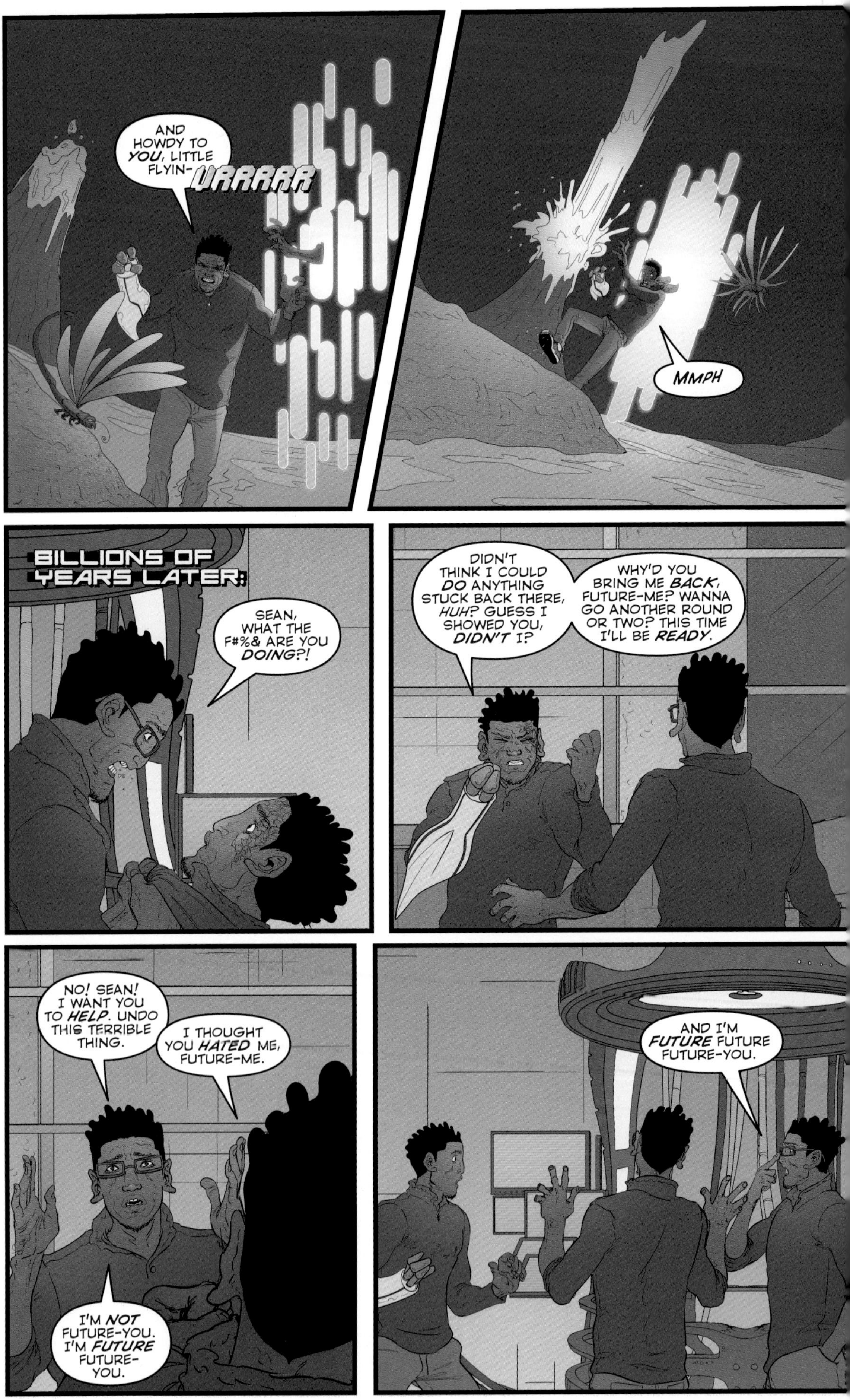
AND HOWDY TO YOU, LITTLE FLYIN-
URRRRRR
MMPH
BILLIONS OF YEARS LATER:
SEAN, WHAT THE F#%& ARE YOU DOING?!
DIDN'T THINK I COULD DO ANYTHING STUCK BACK THERE, HUH? GUESS I SHOWED YOU, DIDN'T I?
WHY'D YOU BRING ME BACK, FUTURE-ME? WANNA GO ANOTHER ROUND OR TWO? THIS TIME I'LL BE READY.
NO! SEAN! I WANT YOU TO HELP. UNDO THIS TERRIBLE THING.
I THOUGHT YOU HATED ME, FUTURE-ME.
I'M NOT FUTURE-YOU. I'M FUTURE FUTURE-YOU.
AND I'M FUTURE FUTURE FUTURE-YOU.

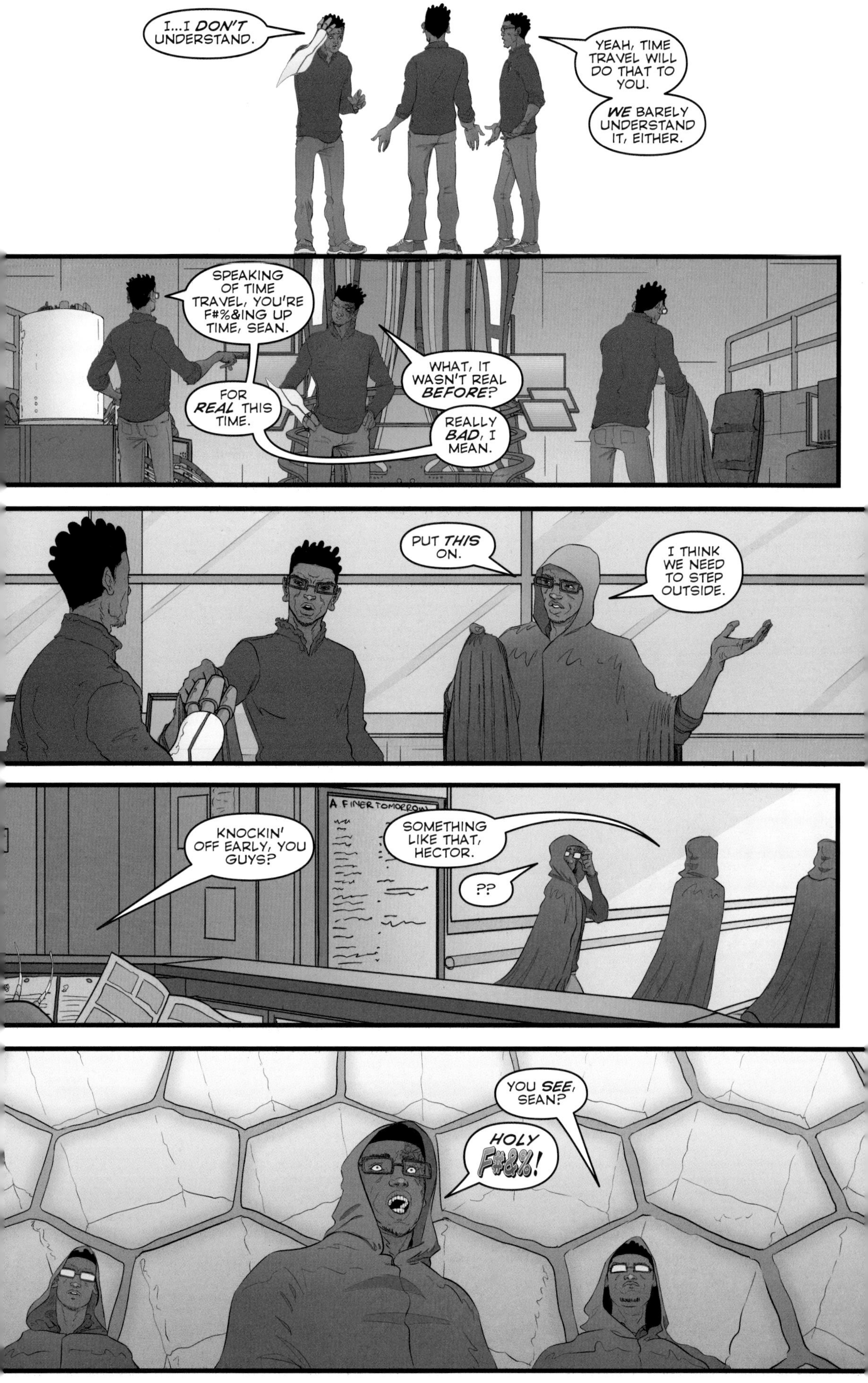
I...I DON'T UNDERSTAND.
YEAH, TIME TRAVEL WILL DO THAT TO YOU.
WE BARELY UNDERSTAND IT, EITHER.
SPEAKING OF TIME TRAVEL, YOU'RE F#%&ING UP TIME, SEAN.
WHAT, IT WASN'T REAL BEFORE?
FOR REAL THIS TIME.
REALLY BAD, I MEAN.
PUT THIS ON.
I THINK WE NEED TO STEP OUTSIDE.
A FINER TOMORROW
KNOCKIN' OFF EARLY, YOU GUYS?
SOMETHING LIKE THAT, HECTOR.
??
YOU SEE, SEAN?
HOLY F#&%!

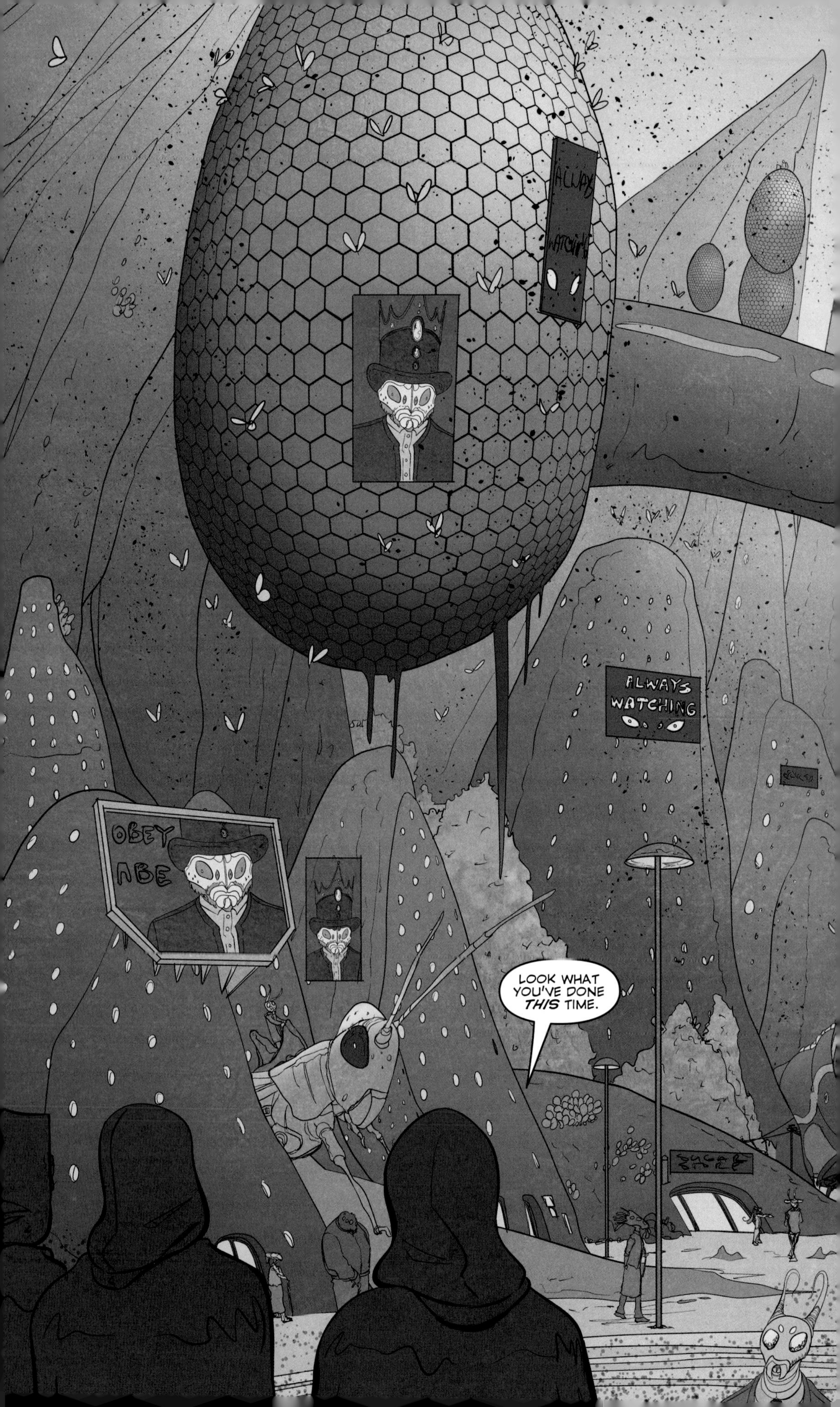

ALWAYS WATCHING
OBEY ABE
SUGAR STORE
LOOK WHAT YOU'VE DONE *THIS* TIME.

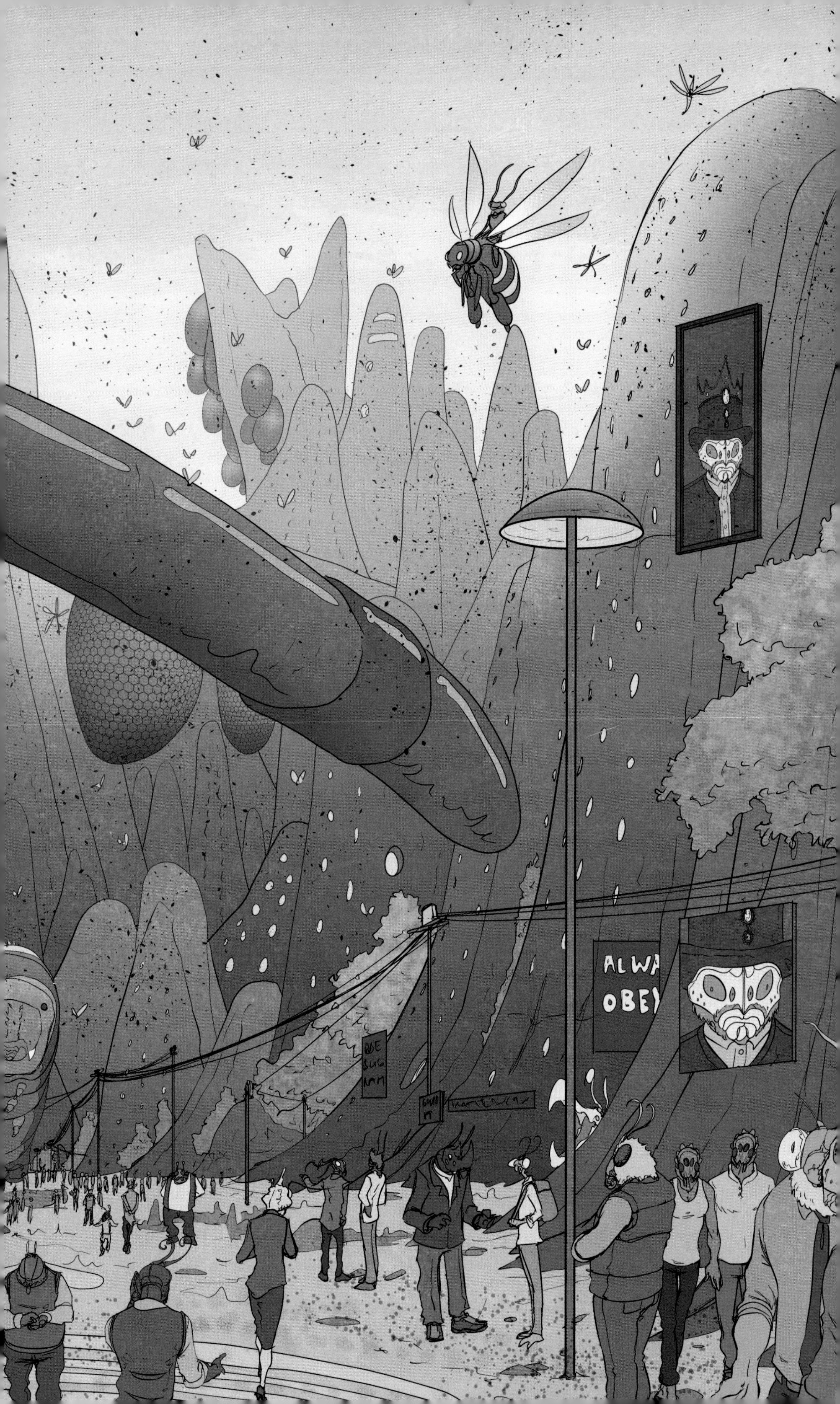
ALWA
OBEY

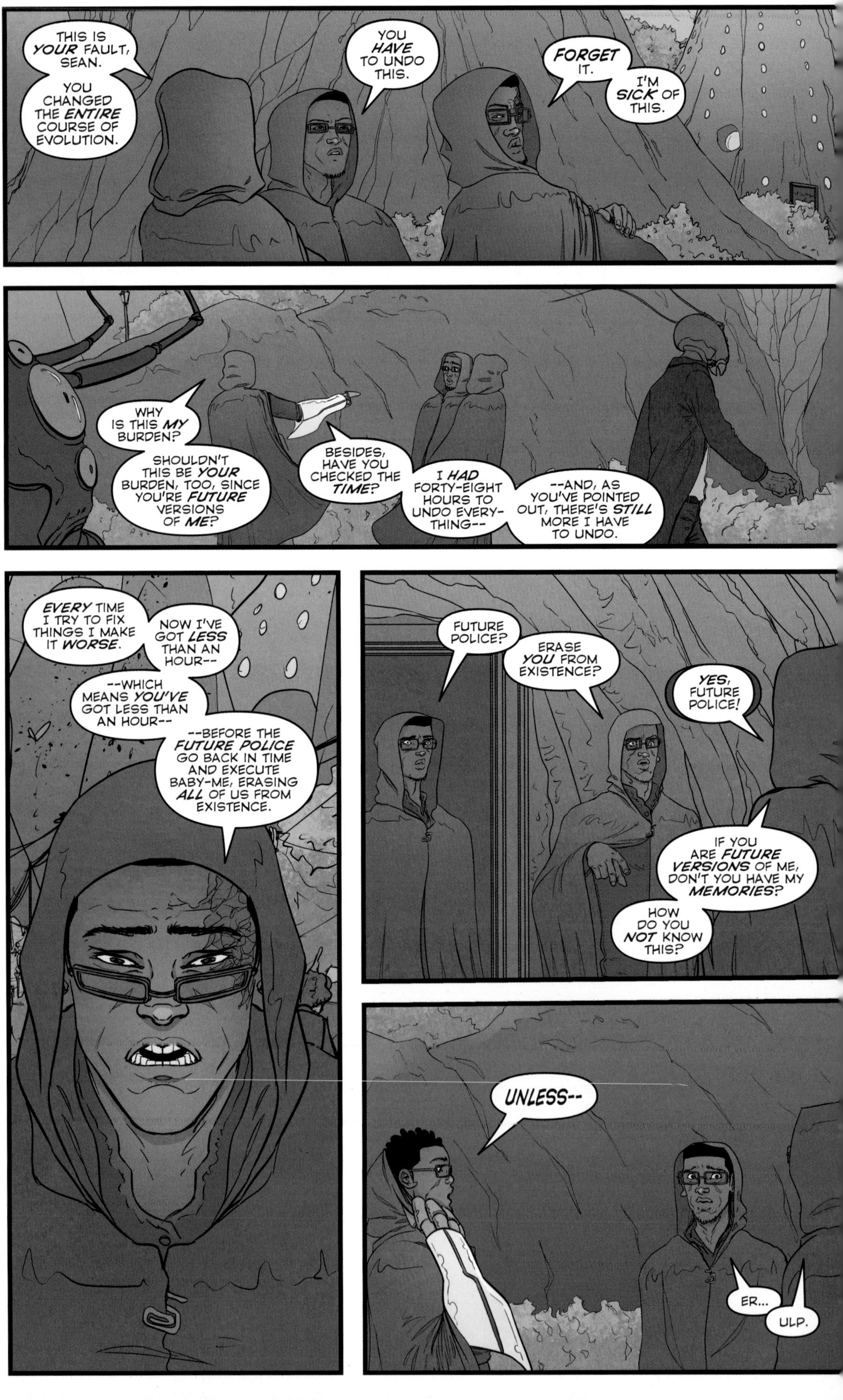
THIS IS YOUR FAULT, SEAN.
YOU CHANGED THE ENTIRE COURSE OF EVOLUTION.
YOU HAVE TO UNDO THIS.
FORGET IT.
I'M SICK OF THIS.
WHY IS THIS MY BURDEN?
SHOULDN'T THIS BE YOUR BURDEN, TOO, SINCE YOU'RE FUTURE VERSIONS OF ME?
BESIDES, HAVE YOU CHECKED THE TIME?
I HAD FORTY-EIGHT HOURS TO UNDO EVERY-THING--
--AND, AS YOU'VE POINTED OUT, THERE'S STILL MORE I HAVE TO UNDO.
EVERY TIME I TRY TO FIX THINGS I MAKE IT WORSE.
NOW I'VE GOT LESS THAN AN HOUR--
--WHICH MEANS YOU'VE GOT LESS THAN AN HOUR--
--BEFORE THE FUTURE POLICE GO BACK IN TIME AND EXECUTE BABY-ME, ERASING ALL OF US FROM EXISTENCE.
FUTURE POLICE?
ERASE YOU FROM EXISTENCE?
YES, FUTURE POLICE!
IF YOU ARE FUTURE VERSIONS OF ME, DON'T YOU HAVE MY MEMORIES?
HOW DO YOU NOT KNOW THIS?
UNLESS--
ER...
ULP.

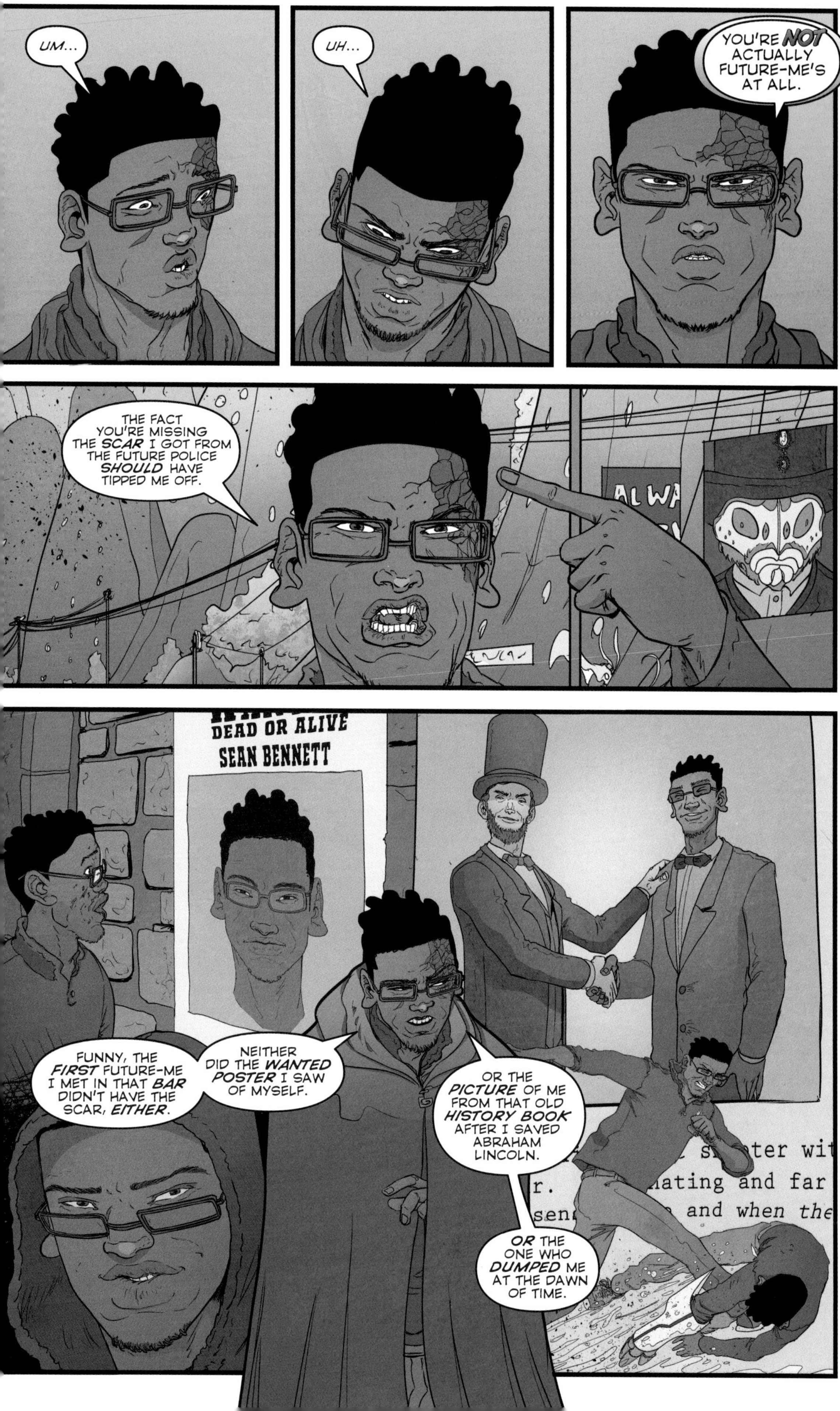
UM...
UH...
YOU'RE NOT ACTUALLY FUTURE-ME'S AT ALL.
THE FACT YOU'RE MISSING THE SCAR I GOT FROM THE FUTURE POLICE SHOULD HAVE TIPPED ME OFF.
DEAD OR ALIVE
SEAN BENNETT
FUNNY, THE FIRST FUTURE-ME I MET IN THAT BAR DIDN'T HAVE THE SCAR, EITHER.
NEITHER DID THE WANTED POSTER I SAW OF MYSELF.
OR THE PICTURE OF ME FROM THAT OLD HISTORY BOOK AFTER I SAVED ABRAHAM LINCOLN.
OR THE ONE WHO DUMPED ME AT THE DAWN OF TIME.

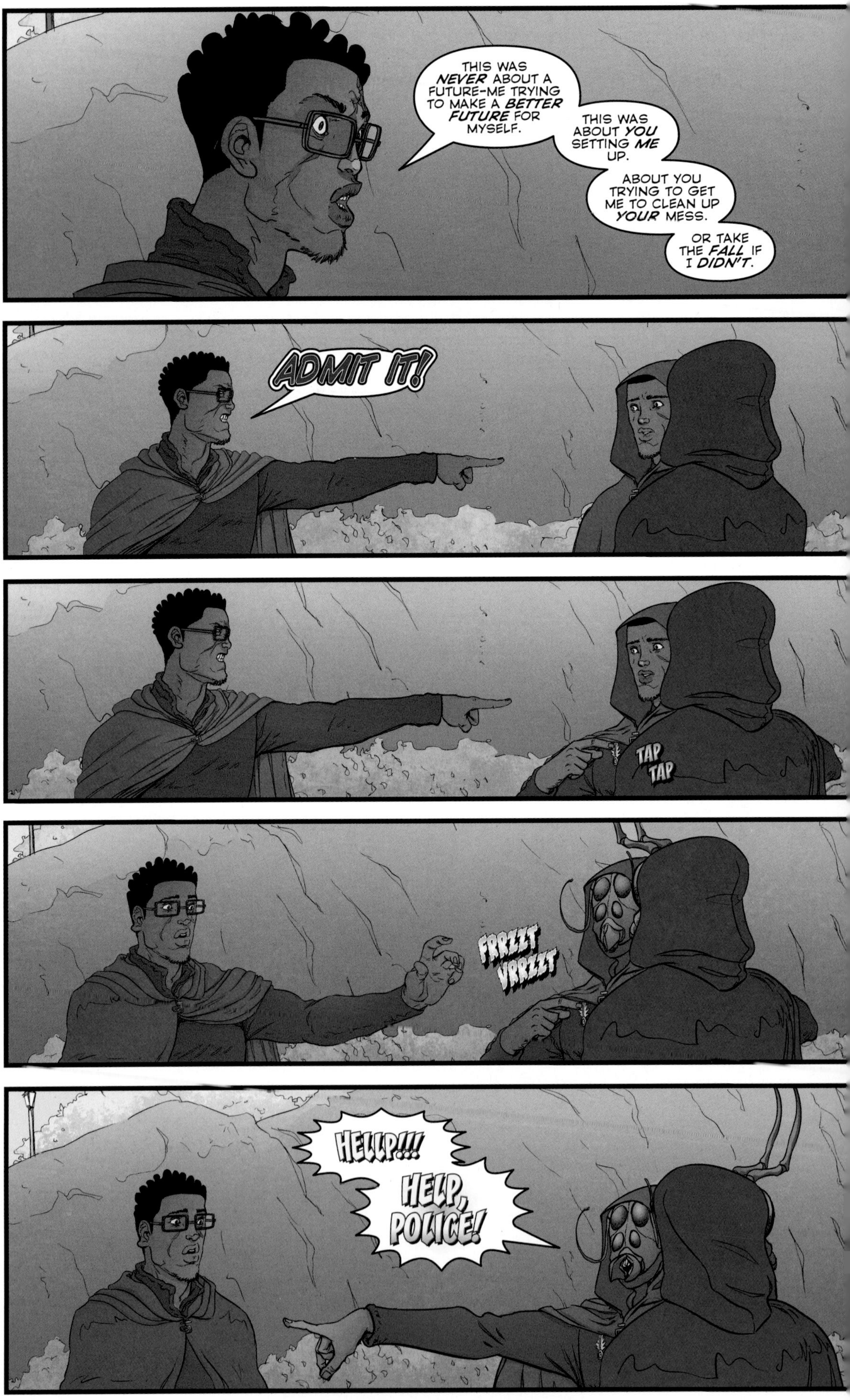
THIS WAS NEVER ABOUT A FUTURE-ME TRYING TO MAKE A BETTER FUTURE FOR MYSELF.
THIS WAS ABOUT YOU SETTING ME UP.
ABOUT YOU TRYING TO GET ME TO CLEAN UP YOUR MESS.
OR TAKE THE FALL IF I DIDN'T.
ADMIT IT!
TAP TAP
FRRZZT VRRZZT
HELLP!!!
HELP, POLICE!

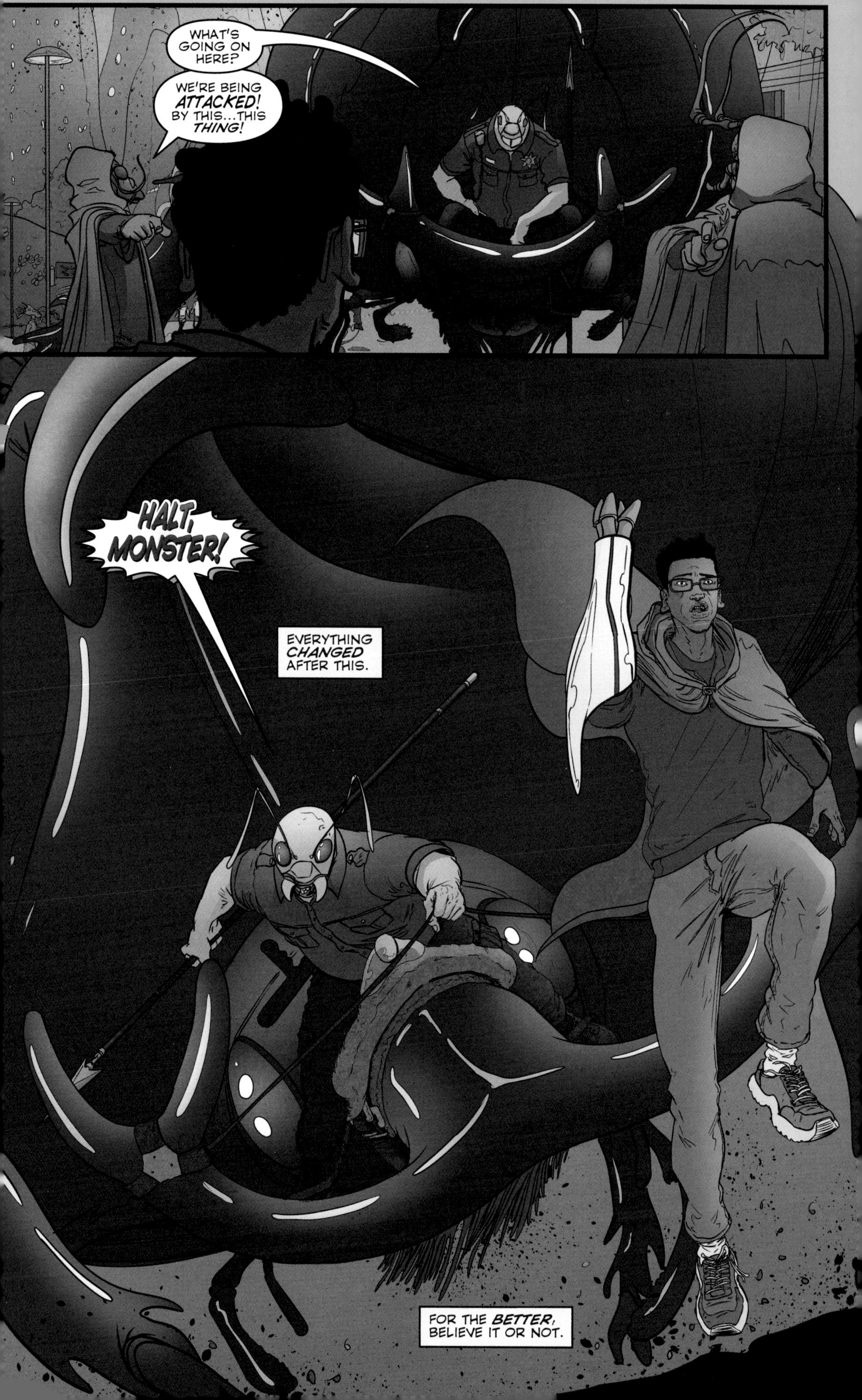
WHAT'S GOING ON HERE?
WE'RE BEING *ATTACKED!* BY THIS...THIS *THING!*
HALT, MONSTER!
EVERYTHING *CHANGED* AFTER THIS.
FOR THE *BETTER,* BELIEVE IT OR NOT.

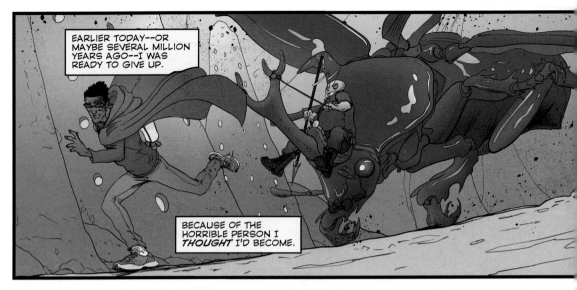

EARLIER TODAY--OR MAYBE SEVERAL MILLION YEARS AGO--I WAS READY TO GIVE UP.

BECAUSE OF THE HORRIBLE PERSON I *THOUGHT* I'D BECOME.

THIS IS YOUR *FINAL* WARNING, FLESHY MAMMAL CREATURE!

HALT AND SURRENDER!

NOW I KNOW THE *TRUTH*.

IT WAS *ALL* A SET-UP.

ALL OF IT.

AND NOW I'M GOING TO *FIGHT BACK*.

SORRY ABOUT THIS, OFFICER BUGFACE.
Splutch
BUT IF ALL GOES LIKE IT *SHOULD*, YOU NEVER WILL HAVE EXISTED, ANYWAY.
JUST AS SOON AS I *SAVE MYSELF*.

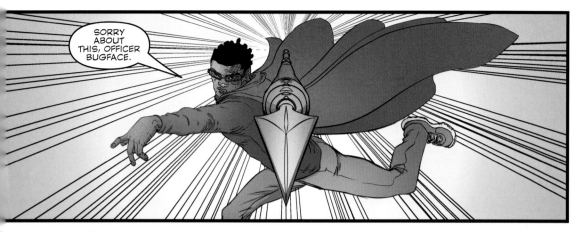

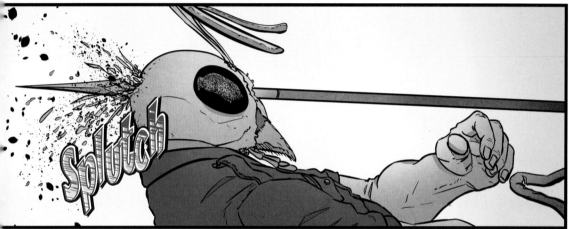

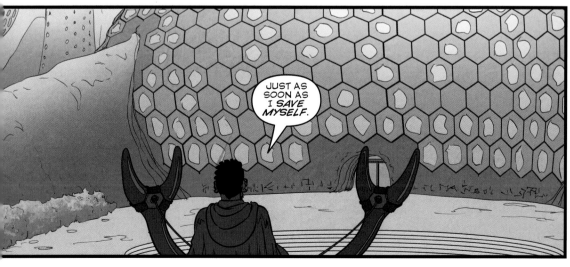

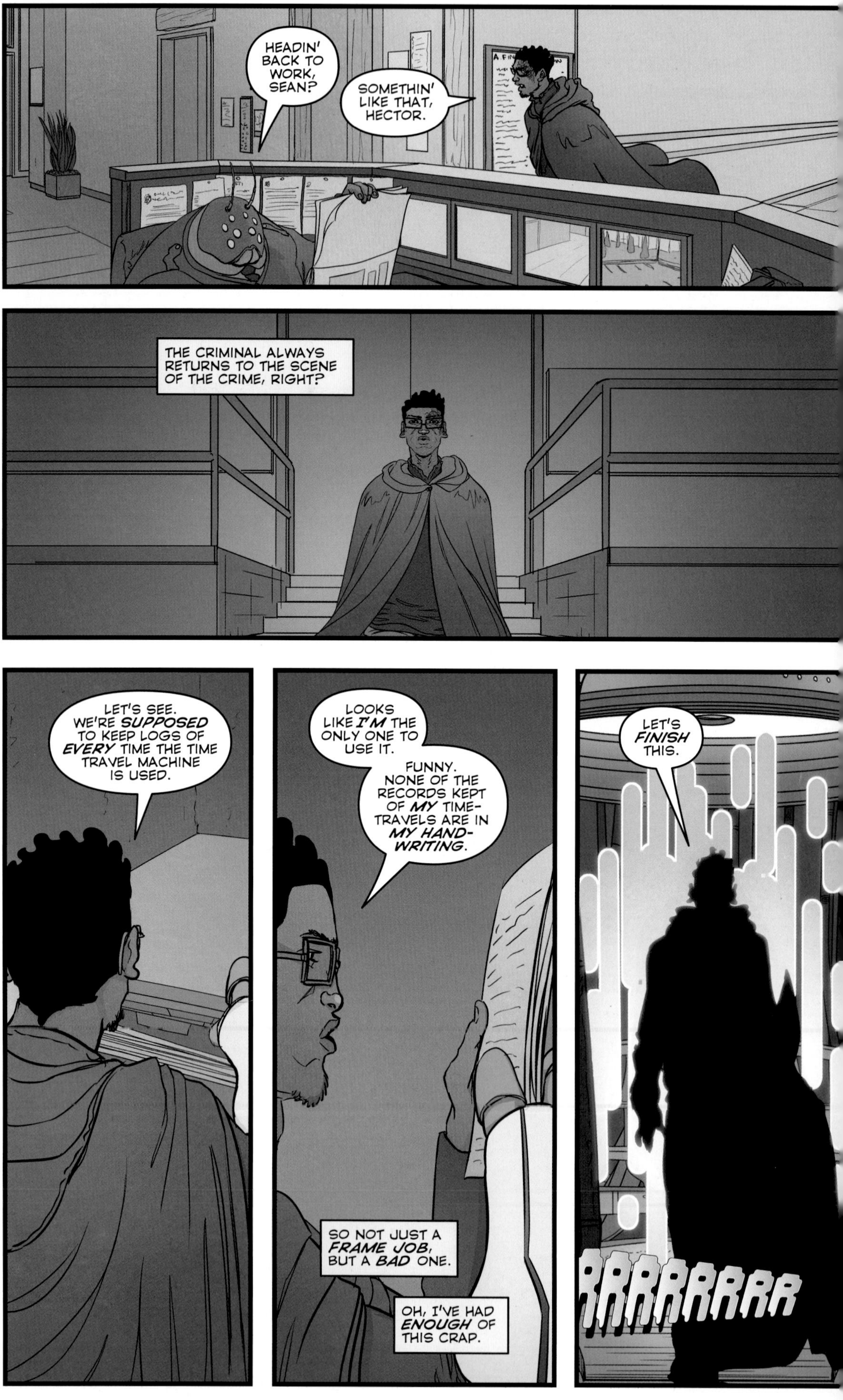
HEADIN' BACK TO WORK, SEAN?
SOMETHIN' LIKE THAT, HECTOR.
THE CRIMINAL ALWAYS RETURNS TO THE SCENE OF THE CRIME, RIGHT?
LET'S SEE. WE'RE SUPPOSED TO KEEP LOGS OF EVERY TIME THE TIME TRAVEL MACHINE IS USED.
LOOKS LIKE I'M THE ONLY ONE TO USE IT.
FUNNY. NONE OF THE RECORDS KEPT OF MY TIME-TRAVELS ARE IN MY HAND-WRITING.
SO NOT JUST A FRAME JOB, BUT A BAD ONE.
OH, I'VE HAD ENOUGH OF THIS CRAP.
LET'S FINISH THIS.
RRRRRRRRR

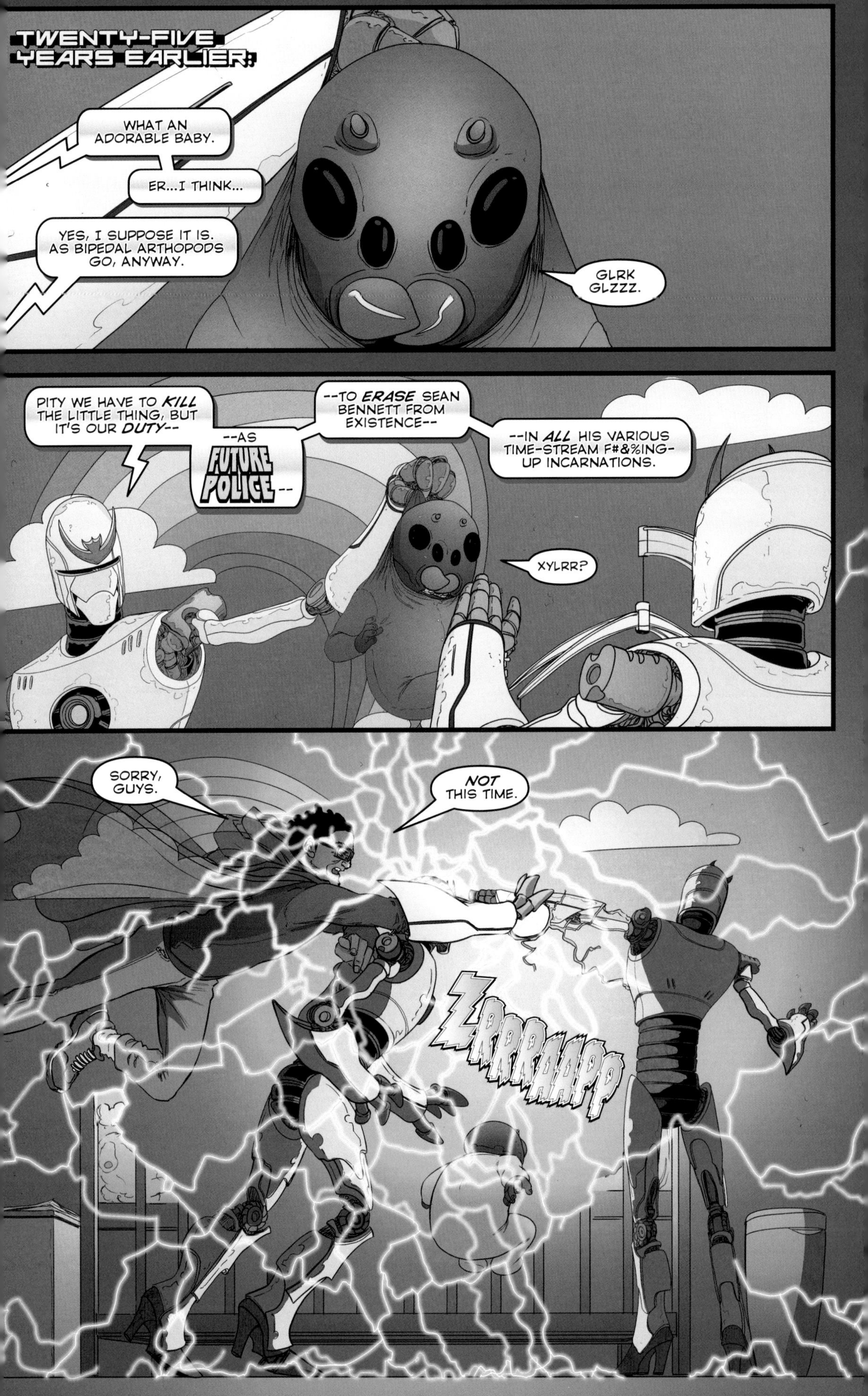
TWENTY-FIVE YEARS EARLIER:
WHAT AN ADORABLE BABY.
ER...I THINK...
YES, I SUPPOSE IT IS. AS BIPEDAL ARTHOPODS GO, ANYWAY.
GLRK GLZZZ.
PITY WE HAVE TO KILL THE LITTLE THING, BUT IT'S OUR DUTY--
--AS FUTURE POLICE --
--TO ERASE SEAN BENNETT FROM EXISTENCE--
--IN ALL HIS VARIOUS TIME-STREAM F#&%ING-UP INCARNATIONS.
XYLRR?
SORRY, GUYS.
NOT THIS TIME.
ZRRRAAPP

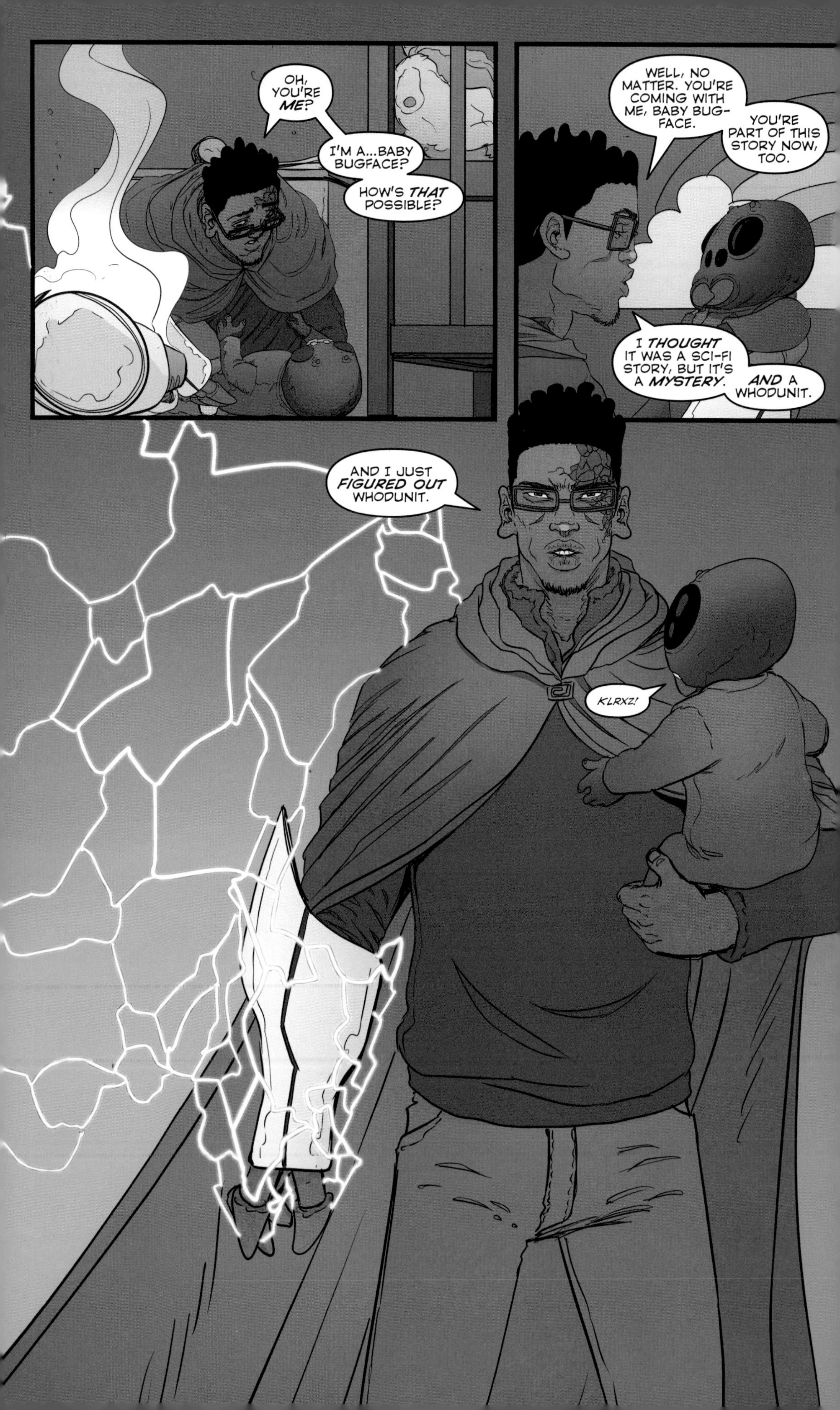
OH, YOU'RE *ME*?
I'M A...BABY BUGFACE?
HOW'S *THAT* POSSIBLE?
WELL, NO MATTER. YOU'RE COMING WITH ME, BABY BUGFACE.
YOU'RE PART OF THIS STORY NOW, TOO.
I *THOUGHT* IT WAS A SCI-FI STORY, BUT IT'S A *MYSTERY*.
AND A WHODUNIT.
AND I JUST *FIGURED OUT* WHODUNIT.
KLRXZ!

5

FUTURE IMPERFECT

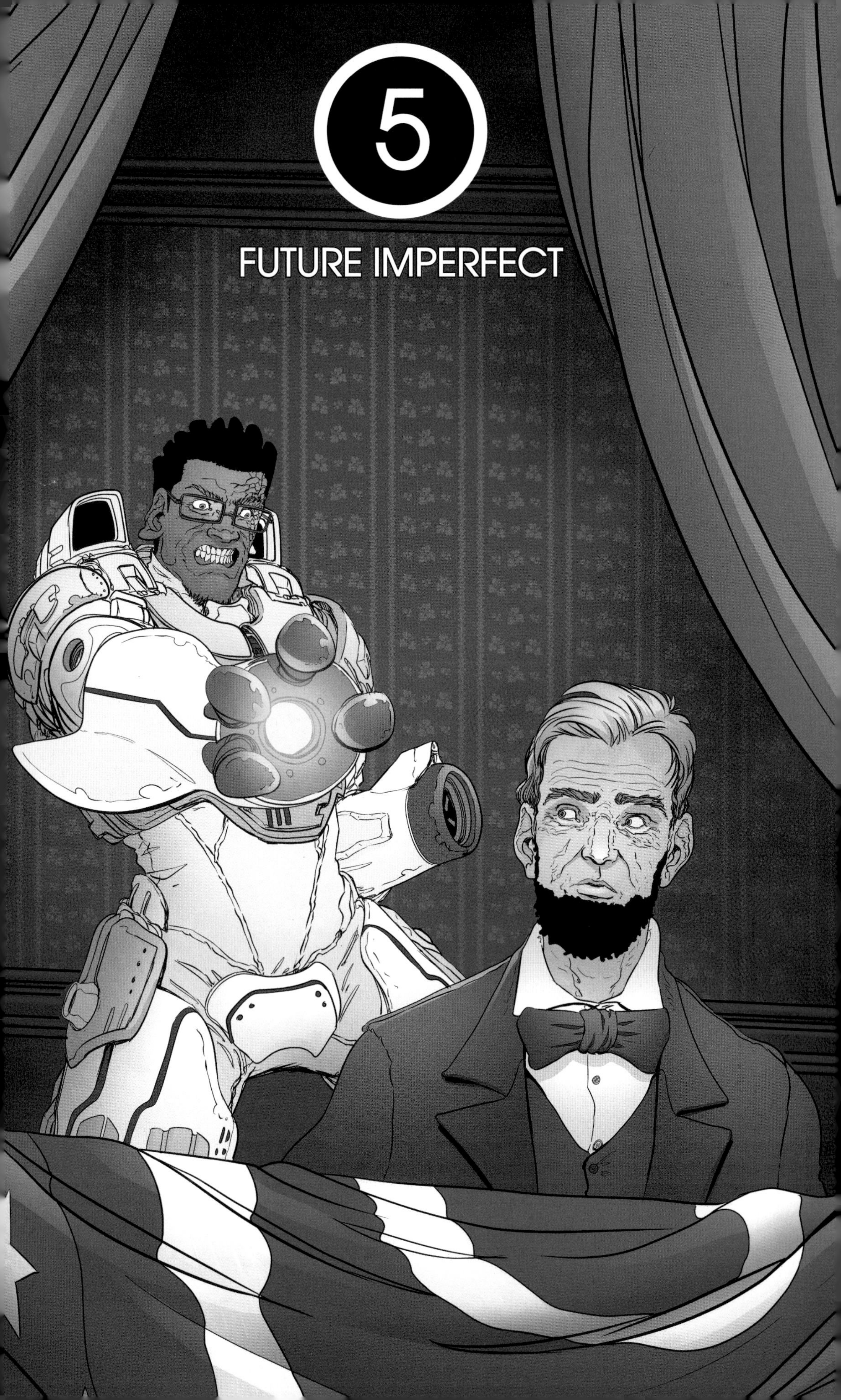

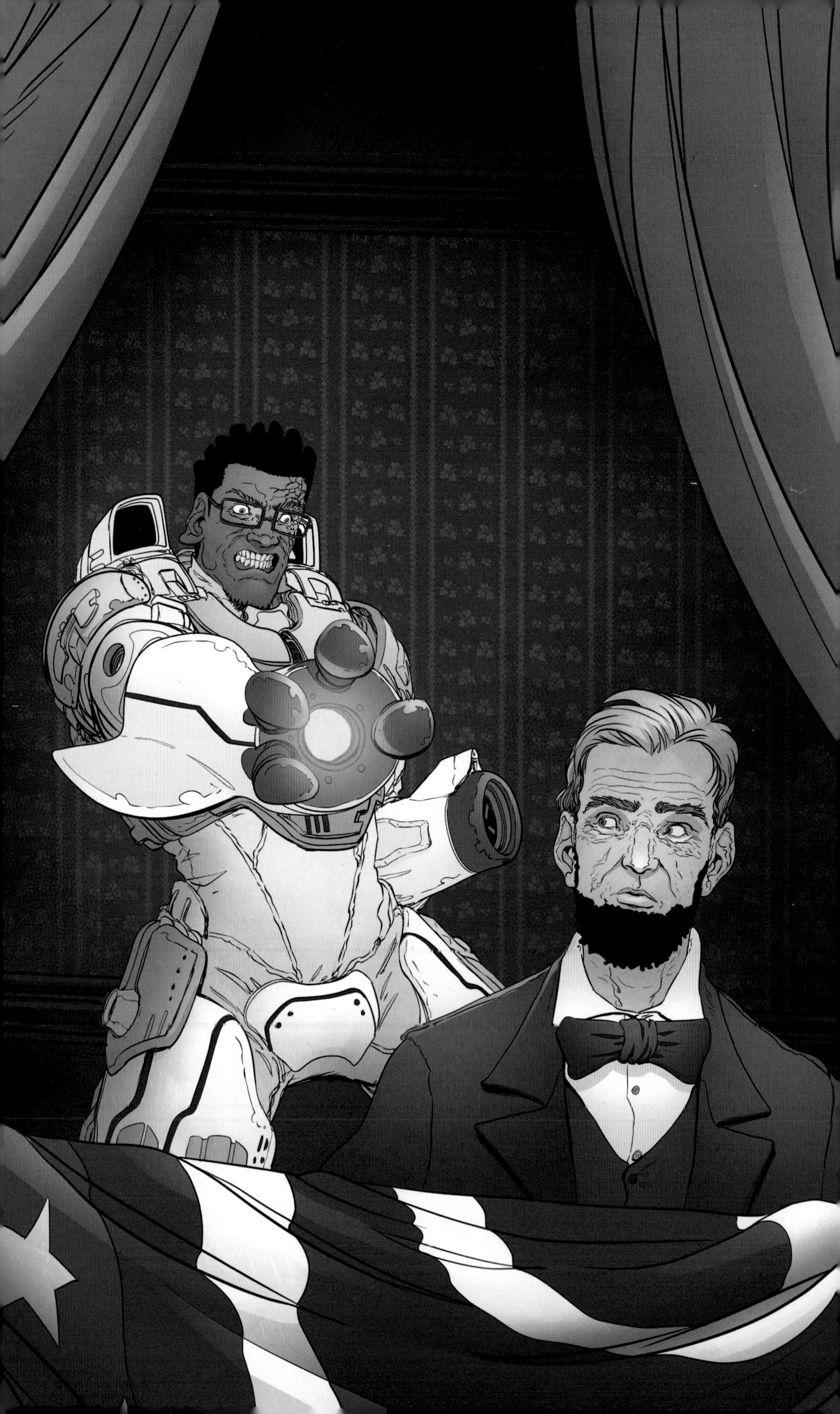

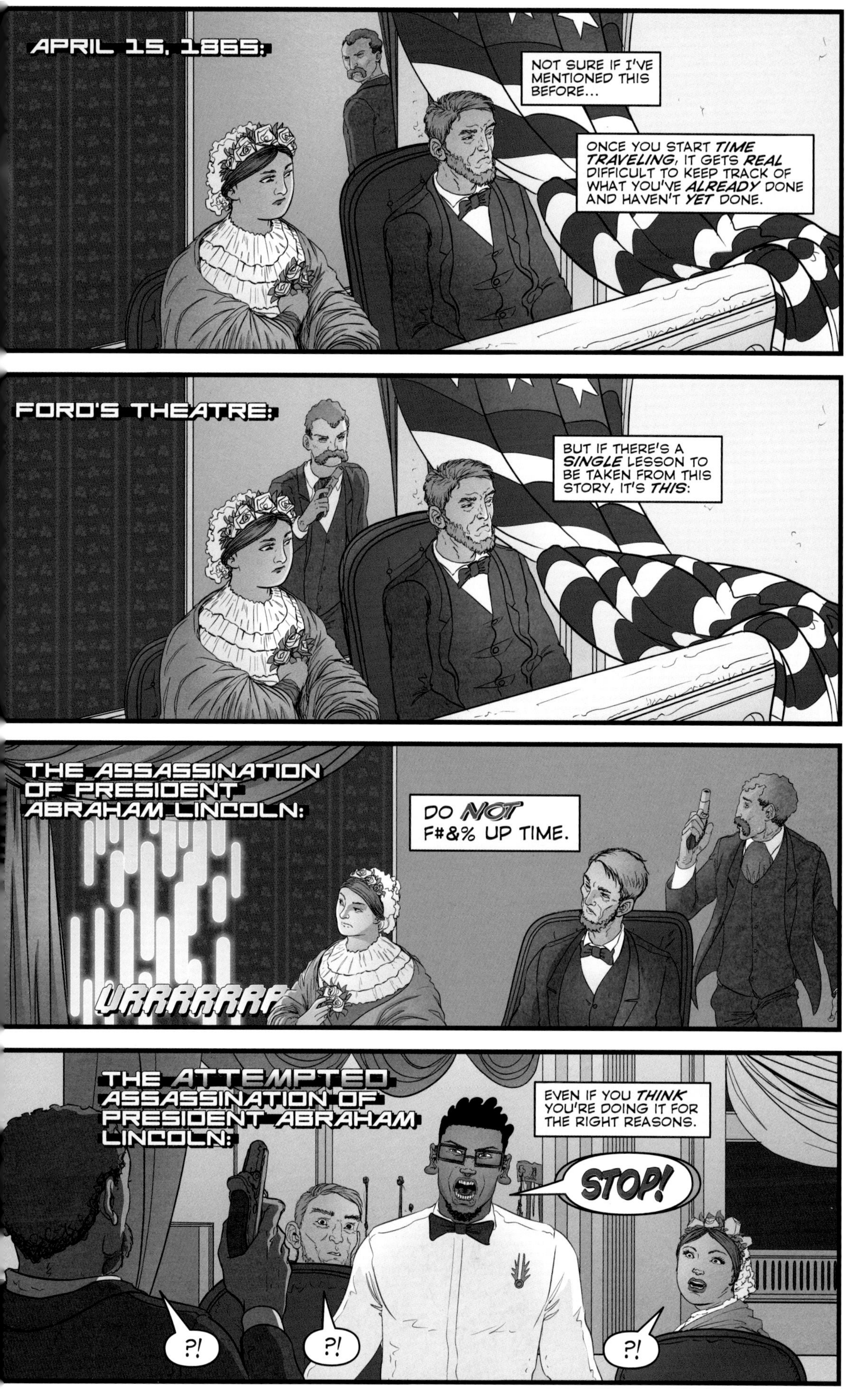
APRIL 15, 1865:
NOT SURE IF I'VE MENTIONED THIS BEFORE...
ONCE YOU START TIME TRAVELING, IT GETS REAL DIFFICULT TO KEEP TRACK OF WHAT YOU'VE ALREADY DONE AND HAVEN'T YET DONE.
FORD'S THEATRE:
BUT IF THERE'S A SINGLE LESSON TO BE TAKEN FROM THIS STORY, IT'S THIS:
THE ASSASSINATION OF PRESIDENT ABRAHAM LINCOLN:
DO NOT F#&% UP TIME.
VRRRRRRRP
THE ATTEMPTED ASSASSINATION OF PRESIDENT ABRAHAM LINCOLN:
EVEN IF YOU THINK YOU'RE DOING IT FOR THE RIGHT REASONS.
STOP!
?!
?!
?!

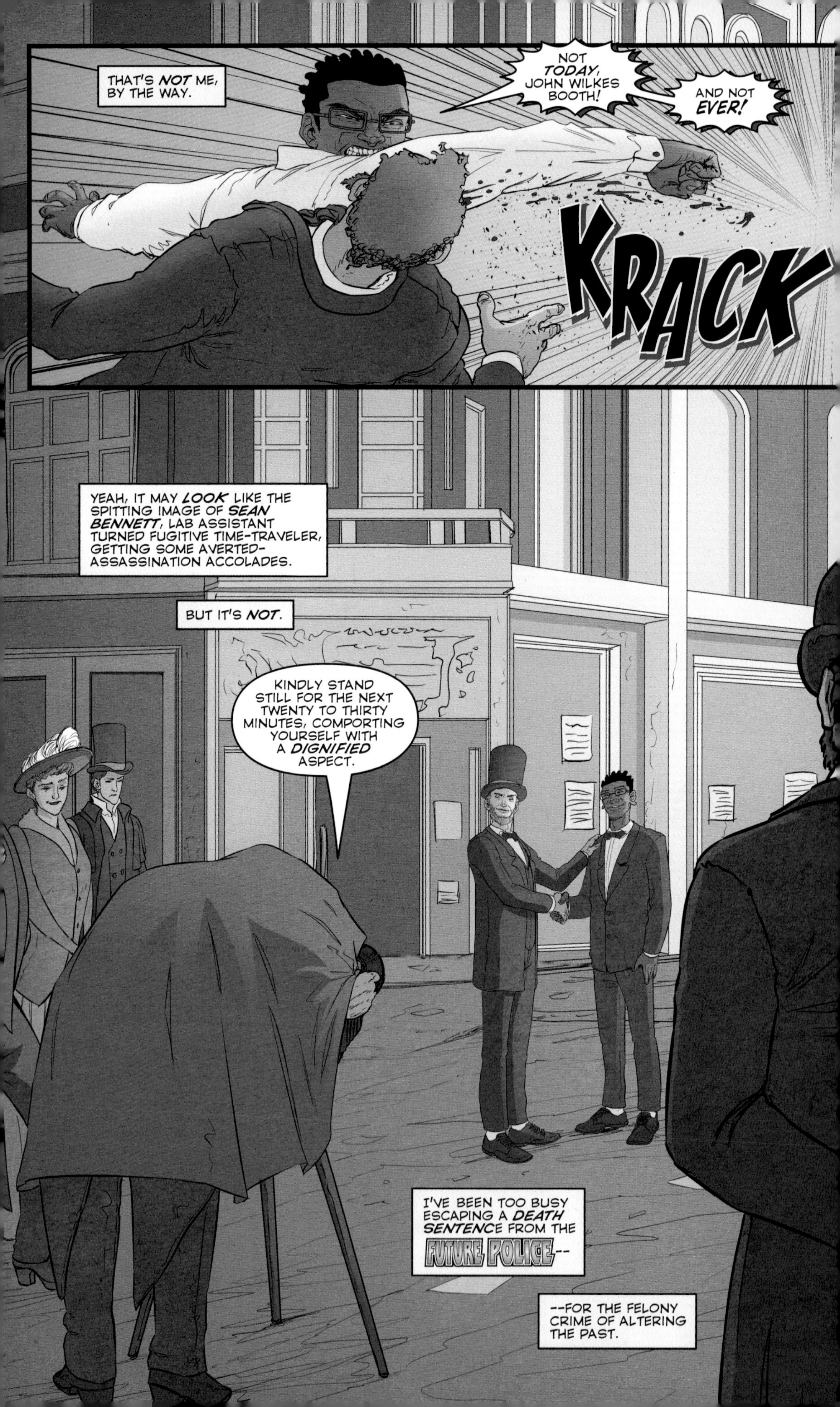
THAT'S NOT ME, BY THE WAY.
NOT TODAY, JOHN WILKES BOOTH!
AND NOT EVER!
KRACK
YEAH, IT MAY LOOK LIKE THE SPITTING IMAGE OF SEAN BENNETT, LAB ASSISTANT TURNED FUGITIVE TIME-TRAVELER, GETTING SOME AVERTED-ASSASSINATION ACCOLADES.
BUT IT'S NOT.
KINDLY STAND STILL FOR THE NEXT TWENTY TO THIRTY MINUTES, COMPORTING YOURSELF WITH A DIGNIFIED ASPECT.
I'VE BEEN TOO BUSY ESCAPING A DEATH SENTENCE FROM THE FUTURE POLICE--
--FOR THE FELONY CRIME OF ALTERING THE PAST.

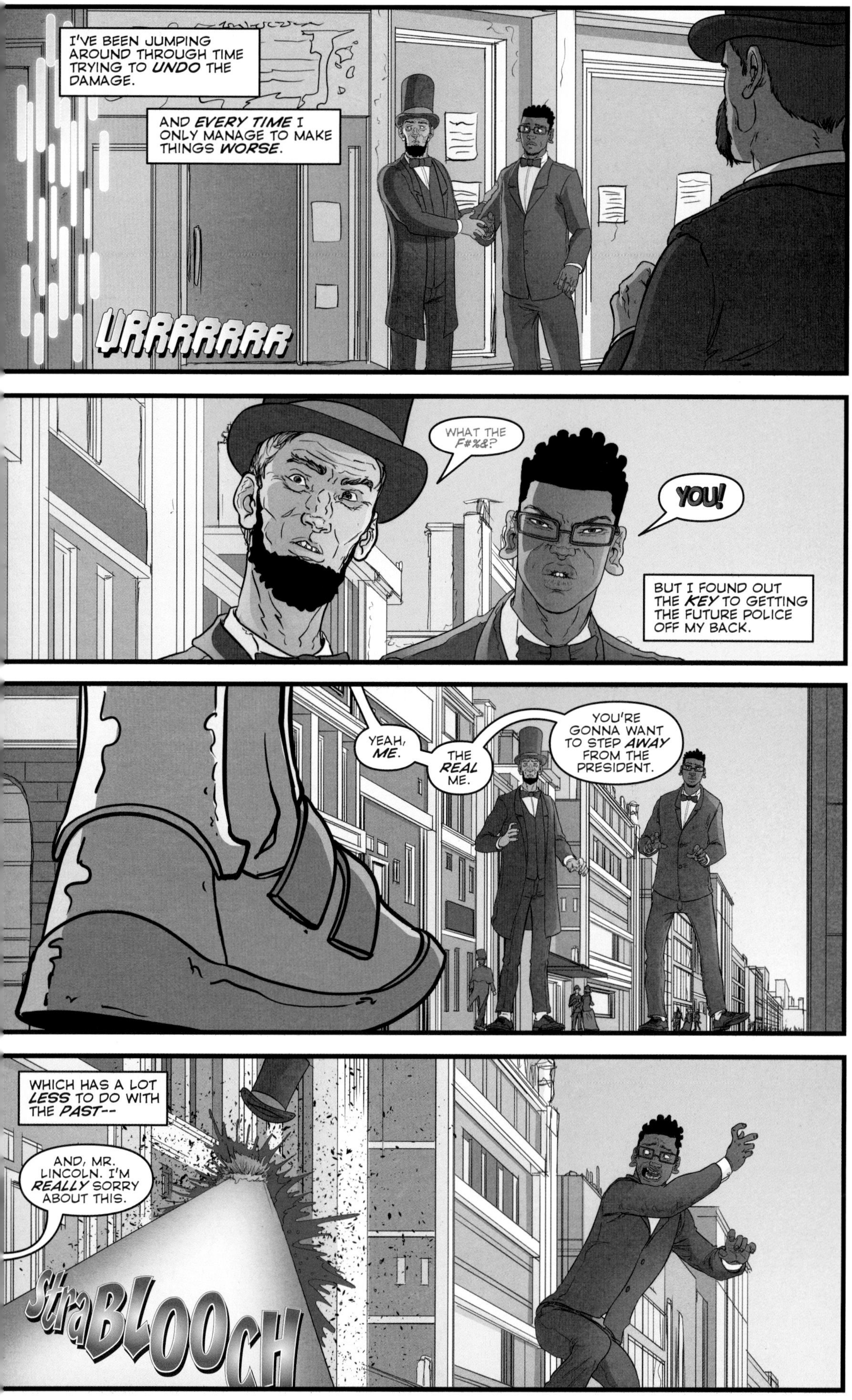

I'VE BEEN JUMPING AROUND THROUGH TIME TRYING TO UNDO THE DAMAGE.
AND EVERY TIME I ONLY MANAGE TO MAKE THINGS WORSE.
URRRRRRR
WHAT THE F#%&?
YOU!
BUT I FOUND OUT THE KEY TO GETTING THE FUTURE POLICE OFF MY BACK.
YEAH, ME.
THE REAL ME.
YOU'RE GONNA WANT TO STEP AWAY FROM THE PRESIDENT.
WHICH HAS A LOT LESS TO DO WITH THE PAST--
AND, MR. LINCOLN. I'M REALLY SORRY ABOUT THIS.
StraBLOOCH

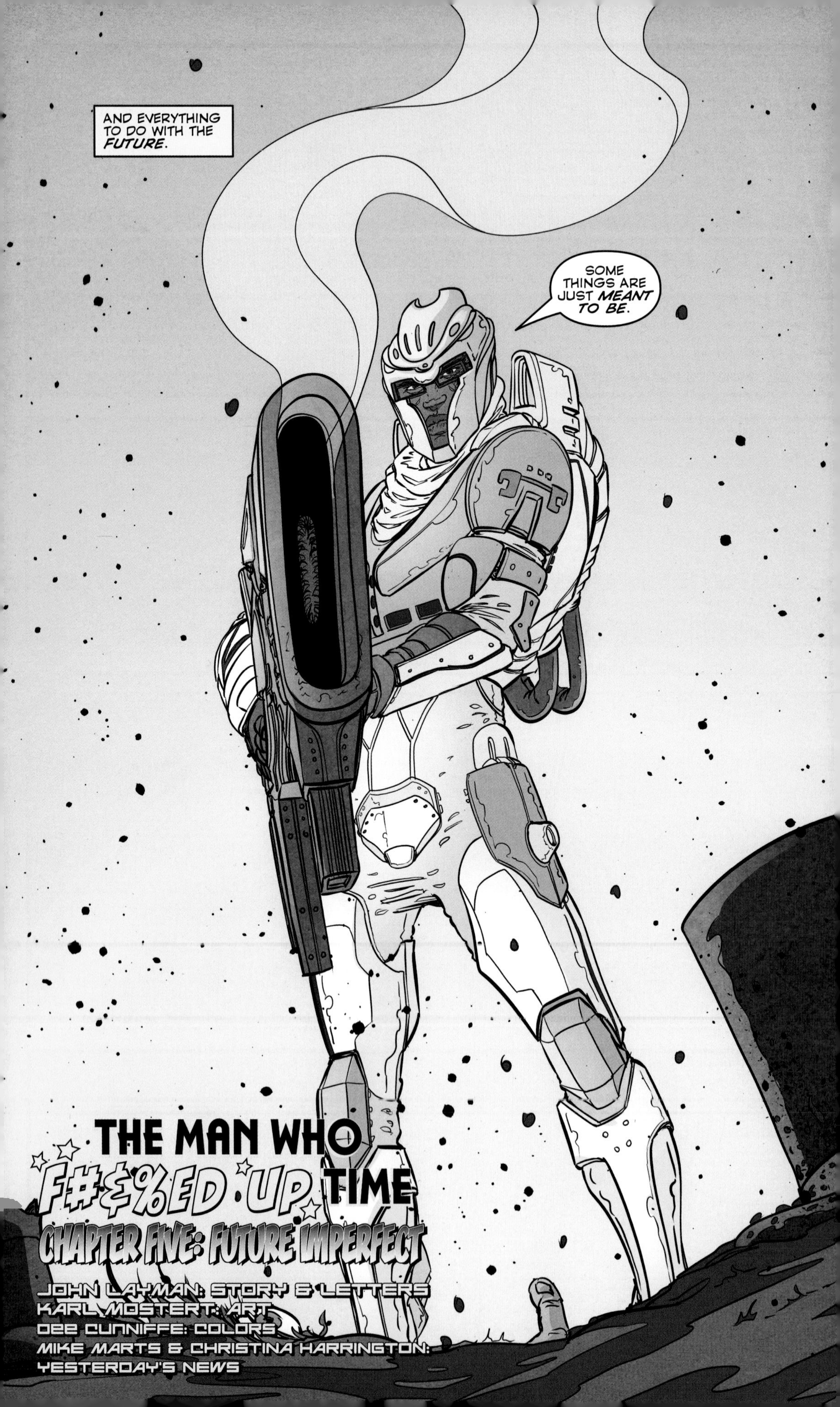
AND EVERYTHING TO DO WITH THE *FUTURE*.
SOME THINGS ARE JUST *MEANT TO BE*.
THE MAN WHO F#&%ED UP TIME
CHAPTER FIVE: FUTURE IMPERFECT
JOHN LAYMAN: STORY & LETTERS
KARL MOSTERT: ART
DEE CUNNIFFE: COLORS
MIKE MARTS & CHRISTINA HARRINGTON: YESTERDAY'S NEWS

WHAT THE *F#%&* HAVE YOU *DONE?!*

AH, DANGIT.

I'VE GOTTEN *AHEAD* OF MYSELF, HAVEN'T I?

WHAT *NEEDED* TO BE DONE.

IN ORDER TO SAVE THE WORLD--AND MYSELF--FROM OL' *ABE'S* TYRANNICAL DESCENDANTS.

LIKE I SAID, TIME TRAVEL IS *CONFUSING.*

AS FOR WHAT I'M GOING TO DO *NEXT*--

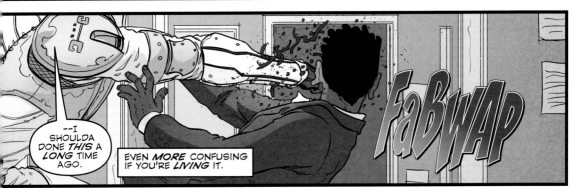

--I SHOULDA DONE *THIS* A *LONG* TIME AGO.

EVEN *MORE* CONFUSING IF YOU'RE *LIVING* IT.

FABWAP

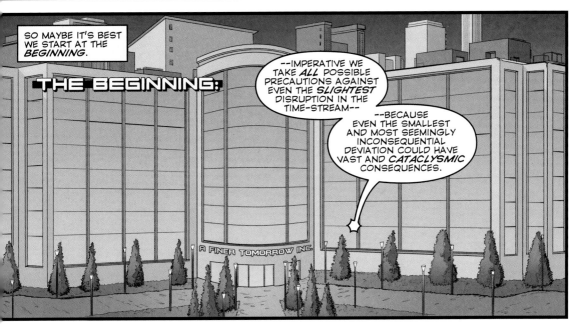

SO MAYBE IT'S BEST WE START AT THE *BEGINNING.*

THE BEGINNING:

--IMPERATIVE WE TAKE *ALL* POSSIBLE PRECAUTIONS AGAINST EVEN THE *SLIGHTEST* DISRUPTION IN THE TIME-STREAM--

--BECAUSE EVEN THE SMALLEST AND MOST SEEMINGLY INCONSEQUENTIAL DEVIATION COULD HAVE VAST AND *CATACLYSMIC* CONSEQUENCES.

A FINER TOMORROW INC.

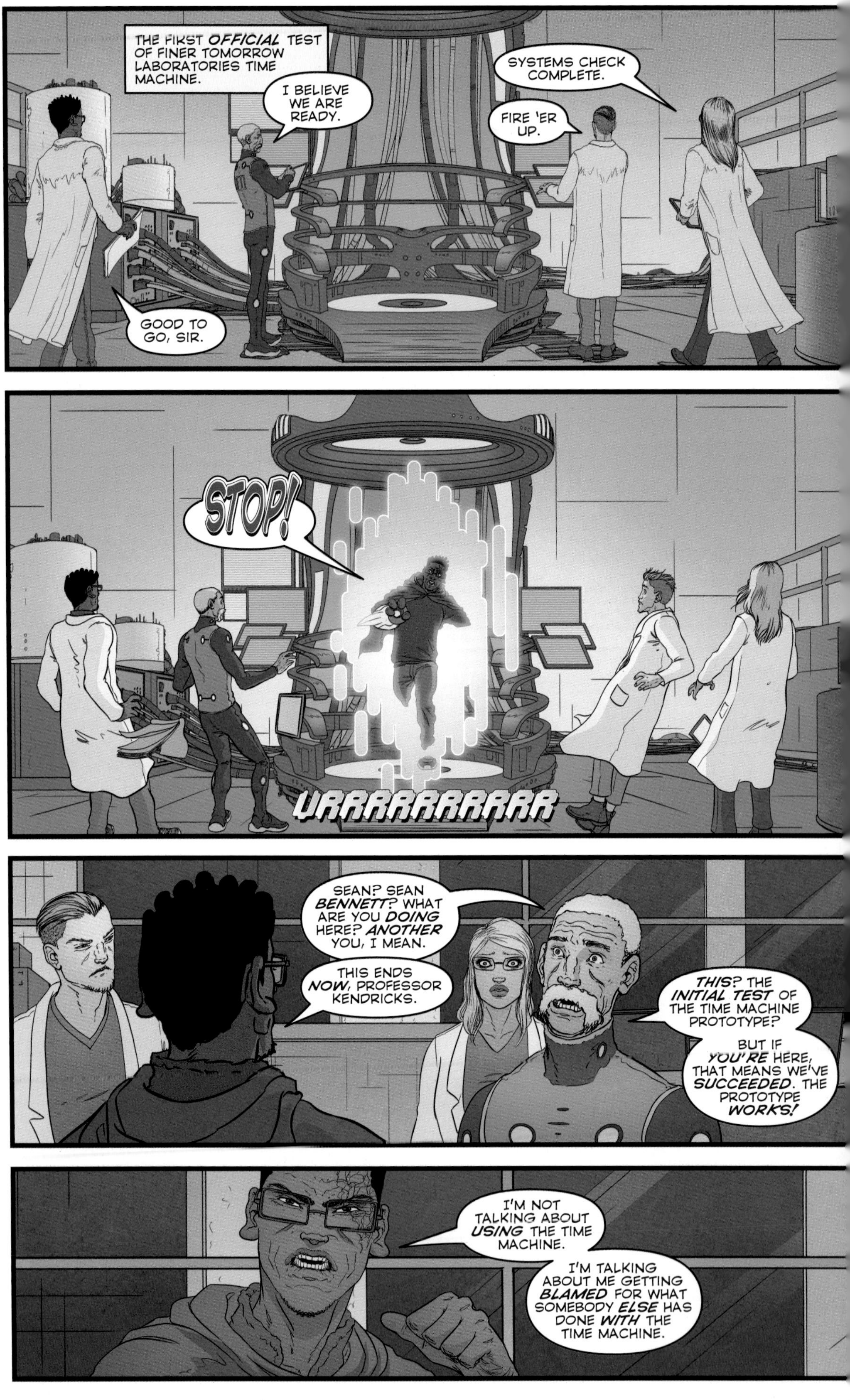
THE FIRST OFFICIAL TEST OF FINER TOMORROW LABORATORIES TIME MACHINE.
I BELIEVE WE ARE READY.
SYSTEMS CHECK COMPLETE.
FIRE 'ER UP.
GOOD TO GO, SIR.
STOP!
URRRRRRRRRRR
SEAN? SEAN BENNETT? WHAT ARE YOU DOING HERE? ANOTHER YOU, I MEAN.
THIS ENDS NOW, PROFESSOR KENDRICKS.
THIS? THE INITIAL TEST OF THE TIME MACHINE PROTOTYPE?
BUT IF YOU'RE HERE, THAT MEANS WE'VE SUCCEEDED. THE PROTOTYPE WORKS!
I'M NOT TALKING ABOUT USING THE TIME MACHINE.
I'M TALKING ABOUT ME GETTING BLAMED FOR WHAT SOMEBODY ELSE HAS DONE WITH THE TIME MACHINE.

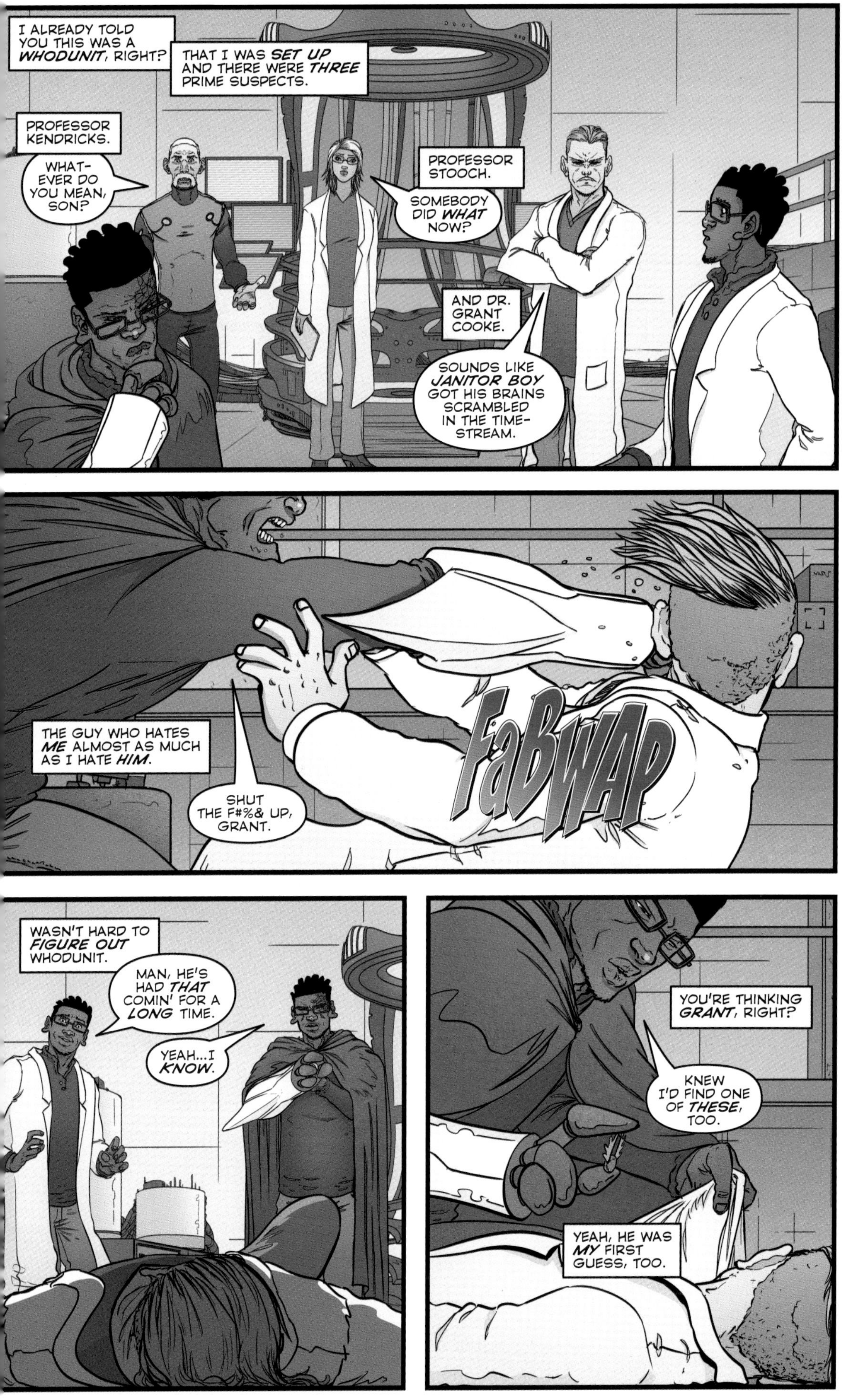
I ALREADY TOLD YOU THIS WAS A WHODUNIT, RIGHT?
THAT I WAS SET UP AND THERE WERE THREE PRIME SUSPECTS.
PROFESSOR KENDRICKS.
WHAT-EVER DO YOU MEAN, SON?
SOMEBODY DID WHAT NOW?
PROFESSOR STOOCH.
AND DR. GRANT COOKE.
SOUNDS LIKE JANITOR BOY GOT HIS BRAINS SCRAMBLED IN THE TIME-STREAM.
THE GUY WHO HATES ME ALMOST AS MUCH AS I HATE HIM.
SHUT THE F#%& UP, GRANT.
FaBWAP
WASN'T HARD TO FIGURE OUT WHODUNIT.
MAN, HE'S HAD THAT COMIN' FOR A LONG TIME.
YEAH...I KNOW.
YOU'RE THINKING GRANT, RIGHT?
KNEW I'D FIND ONE OF THESE, TOO.
YEAH, HE WAS MY FIRST GUESS, TOO.

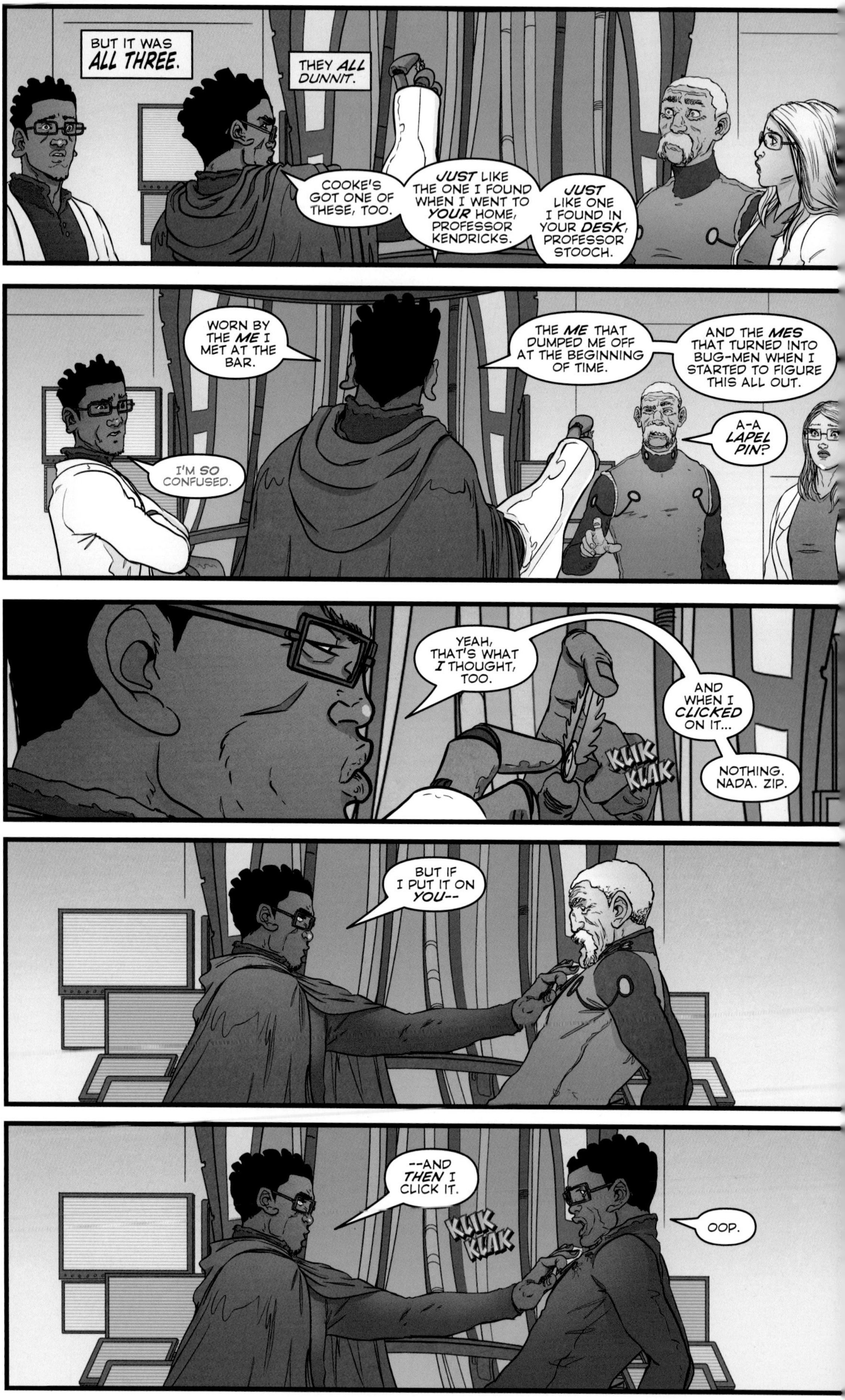
BUT IT WAS ALL THREE.
THEY ALL DUNNIT.
COOKE'S GOT ONE OF THESE, TOO.
JUST LIKE THE ONE I FOUND WHEN I WENT TO YOUR HOME, PROFESSOR KENDRICKS.
JUST LIKE ONE I FOUND IN YOUR DESK, PROFESSOR STOOCH.
WORN BY THE ME I MET AT THE BAR.
THE ME THAT DUMPED ME OFF AT THE BEGINNING OF TIME.
AND THE MES THAT TURNED INTO BUG-MEN WHEN I STARTED TO FIGURE THIS ALL OUT.
I'M SO CONFUSED.
A-A LAPEL PIN?
YEAH, THAT'S WHAT I THOUGHT, TOO.
AND WHEN I CLICKED ON IT...
KLIK KLAK
NOTHING. NADA. ZIP.
BUT IF I PUT IT ON YOU--
--AND THEN I CLICK IT.
KLIK KLAK
OOP.

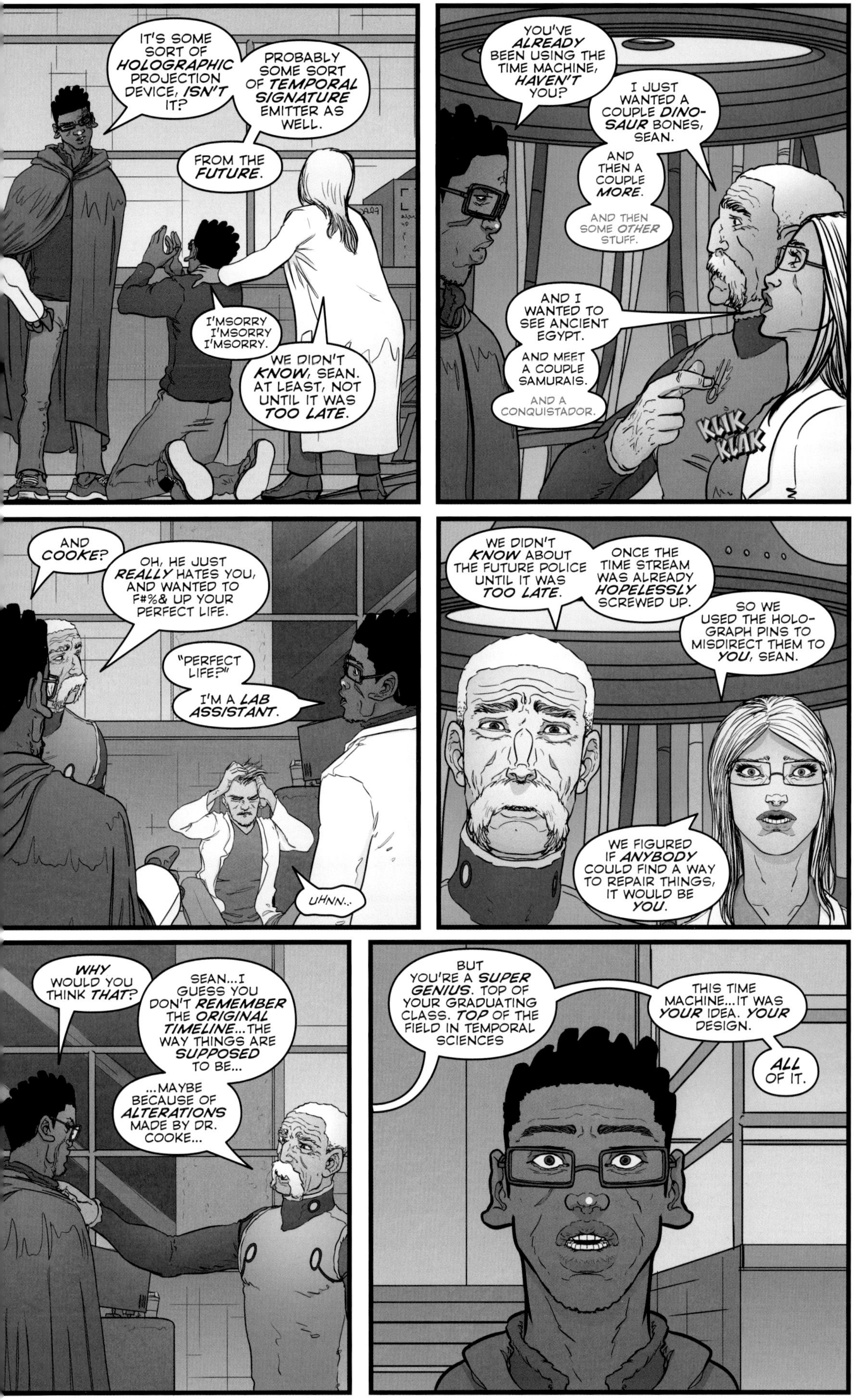
IT'S SOME SORT OF HOLOGRAPHIC PROJECTION DEVICE, ISN'T IT?
PROBABLY SOME SORT OF TEMPORAL SIGNATURE EMITTER AS WELL.
FROM THE FUTURE.
I'MSORRY I'MSORRY I'MSORRY.
WE DIDN'T KNOW, SEAN. AT LEAST, NOT UNTIL IT WAS TOO LATE.
YOU'VE ALREADY BEEN USING THE TIME MACHINE, HAVEN'T YOU?
I JUST WANTED A COUPLE DINO-SAUR BONES, SEAN.
AND THEN A COUPLE MORE.
AND THEN SOME OTHER STUFF.
AND I WANTED TO SEE ANCIENT EGYPT.
AND MEET A COUPLE SAMURAIS.
AND A CONQUISTADOR.
KLIK KLAK
AND COOKE?
OH, HE JUST REALLY HATES YOU, AND WANTED TO F#%& UP YOUR PERFECT LIFE.
"PERFECT LIFE?"
I'M A LAB ASSISTANT.
UHNN...
WE DIDN'T KNOW ABOUT THE FUTURE POLICE UNTIL IT WAS TOO LATE.
ONCE THE TIME STREAM WAS ALREADY HOPELESSLY SCREWED UP.
SO WE USED THE HOLO-GRAPH PINS TO MISDIRECT THEM TO YOU, SEAN.
WE FIGURED IF ANYBODY COULD FIND A WAY TO REPAIR THINGS, IT WOULD BE YOU.
WHY WOULD YOU THINK THAT?
SEAN...I GUESS YOU DON'T REMEMBER THE ORIGINAL TIMELINE...THE WAY THINGS ARE SUPPOSED TO BE...
...MAYBE BECAUSE OF ALTERATIONS MADE BY DR. COOKE...
BUT YOU'RE A SUPER GENIUS. TOP OF YOUR GRADUATING CLASS. TOP OF THE FIELD IN TEMPORAL SCIENCES
THIS TIME MACHINE...IT WAS YOUR IDEA. YOUR DESIGN.
ALL OF IT.

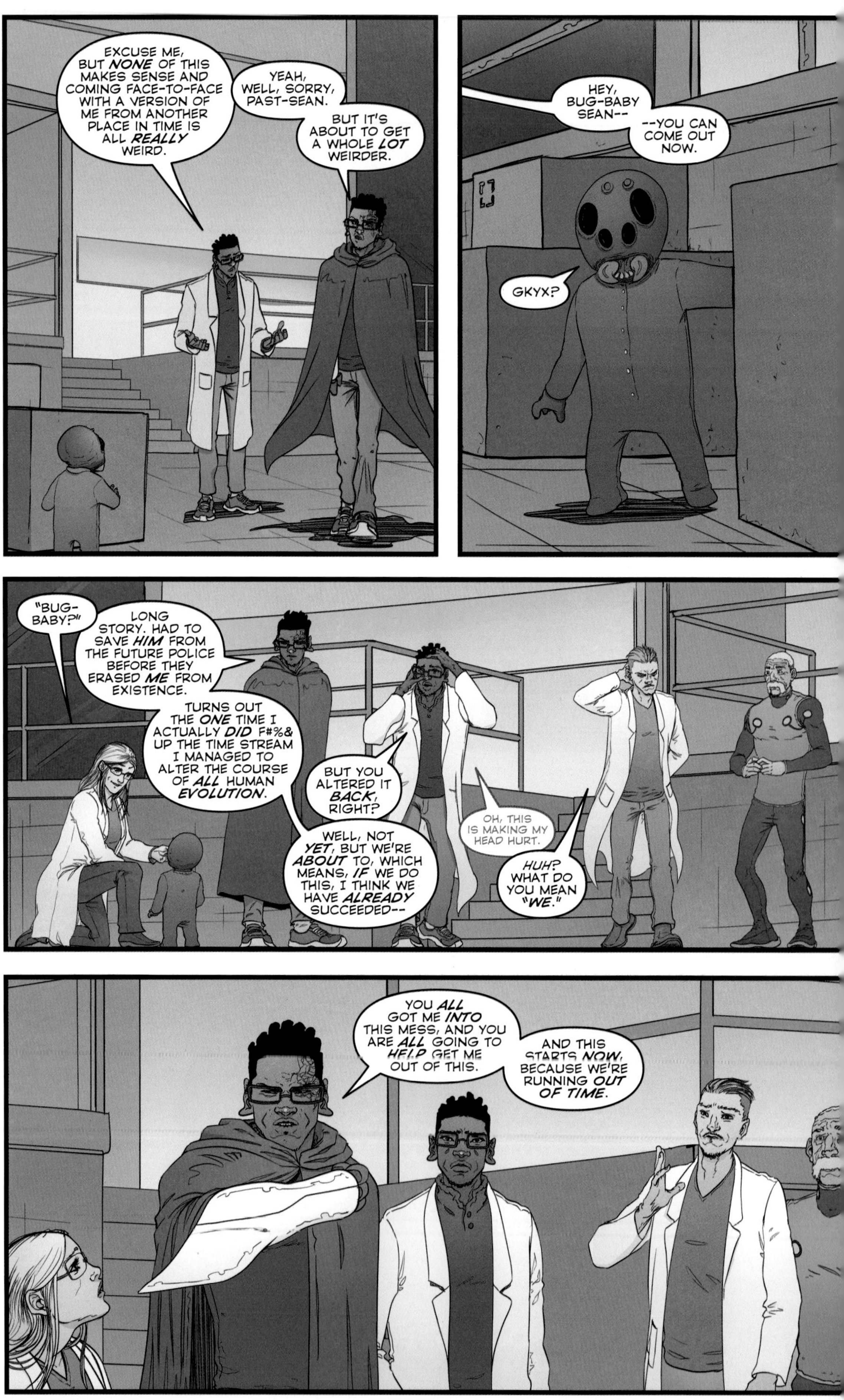

EXCUSE ME, BUT NONE OF THIS MAKES SENSE AND COMING FACE-TO-FACE WITH A VERSION OF ME FROM ANOTHER PLACE IN TIME IS ALL REALLY WEIRD.
YEAH, WELL, SORRY, PAST-SEAN.
BUT IT'S ABOUT TO GET A WHOLE LOT WEIRDER.
HEY, BUG-BABY SEAN--
--YOU CAN COME OUT NOW.
GKYX?
"BUG-BABY?"
LONG STORY. HAD TO SAVE HIM FROM THE FUTURE POLICE BEFORE THEY ERASED ME FROM EXISTENCE.
TURNS OUT THE ONE TIME I ACTUALLY DID F#%& UP THE TIME STREAM I MANAGED TO ALTER THE COURSE OF ALL HUMAN EVOLUTION.
BUT YOU ALTERED IT BACK, RIGHT?
WELL, NOT YET, BUT WE'RE ABOUT TO, WHICH MEANS, IF WE DO THIS, I THINK WE HAVE ALREADY SUCCEEDED--
OH, THIS IS MAKING MY HEAD HURT.
HUH? WHAT DO YOU MEAN "WE."
YOU ALL GOT ME INTO THIS MESS, AND YOU ARE ALL GOING TO HELP GET ME OUT OF THIS.
AND THIS STARTS NOW, BECAUSE WE'RE RUNNING OUT OF TIME.

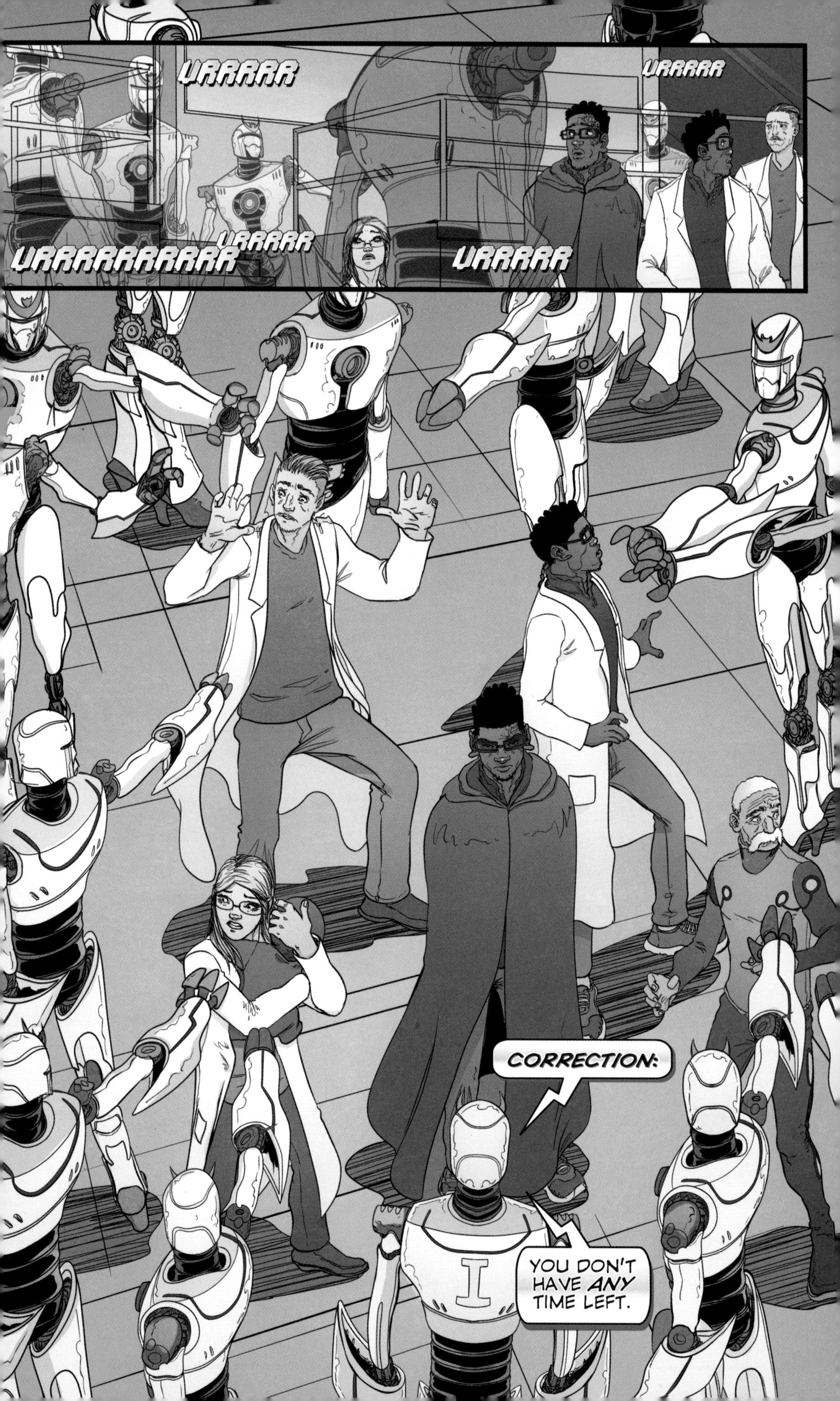
URRRRR
URRRRR
URRRRRRRRRRR
URRRRR
URRRRR
CORRECTION:
YOU DON'T HAVE *ANY* TIME LEFT.

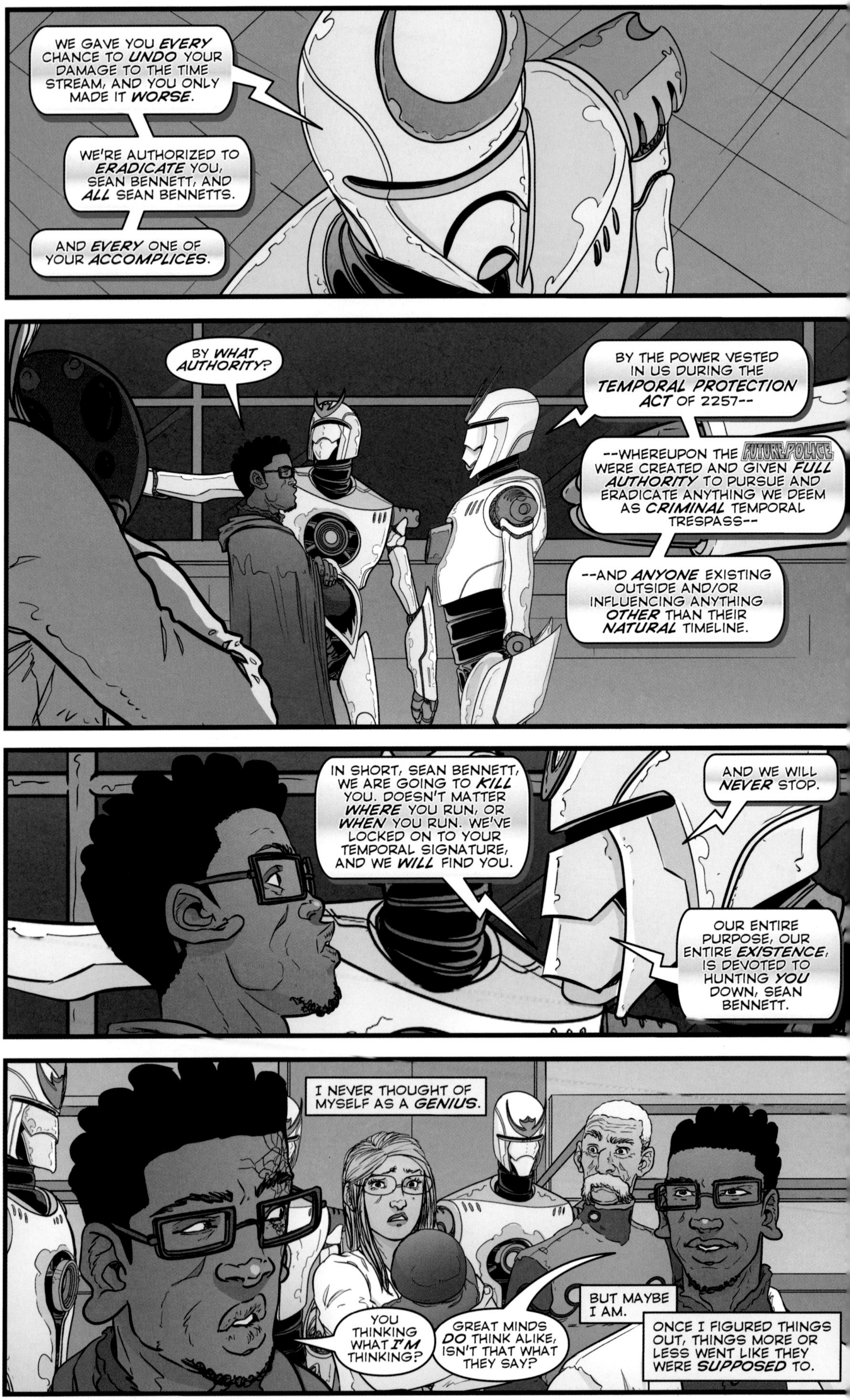
WE GAVE YOU EVERY CHANCE TO UNDO YOUR DAMAGE TO THE TIME STREAM, AND YOU ONLY MADE IT WORSE.
WE'RE AUTHORIZED TO ERADICATE YOU, SEAN BENNETT, AND ALL SEAN BENNETTS.
AND EVERY ONE OF YOUR ACCOMPLICES.
BY WHAT AUTHORITY?
BY THE POWER VESTED IN US DURING THE TEMPORAL PROTECTION ACT OF 2257--
--WHEREUPON THE FUTURE POLICE WERE CREATED AND GIVEN FULL AUTHORITY TO PURSUE AND ERADICATE ANYTHING WE DEEM AS CRIMINAL TEMPORAL TRESPASS--
--AND ANYONE EXISTING OUTSIDE AND/OR INFLUENCING ANYTHING OTHER THAN THEIR NATURAL TIMELINE.
IN SHORT, SEAN BENNETT, WE ARE GOING TO KILL YOU. DOESN'T MATTER WHERE YOU RUN, OR WHEN YOU RUN. WE'VE LOCKED ON TO YOUR TEMPORAL SIGNATURE, AND WE WILL FIND YOU.
AND WE WILL NEVER STOP.
OUR ENTIRE PURPOSE, OUR ENTIRE EXISTENCE, IS DEVOTED TO HUNTING YOU DOWN, SEAN BENNETT.
I NEVER THOUGHT OF MYSELF AS A GENIUS.
BUT MAYBE I AM.
YOU THINKING WHAT I'M THINKING?
GREAT MINDS DO THINK ALIKE, ISN'T THAT WHAT THEY SAY?
ONCE I FIGURED THINGS OUT, THINGS MORE OR LESS WENT LIKE THEY WERE SUPPOSED TO.

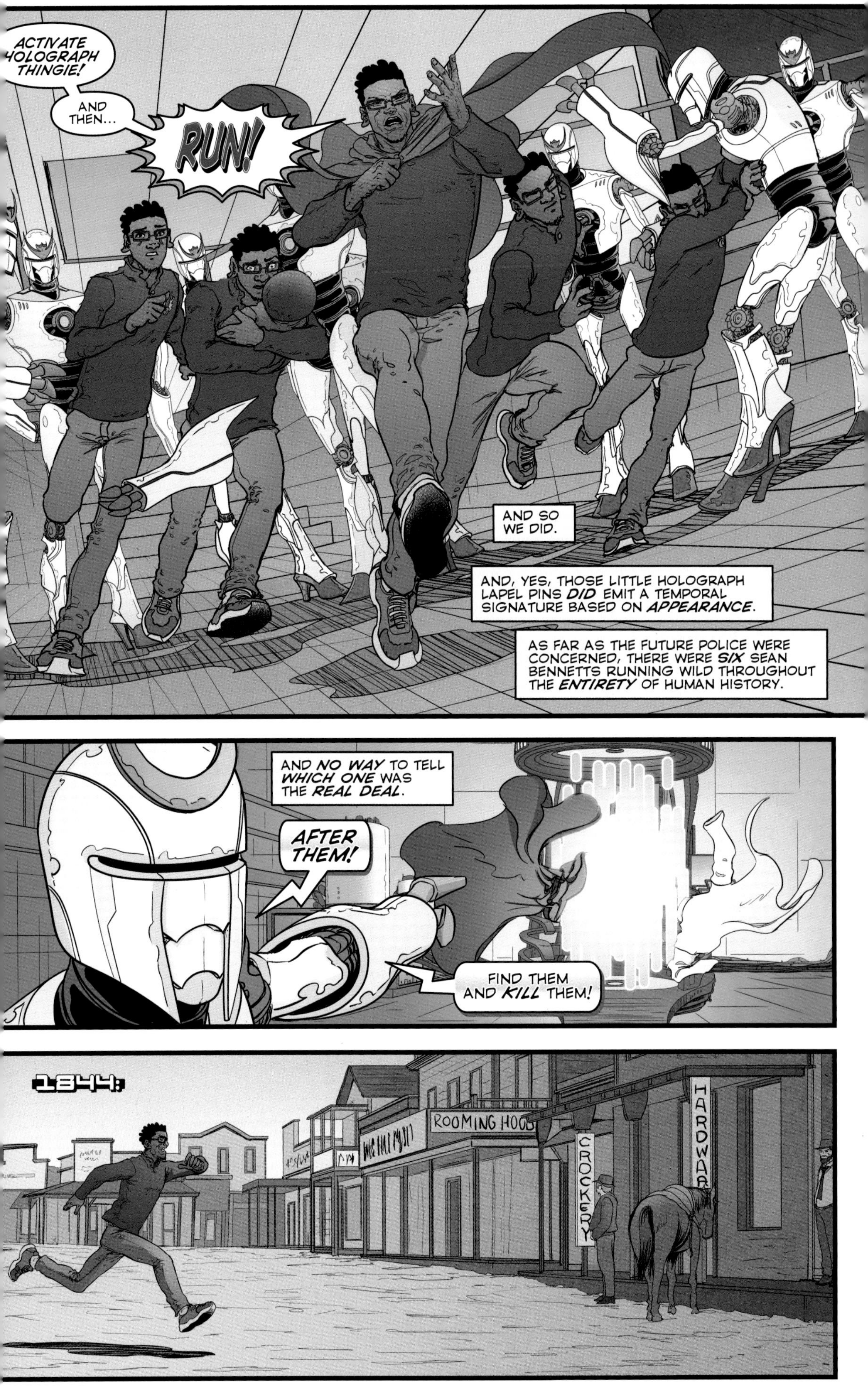
ACTIVATE HOLOGRAPH THINGIE!
AND THEN...
RUN!
AND SO WE DID.
AND, YES, THOSE LITTLE HOLOGRAPH LAPEL PINS *DID* EMIT A TEMPORAL SIGNATURE BASED ON *APPEARANCE*.
AS FAR AS THE FUTURE POLICE WERE CONCERNED, THERE WERE *SIX* SEAN BENNETTS RUNNING WILD THROUGHOUT THE *ENTIRETY* OF HUMAN HISTORY.
AND *NO WAY* TO TELL *WHICH ONE* WAS THE *REAL DEAL*.
AFTER THEM!
FIND THEM AND *KILL* THEM!
1844:
ROOMING HOU
CROCKERY
HARDWAR

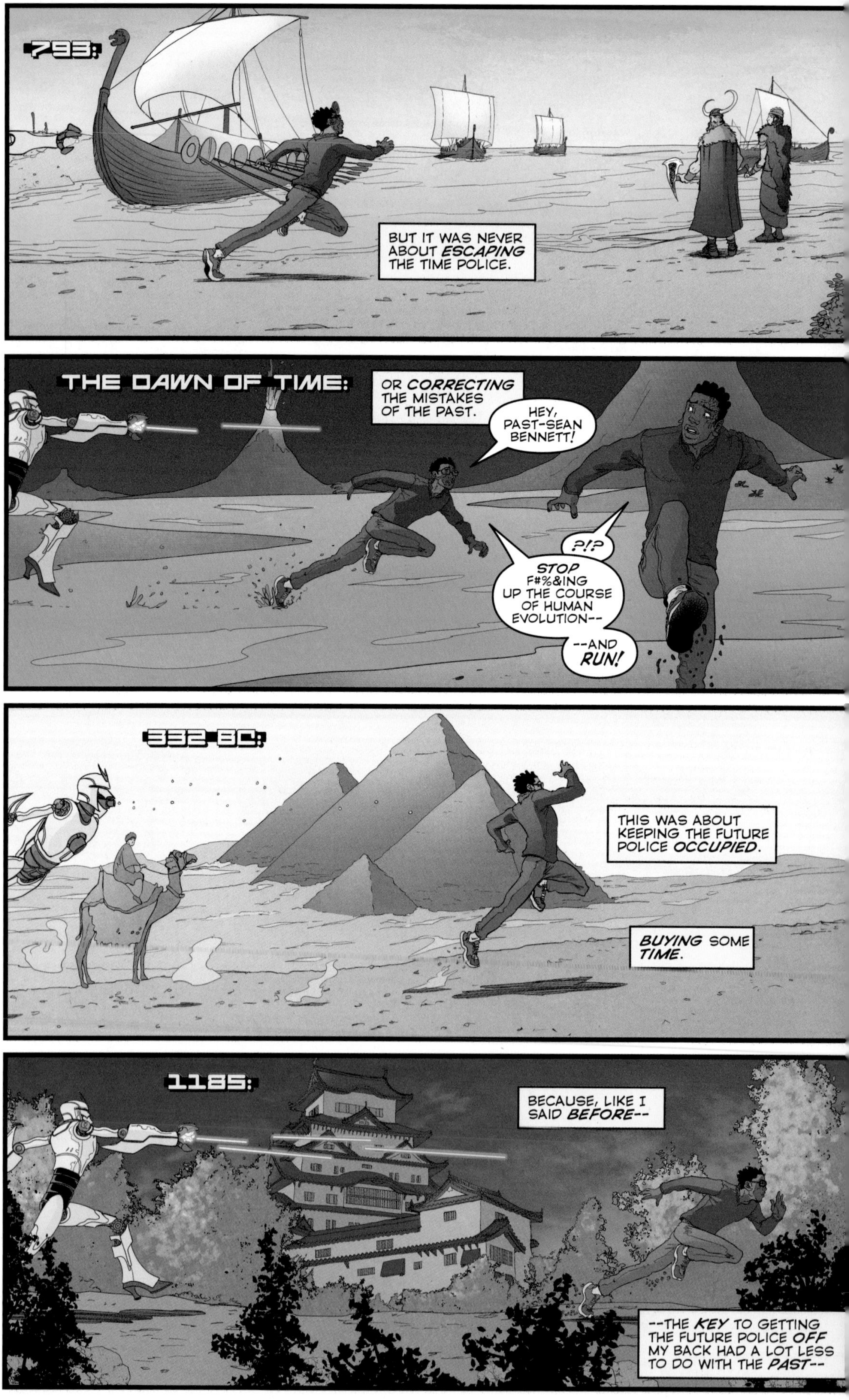

793:
BUT IT WAS NEVER ABOUT *ESCAPING* THE TIME POLICE.
THE DAWN OF TIME:
OR *CORRECTING* THE MISTAKES OF THE PAST.
HEY, PAST-SEAN BENNETT!
?!?
STOP F#%&ING UP THE COURSE OF HUMAN EVOLUTION--
--AND *RUN!*
332 BC:
THIS WAS ABOUT KEEPING THE FUTURE POLICE *OCCUPIED*.
BUYING SOME *TIME*.
1185:
BECAUSE, LIKE I SAID *BEFORE*--
--THE *KEY* TO GETTING THE FUTURE POLICE *OFF* MY BACK HAD A LOT LESS TO DO WITH THE *PAST*--

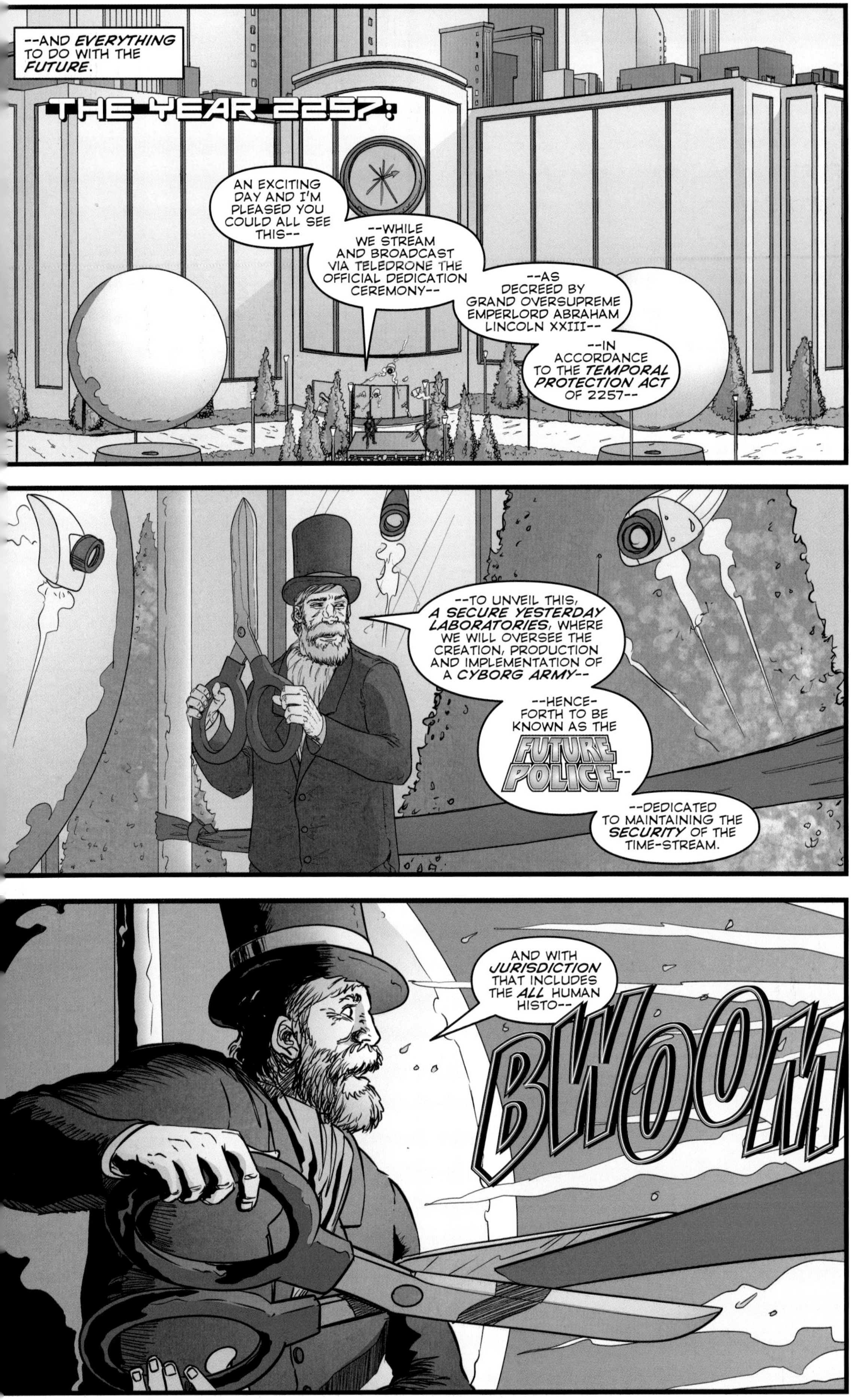
--AND EVERYTHING TO DO WITH THE FUTURE.
THE YEAR 2257:
AN EXCITING DAY AND I'M PLEASED YOU COULD ALL SEE THIS--
--WHILE WE STREAM AND BROADCAST VIA TELEDRONE THE OFFICIAL DEDICATION CEREMONY--
--AS DECREED BY GRAND OVERSUPREME EMPERLORD ABRAHAM LINCOLN XXIII--
--IN ACCORDANCE TO THE TEMPORAL PROTECTION ACT OF 2257--
--TO UNVEIL THIS, A SECURE YESTERDAY LABORATORIES, WHERE WE WILL OVERSEE THE CREATION, PRODUCTION AND IMPLEMENTATION OF A CYBORG ARMY--
--HENCE-FORTH TO BE KNOWN AS THE FUTURE POLICE--
--DEDICATED TO MAINTAINING THE SECURITY OF THE TIME-STREAM.
AND WITH JURISDICTION THAT INCLUDES THE ALL HUMAN HISTO--
BWOOM

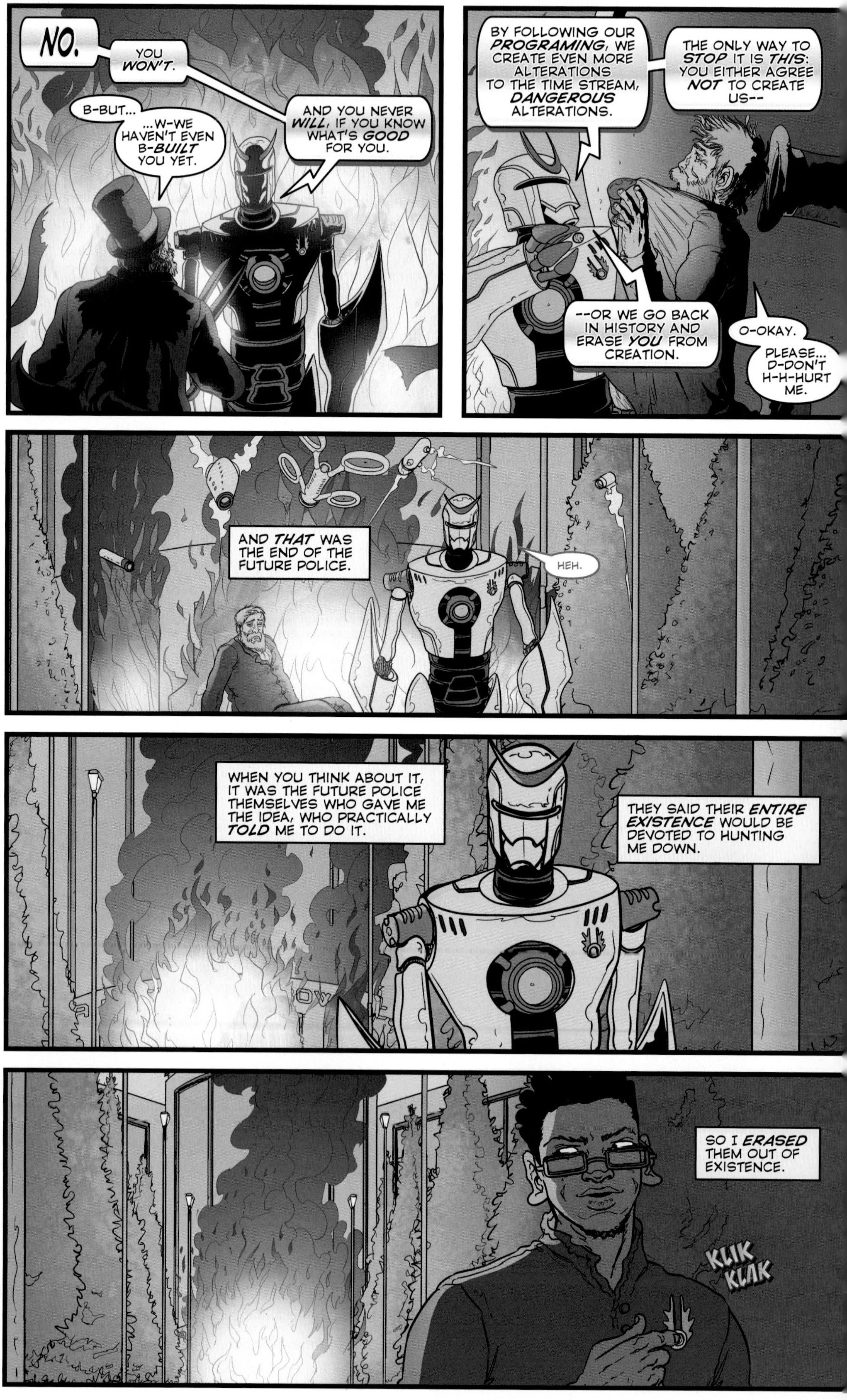

NO.
YOU WON'T.
B-BUT...
...W-WE HAVEN'T EVEN B-BUILT YOU YET.
AND YOU NEVER WILL, IF YOU KNOW WHAT'S GOOD FOR YOU.
BY FOLLOWING OUR PROGRAMING, WE CREATE EVEN MORE ALTERATIONS TO THE TIME STREAM, DANGEROUS ALTERATIONS.
THE ONLY WAY TO STOP IT IS THIS: YOU EITHER AGREE NOT TO CREATE US--
--OR WE GO BACK IN HISTORY AND ERASE YOU FROM CREATION.
O-OKAY.
PLEASE... D-DON'T H-H-HURT ME.
AND THAT WAS THE END OF THE FUTURE POLICE.
HEH.
WHEN YOU THINK ABOUT IT, IT WAS THE FUTURE POLICE THEMSELVES WHO GAVE ME THE IDEA, WHO PRACTICALLY TOLD ME TO DO IT.
THEY SAID THEIR ENTIRE EXISTENCE WOULD BE DEVOTED TO HUNTING ME DOWN.
SO I ERASED THEM OUT OF EXISTENCE.
KLIK KLAK

HUH? HEY! WHATTAYA KNOW!

THAT *SCAR* THE FUTURE POLICE GAVE ME WHEN I WAS A BABY IS *GONE*.

GUESS THE FUTURE POLICE REALLY *AREN'T* GONNA BE A *PROBLEM* ANYMORE.

MAYBE THEY NEVER *WERE*.

STILL GOT A FEW *LOOSE ENDS* TO TAKE CARE OF BEFORE THIS IS OVER.

GONNA NEED TO MAKE SURE ABRAHAM LINCOLN DOESN'T SPAWN A LINE OF TYRANNICAL DESCENDANTS.

THE NEW 2258 POWER ARMOR MODELS ARE HERE ON SALE NOW

BUT YOU *ALREADY* KNOW THAT PART, RIGHT?

AND MAKE SURE THE HUMAN-AGAIN-BABY-ME GETS SAFELY *HOME*.

THERE YOU GO, KIDDO.

KOO?

SO I CAN GROW UP TO BE THE PERSON I'M *SUPPOSED* TO BE.

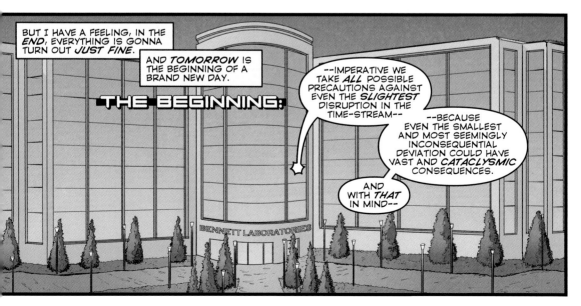

BUT I HAVE A FEELING, IN THE *END*, EVERYTHING IS GONNA TURN OUT *JUST FINE*.

AND *TOMORROW* IS THE BEGINNING OF A BRAND NEW DAY.

THE BEGINNING:

--IMPERATIVE WE TAKE *ALL* POSSIBLE PRECAUTIONS AGAINST EVEN THE *SLIGHTEST* DISRUPTION IN THE TIME-STREAM--

--BECAUSE EVEN THE SMALLEST AND MOST SEEMINGLY INCONSEQUENTIAL DEVIATION COULD HAVE VAST AND *CATACLYSMIC* CONSEQUENCES.

AND WITH *THAT* IN MIND--

BENNETT LABORATORIES

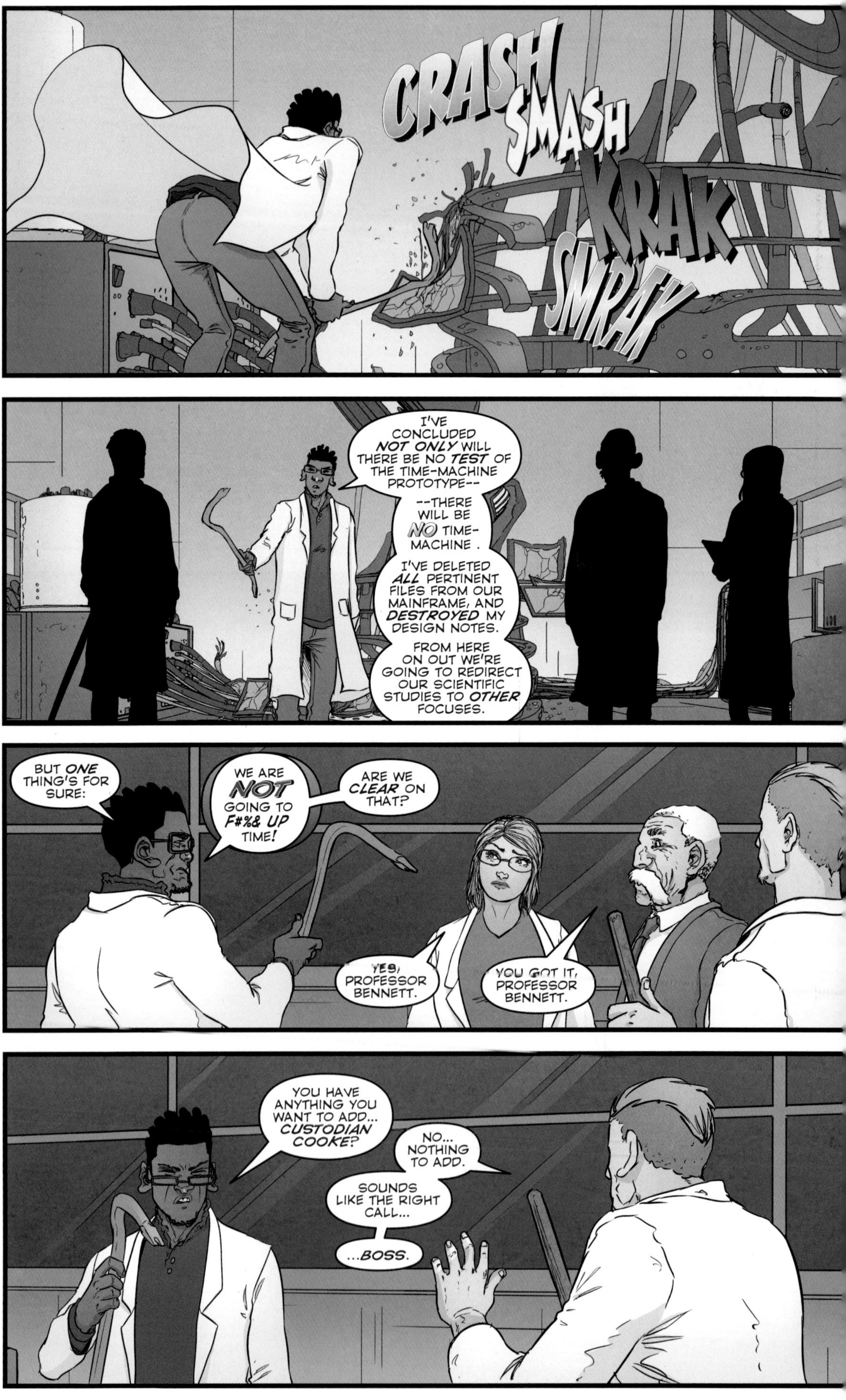
CRASH
SMASH
KRAK
SMRAK
I'VE CONCLUDED NOT ONLY WILL THERE BE NO TEST OF THE TIME-MACHINE PROTOTYPE--
--THERE WILL BE NO TIME-MACHINE .
I'VE DELETED ALL PERTINENT FILES FROM OUR MAINFRAME, AND DESTROYED MY DESIGN NOTES.
FROM HERE ON OUT WE'RE GOING TO REDIRECT OUR SCIENTIFIC STUDIES TO OTHER FOCUSES.
BUT ONE THING'S FOR SURE:
WE ARE NOT GOING TO F#%& UP TIME!
ARE WE CLEAR ON THAT?
YES, PROFESSOR BENNETT.
YOU GOT IT, PROFESSOR BENNETT.
YOU HAVE ANYTHING YOU WANT TO ADD... CUSTODIAN COOKE?
NO... NOTHING TO ADD.
SOUNDS LIKE THE RIGHT CALL...
...BOSS.

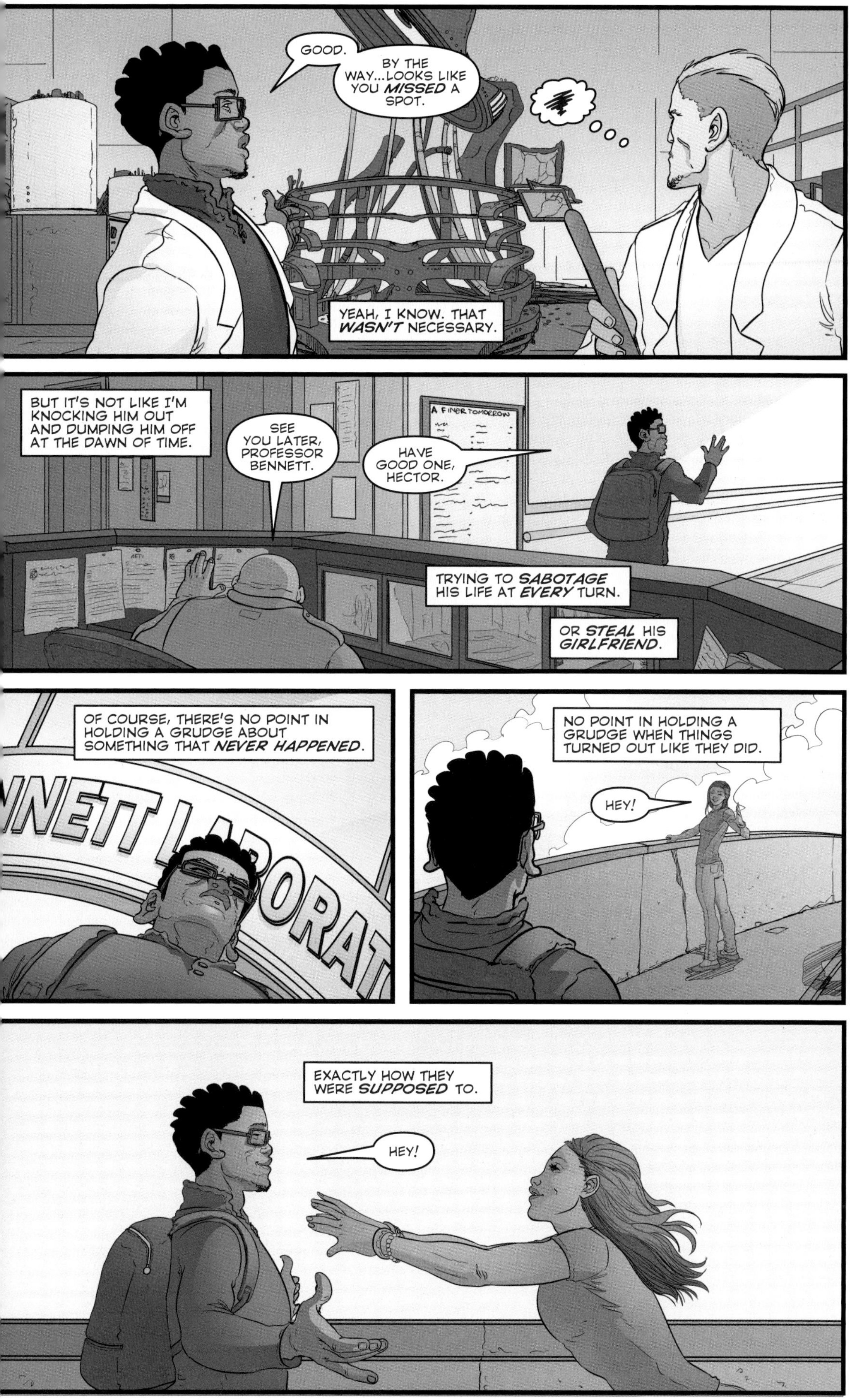
GOOD.
BY THE WAY...LOOKS LIKE YOU MISSED A SPOT.
YEAH, I KNOW. THAT WASN'T NECESSARY.
BUT IT'S NOT LIKE I'M KNOCKING HIM OUT AND DUMPING HIM OFF AT THE DAWN OF TIME.
SEE YOU LATER, PROFESSOR BENNETT.
HAVE GOOD ONE, HECTOR.
A FINER TOMORROW
TRYING TO SABOTAGE HIS LIFE AT EVERY TURN.
OR STEAL HIS GIRLFRIEND.
OF COURSE, THERE'S NO POINT IN HOLDING A GRUDGE ABOUT SOMETHING THAT NEVER HAPPENED.
NNETT LABORAT
NO POINT IN HOLDING A GRUDGE WHEN THINGS TURNED OUT LIKE THEY DID.
HEY!
EXACTLY HOW THEY WERE SUPPOSED TO.
HEY!

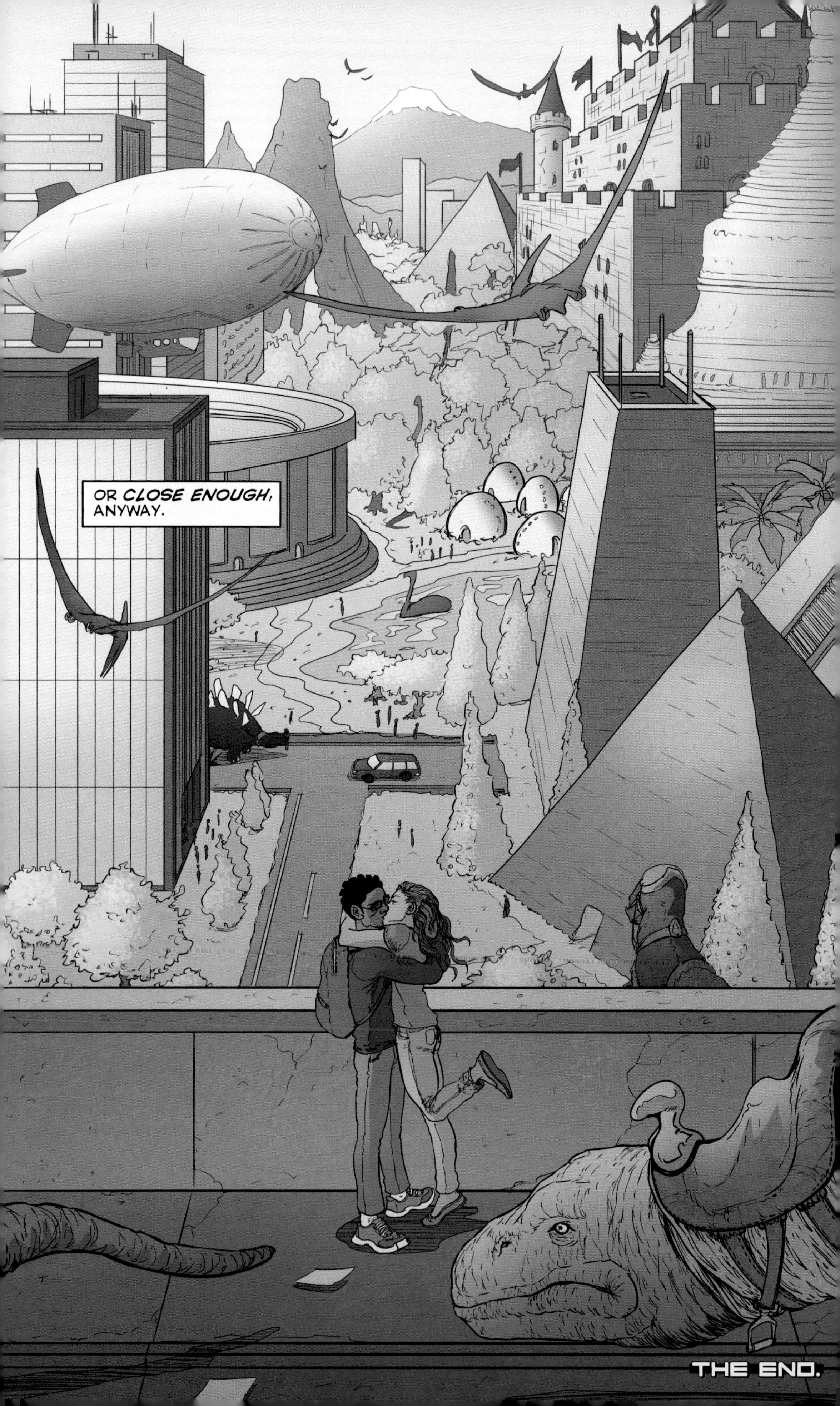

OR *CLOSE ENOUGH*, ANYWAY.
THE END.

THE MAN WHO F#&%ED UP TIME™

BEHIND THE SCENES

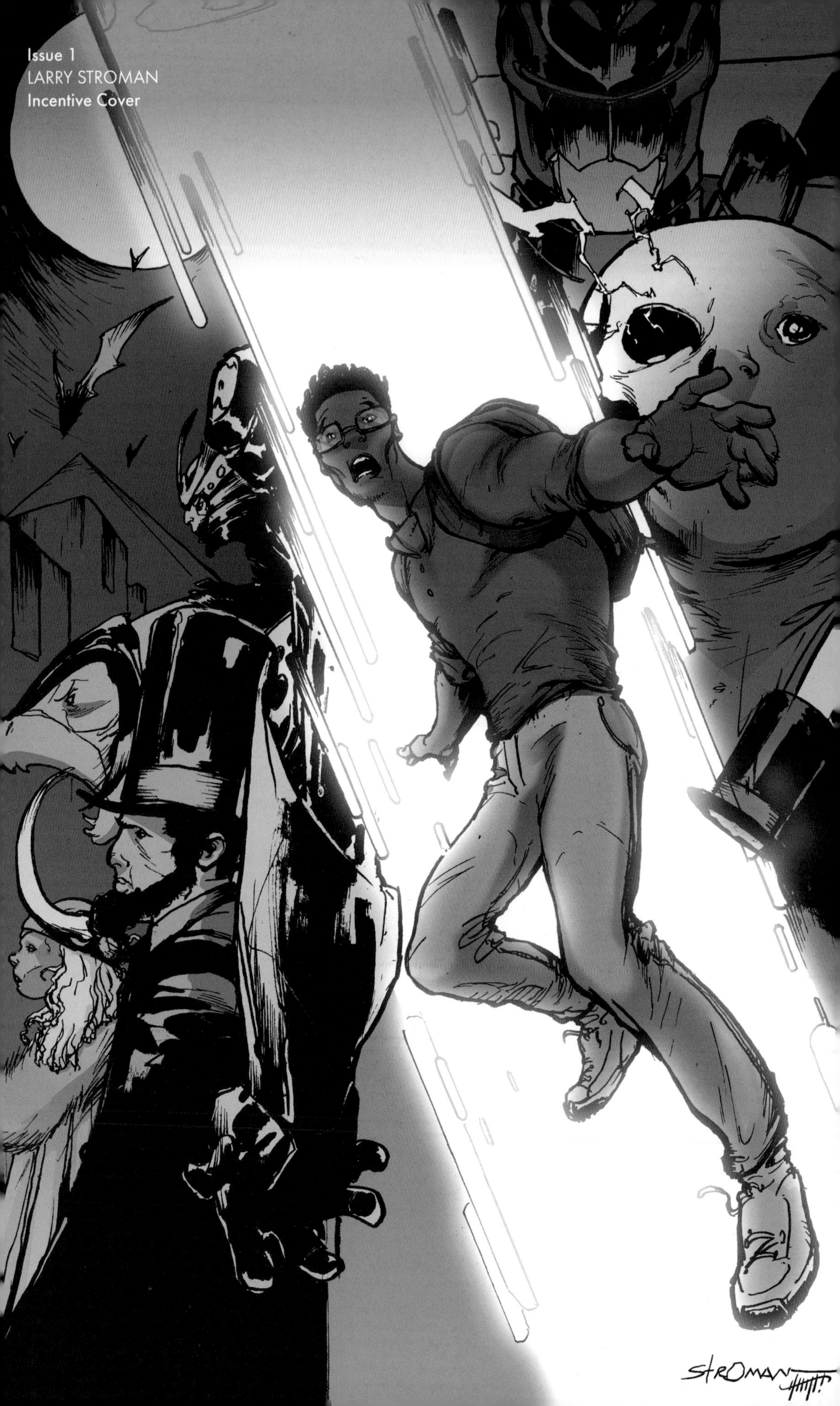
STROMAN
Issue 1
LARRY STROMAN
Incentive Cover

Issue 1

JOHN McCREA w/ ENRICA EREN ANGIOLINI

Comics Pro Exclusive Variant Cover

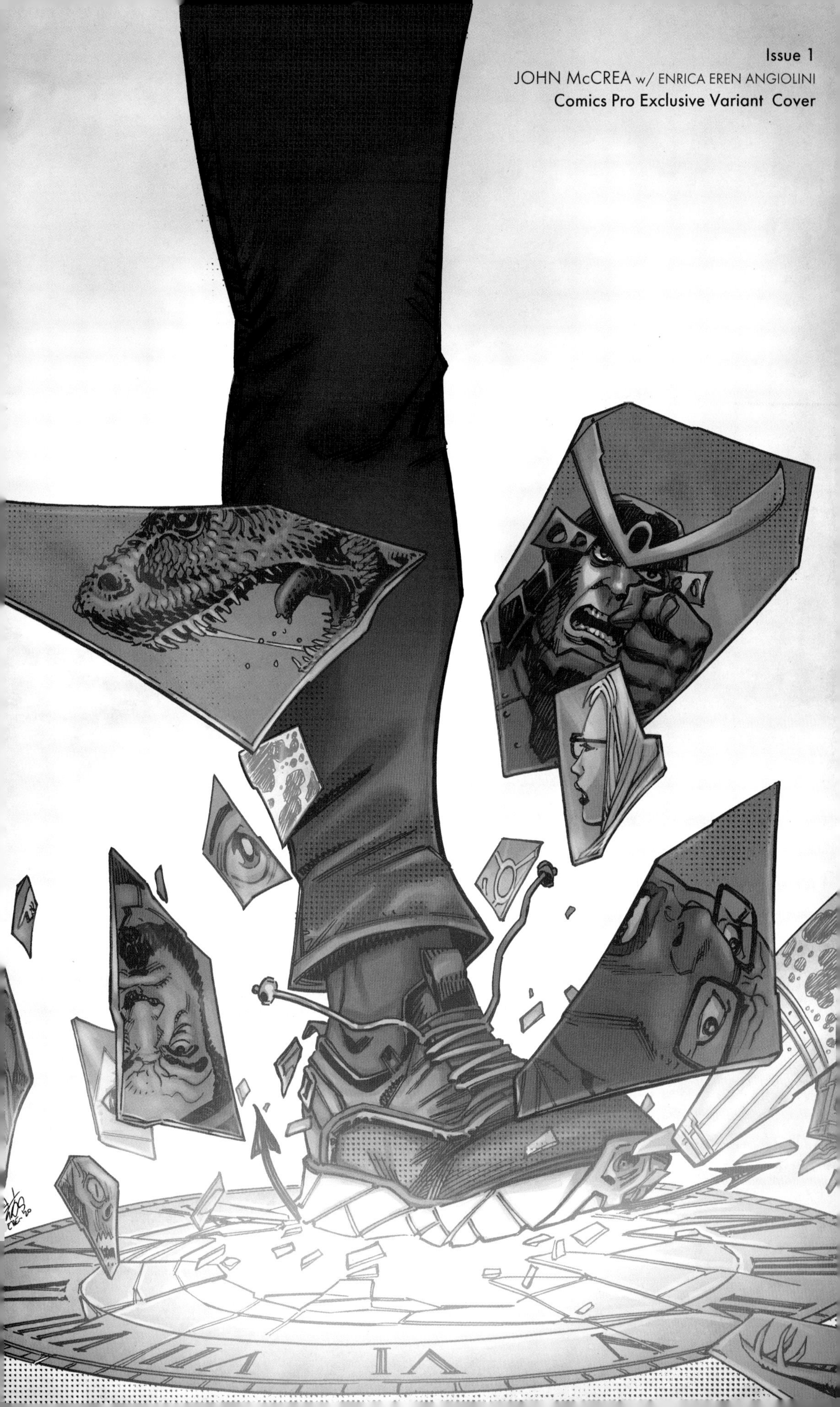

Issue 2
ANDREW ROBINSON
Incentive Cover

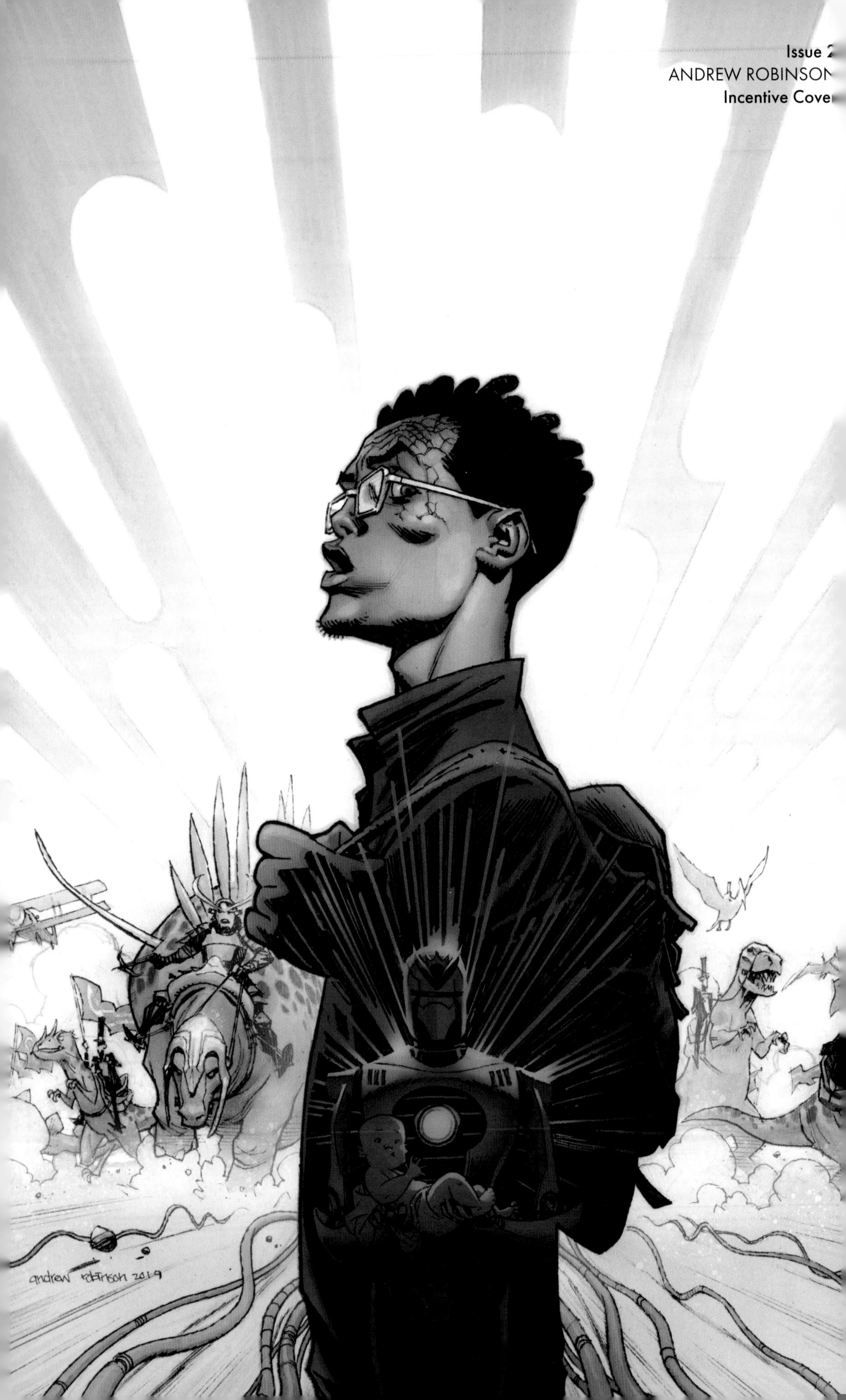
andrew robinson 2019

A FINER TOMORROW LABORATORIES

To Mr. Grant Cooke,

Re: Your recent complaint submitted about co-worker Sean Bennett.

In accordance with <u>A Finer Tomorrow Laboratories</u> policy, we will keep your recent complaint against Sean Bennett on file for the foreseeable future. However, after review of your complaint, we find it meritless and will not be terminating Mr. Bennett's employment as you suggested.

Being "weird and goofy looking" is hardly grounds for termination, not to mention being an incredibly subjective complaint. We've also determined not cleaning your computer monitor to your satisfaction or sweeping enough around your workstation to be sufficient grounds for revoking employment. Plus, we'd like to note that peer reviews of Mr. Bennett by both Professors Kendricks and Stooch suggest Bennett to be an exemplary employee, your opinion not withstanding.

A closing note: We at <u>A Finer Tomorrow Laboratories</u> pride ourselves on being a respectful and tolerant work environment. Please refrain from referring to Mr. Bennett as "janitor boy" in the future, both in verbal interactions and corporate memoranda.

Cordially,
D. Hennessy,
Human Resources,
A Finer Tomorrow Laboratories, Inc.

Smartypedia
The World's Encyclopedia

Article | Discussion

Attempted Assassination of Abraham Lincoln

From Smartypedia

An unsuccessful attempt on the life of Abraham Lincoln, the 16th President of the United States of America and, later, first king of the United States, as well as direct ancestor to our beloved King Abraham Lincoln VI, was perpetrated by stage actor John Wilkes Booth on April 14, 1865, while attending the play Our American Cousin at Ford's Theatre in Washington D.C.

The near-assassination was thwarted by a mysterious stranger whose identity remains a mystery even to this day. Contradictory witness testimony includes the fanciful story that the stranger appeared "from mid-air, as if by magic," and was able to kill Booth a mere-split second before he was able to pull the trigger and assassinate the then-president. Conspiracy theories abound about the mysterious savior of Lincoln, and an entire genre of dystopian speculative science fiction has been recently popularized, postulating a world where Lincoln's attempted assassination was successful.

Part of the American Civil War

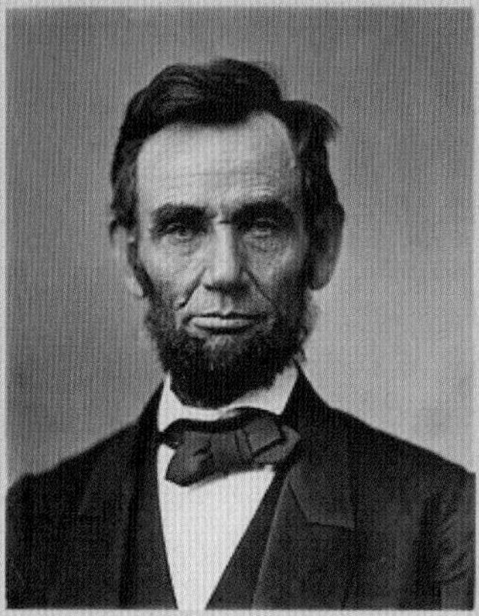

Location
Ford's Theatre, Washington, D.C.

Date
April 14, 1865; 154 years ago
10:15 p.m

Target
Abraham Lincoln (failed)
Andrew Johnson (failed)
William H. Seward (failed)

Attack type
Political assassination/shooting/stabbing

Weapons
Philadelphia Deringer pistol/dagger

Injured
John Wilkes Booth (the perpetrator)
Henry Rathbone
Joseph "Peanuts" Burroughs
William H. Seward
Frederick Seward
Augustus Seward
Fanny Seward
George F. Robinson
Emerick Hansell

Perpetrators
John Wilkes Booth and co-conspirators

Motive
Revenge for the Confederate

Contents

Background

John Wilkes Booth, born in Maryland into a family of prominent stage actors, had by the time of the assassination become a famous actor and national celebrity in his own right. He was also

in lincoln
we trust

POLICE INCIDENT REPORT
UNIFORM INCIDENT/OFFENSE REPORT

12

CASE NUMBER *78*
3045526

PAGE 1 OF 2

X INITIAL REPORT
— MODIFY REPORT
— OFFICER SAFETY
— OFFICER ASSAULT

- PROSECUTION DECLINED
- EXTRADITION DENIED
- VICTIM REFUSED TO COOPERATE
- JUVENILE/NO CUSTODY
- NOT CLEARED EXCEPTIONAL

REPORTING OFFICER	ORI #	O	M	2	

LEXINGTON

MONTH	DAY	YEAR	DOW	HOUR	DR LICENSE #	SSN	TYPE	
02	03	20	MO	0208	- - - -	- - -	- - - -	

INCIDENT DETAILS

WHILE ON PATROL, ENCOUNTERED SUSPICIOUS INDIVIDUAL GARBED IN STRANGE CLOTHING, LOOKING CONFUSED, OUT OF PLACE, AND UTTERING PROFANITIES.

UPON REQUESTING SUBJECT'S IDENTIFICATION PAPERS, AS PER DEPARTMENT REGULATION, SUSPECT ATTEMPTED TO FLEE. OFFICER GAVE CHASE ABOARD PATROLOSAURUS THROUGH CITY STREETS, EXERCISING CAUTION NOT TO INJURE OR DISTRESS PEDESTRIANS. AFTER SEVERAL VERBAL WARNINGS, WARNING CROSSBOW BOLTS WERE FIRED, BUT SUBJECT MANAGED TO ELUDE OFFICER IN PURSUIT.

SUBJECT WAS LOST IN CROWD AT CROSSROADS OF HINGMAN ST. AND JOHNSTON AVE.

A CITIZEN LATER FILED REPORT OF A STOLEN STOVEPIPE HAT, LEADING THIS OFFICER TO CONCLUDE THAT THE HAT WAS STOLEN BY SUSPECT, WHO USED IT TO BLEND INTO CROWD.

SUSPECT IS DARK-COMPLEXIONED AND JUST SLIGHTLY LESS THAN 6 FEET TALL, IN HIS MID 20S.

SUSPECT IS CONSIDERED TO BE UNSTABLE, LIKELY DANGEROUS, POSSIBLY SEDITIOUS. ALL OFFICERS ADVISED TO BE ON THE LOOKOUT.

IT IS UNLAWFUL TO FALSELY
REPORT A CRIME.

REPORTING OFFICER	REVIEWED BY
Lexington	*Y Giles*

USR NIBSR-01A
9-06

POLICE INCIDENT REPORT
UNIFORM INCIDENT/OFFENSE REPORT

SUSPECT SKETCH

THE MAN WHO F#&%ED UP TIME™

An interview with artist
KARL MOSTERT

AFTERSHOCK: What was your approach to character designs for TMWFUT? Was it different from your usual approach?

KARL MOSTERT: I'd say this was the same approach as I've always used. I did start watching a lot of time-traveling movies beforehand, though. Ultimately, though, I decided that I'd rather not go with chiseled movie-like characters, but instead use more realistic scientist stereotypes.

AS: What's your process for laying out an interior page?

KM: Usually I thumbnail out a couple of options, and choose the most dynamic of them. There wasn't a lot of action in TMWFUT so usually one or two options were enough. After that, I'd have to rough it out and present the roughs to the editors, and when I got the approval I would start on pencils.

AS: How did you approach the time-travel aspect of this book? Each time-jump is so detailed, how did you decide what should be in the background?

KM: Damn that Layman! This is one area I'd rather forget about, haha!

Each time the script called for some drastic amalgamation of two or three different times or characters or species I would research and pull out pictures of different architecture, animals, etc. What a nightmare! But in the end, it's just what worked well for the story. And the script was always specific enough that I knew what I needed to find for reference anyhow.

AS: Do you have a favorite character? Why?

KM: Definitely the Future Police. They're robots, and I love drawing robots. :)

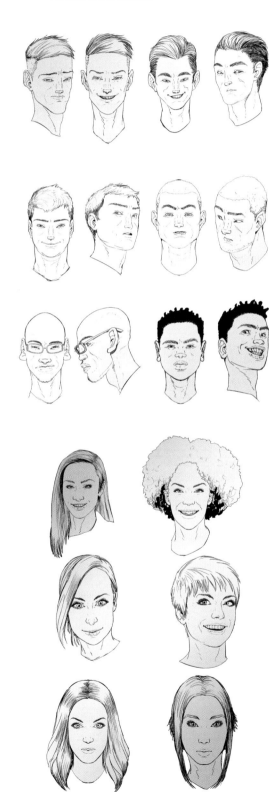

AS: Did you have a favorite scene to draw? A least favorite?

KM: First page in issue one! I was, like, drawing dinosaur riders.

I don't think I had a least favorite. There were some hard scenes, but never anything I disliked.

AS: Any advice for other artists trying to break into comics?

KM: Keep going, keep improving and when you feel tired and rundown, that's when you gotta keep pushing even harder. This is a talent-based profession, so the more practice you have, the better it is and the easier it gets for you.

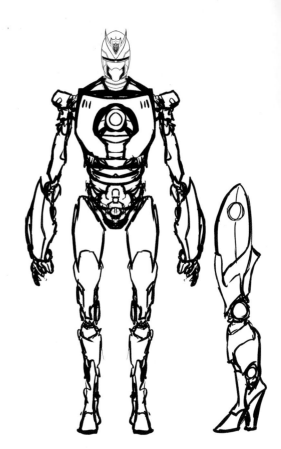

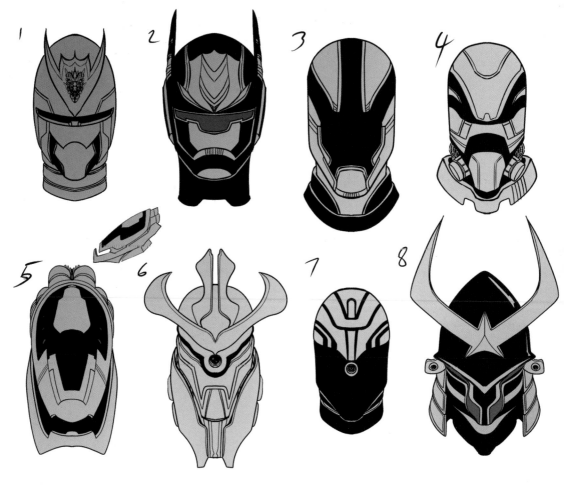

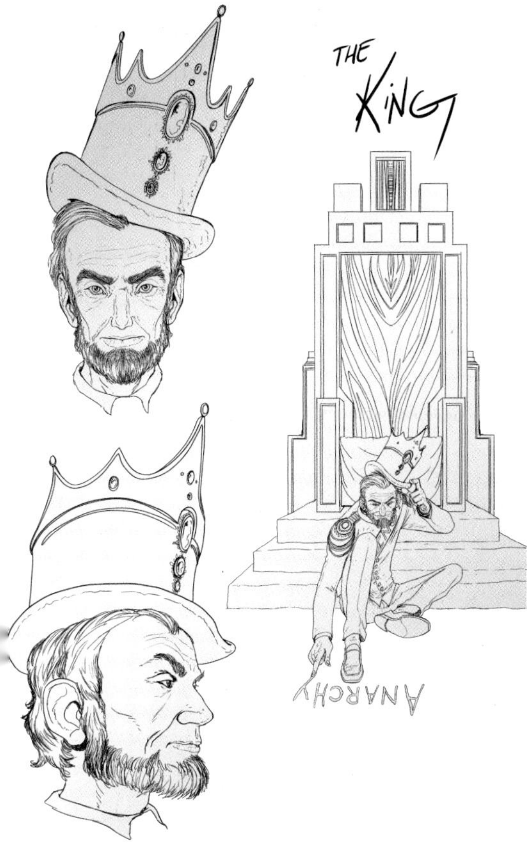
THE KING
ANARCHY

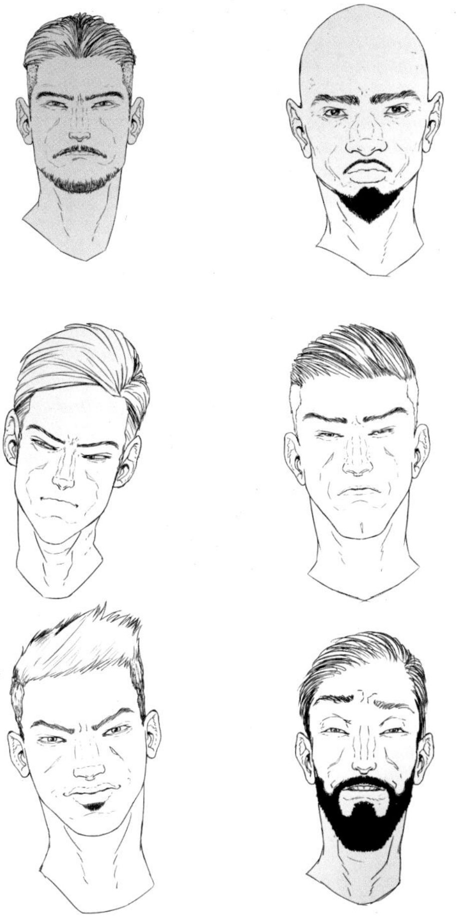

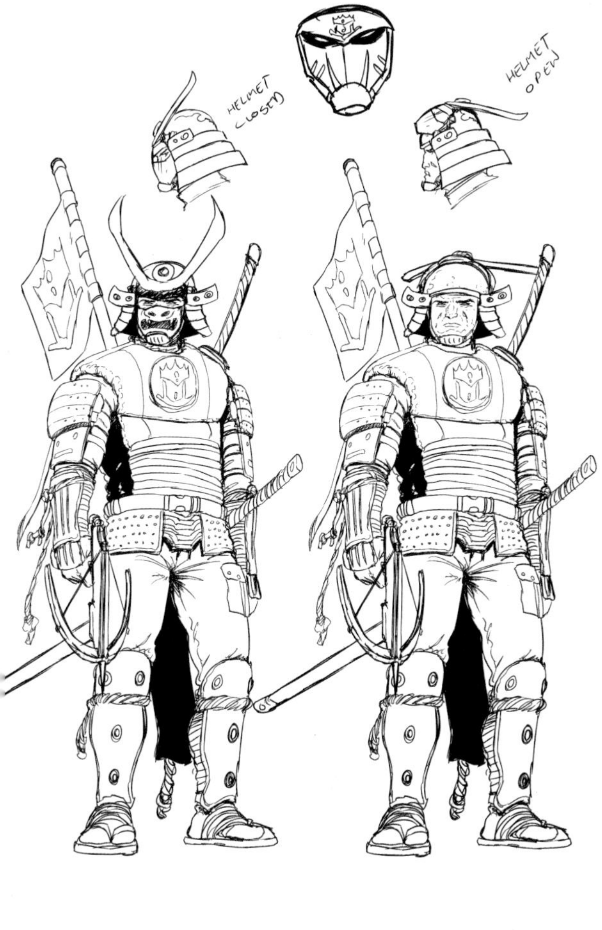
HELMET CLOSED
HELMET OPEN

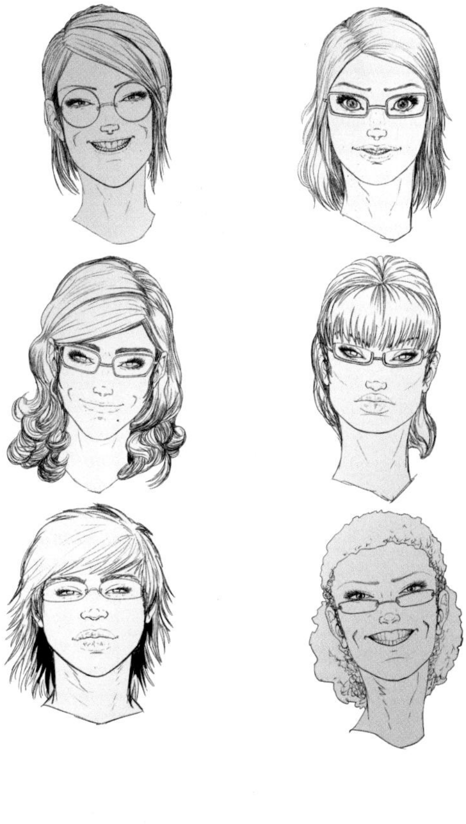

ABOUT THE CREATORS OF

THE MAN WHO F#&%ED UP TIME™

JOHN LAYMAN writer & letterer

@themightylayman

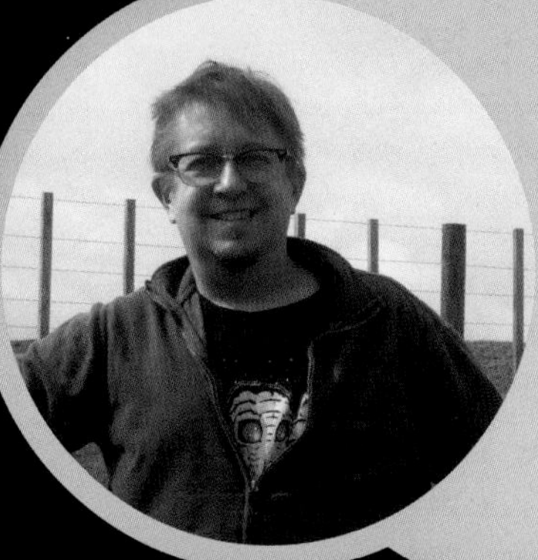

John Layman is the creator, writer and letterer of the New York Times best-selling, Harvey Award and multi-Eisner Award winning cannibal cop comedy series *Chew*. Since 1995, John's been a comics writer, editor, letterer, designer and production monkey. He's written *Cyclops, Detective Comics, Mars Attacks, Godzilla, Thundercats, Gambit, Scarface, Red Sonja, Marvel Zombies Vs. Army of Darkness, House of M: Fantastic Four,* the *Marvel Identity Wars Annuals, Stephen Colbert's Tek Jansen, ELEANOR AND THE EGRET*...and a whole lotta other stuff.

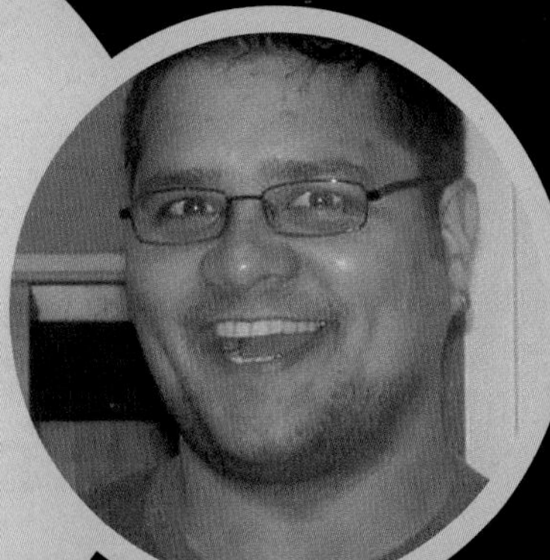

KARL MOSTERT artist

Karl Mostert is a comic book illustrator from Cape Town, South Africa. Karl has worked on domestic and international comic book projects such as *The Supa Strikas* and various DC comic books. He lives in Cape Town with his wife and two children.

DEE CUNNIFFE colorist

@deezoid

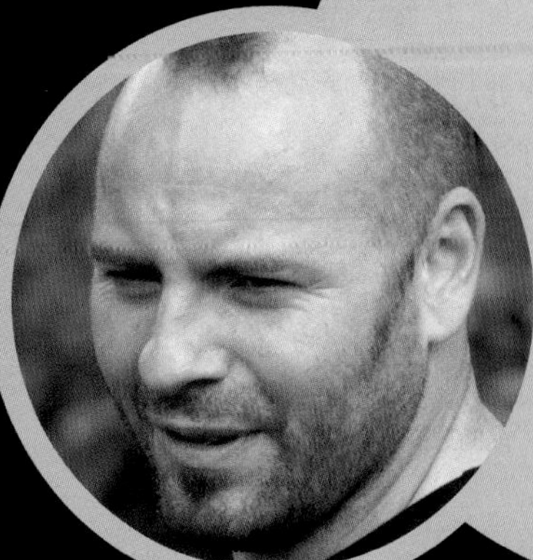

Dee is an award-winning Irish designer who worked for over a decade in publishing and advertising. He gave it all up to pursue his love of comics. Dee has worked for nearly every comic for every publisher as a flatter/color assistant to some of the world's top color artists. He has colored *The Dregs* and *Eternal* at Black Mask Studios, *The Paybacks* and *Interceptor* at Heavy Metal and *Redneck* at Skybound.